O9-AHV-851

My Guantánamo Diary

My
GUANTÁNAMO DIARY
The Detainees and the Stories They Told Me

Mahvish Rukhsana Khan

WITHDRAWN

Mount Laurel Library
100 Walt Whitman Avenue
Mount Laurel, NJ 08054-9539
856-234-7319
www.mtlaurel.lib.nj.us

BBS

PUBLICAFFAIRS
NEW YORK

Copyright © 2008 by Mahvish Rukhsana Khan

Published in the United States by PublicAffairs™, a member of the Perseus Books Group.

All rights reserved.
Printed in the United States of America.

No part of this book may be reproduced in any manner whatsoever without written permission except in the case of brief quotations embodied in critical articles and reviews. For information, address PublicAffairs, 250 West 57th Street, Suite 1321, New York, NY 10107.

PublicAffairs books are available at special discounts for bulk purchases in the U.S. by corporations, institutions, and other organizations. For more information, please contact the Special Markets Department at the Perseus Books Group, 2300 Chestnut Street, Suite 200, Philadelphia, PA 19103, call (800) 810-4145, extension 5000, or e-mail special.markets@perseusbooks.com.

Designed by Timm Bryson
Text set in 11 point Dante by the Perseus Books Group

A CIP catalog record is available from the Library of Congress
ISBN: 978-1-58648-498-9
First Edition
10 9 8 7 6 5 4 3 2 1

This book is dedicated to the loving memory of my younger brother, Hassan-jaan, and to my friends behind the wire.

"Feed the hungry and visit the sick, free the captive if he is unjustly confined, and assist the oppressed."

—THE PROPHET MOHAMMAD

CONTENTS

ACKNOWLEDGMENTS

I would like to thank Peter Ryan, Rebecca Dick, and Carolyn Welshhans of Dechert. I would not have been able to accomplish this without them and am grateful for their unwavering support, meaningful feedback, and friendship. (Do not feed iguanas baklava in open-toe shoes.) A big thank you to Zofia Smardz of the *Washington Post*, my gracious and gifted editor, whose insight and genius helped me hone these stories. A special thank you to BBC reporter Rahman Ullah, to Munir Mujadidi of USAID in Kabul, and to Lal Gul, director of the Afghan Human Rights Organization. I would also like to thank my agent, Lynn Franklin, and I am grateful to Clive Priddle and to the folks at PublicAffairs for giving me a chance and for publishing this book. I am indebted to the following individuals for their help: Tom Wilner of Shearman and Sterling, Sam Zarifi of Human Rights Watch, John Sifton of One World Research, Clive Stafford Smith and Zachary Katznelson of Reprieve, Emi Maclean of the Center for Constitutional Rights, Dicky Grigg of Spivey and Grigg, and federal defenders Bryan Lessley and Chris Schatz. Thanks also to David Sylvester for his immense help with the poets and Salah. I am grateful to Dean William VanderWyden for his support during law school and beyond. I must also give thanks to my inspiring professors for all they have taught me over many years:

Lee C. Bollinger now at Columbia University, and Michael Froomkin and Bruce Winnick at the University of Miami School of Law. Thanks also to Carlos Lozada of the *Washington Post*, who accepted my pitch for "My Guantánamo Diary," the article. Most importantly, I would like to thank my parents, Baba-jaan (the most handsome doctor in the hospital) and Mumma (the most selfless individual I know), for pushing me and loving me. I am grateful for all that you have taught me. Many salaams go to my other mothers, my grandmother, Amiji, and to my beautiful aunties, Aunty gul, and Gulli. Thanks also to Wes and Susan Anson and Joanne Corn.

Finally, a special thank you to Poe for your kindness, love, and generosity. Thank you for listening to drafts out loud—ad nauseam. Oh yeah, and sorry I threatened not to put you in the acknowledgments if you didn't sit through another draft.

AUTHOR'S NOTE

The U.S. prison camp at Guantánamo Bay stands as a challenge to our nation. It challenges our readiness to do the right thing in times of crisis, the times when it's most important, and most difficult, to adhere to our founding principles and to follow the rule of law. What lies at the heart of the Gitmo debate are the beliefs upon which the United States of America was founded and for which it has long been celebrated: the conviction that no one should be imprisoned without charge and that everyone has a right to defend him- or herself in a fair and impartial trial.

The prisoners at Gitmo never had the chance to prove their innocence. They were never told why they'd been brought to Cuba. They were never allowed to be heard in open court. But their perspectives must be aired.

In selecting prisoners to profile, I've tried to present a range of individuals of varied backgrounds. The first detainees I met have had a lasting personal impact. Others offered compelling stories, unique personalities, or distinctive experiences. I did not have access to any of the fifteen "high-value" detainees, such as alleged September 11 mastermind Khaled Sheikh Mohammad.

Though it may appear to some readers that I give ample, and perhaps naïve, credence to the prisoners' points of view, I have made every effort to verify their accounts and to explore the military's contrasting perspective. Some readers may also argue that detainees, or "enemy combatants," as the Defense Department calls them, aren't entitled to the protections of U.S. law. This is an argument I reject. While I believe that Guantánamo may hold evil men as well as innocent ones, I also believe that only a full and fair hearing can separate the good from bad.

Readers may judge for themselves the merits of each tale recounted here. My objective is simply to tell the stories of some of the men held captive by the United States at Guantá-namo Bay, the stories they themselves have never been able to tell.

PROLOGUE

Tehran, August 28, 2003

The phone rings a little after 11 PM. Waheeda knows something is wrong the minute she hears the voice on the other end. It's her brother-in-law, Hayat. She stands in the living room, holding the receiver to her ear with both hands.

"Doctor Sahib has been arrested," Hayat says. He is calling from Gardez, Afghanistan, the hometown of her husband, Ali Shah. Waheeda has not spoken to Ali for more than two months, but his family in Afghanistan has sworn to her repeatedly that everything is fine.

"Khanum, don't worry yourself so much," they say. "He is very busy setting up the clinic and traveling for work on the parliamentary elections. He can't call you in Iran right now because the telephone reception in rural areas here is awful."

But now Waheeda is hearing what she has dreaded all along. "He was arrested on his second night here," Hayat is saying. "The Americans came to the house. . . . They came here and arrested everyone. They took him, Sayed, Ismael, and Reza, too."

Then, he stammers, "Everyone has been released—except Ali."

Waheeda feels the floor sway beneath her.

"What are you saying to me?" she demands. There is a short silence. Then, Hayat says that he had hoped Ali would be released like

---

This account has been reconstructed with the help of Dr. Ali Shah Mousovi's family.

the others. But it has been several months now, and he can no longer hide the truth.

"Oh, Allah," Waheeda says. "What did they say? Why?"

But Hayat knows nothing, can tell her nothing. The rest of the call is a blur. Waheeda hangs up and sits staring at the maroon rug under her feet for a very long time. Hayat's words have descended upon her like the weight of the world. She remembers the last time she spoke to Ali, just hours before his arrest. He was happy to be in Afghanistan again. All was well; his family was happy to have him back.

After more than a decade as a refugee in Iran, Ali Shah had returned to Afghanistan to open a clinic after the fall of the Taliban. Now was the time to go back, he had told her. Once the clinic was up and running, he'd come to fetch her and the children. As the son of a prominent Gardez family, he also planned to run for parliament in the new government led by President Hamid Karzai. And he wanted her, an economist, to fulfill her own dream of working in a free Afghanistan.

She remembers him standing by the door before he left. He'd held her close, told her there was nothing to worry about, that the Taliban were gone now. Their eight-year-old daughter, Hajar, ran to him, and he pulled the child onto his lap, kissing her face and asking what she wanted him to bring her from Afghanistan.

Those images collide with Hayat's words, echoing in her head. She can only remember fragments: Twenty or thirty American soldiers, military uniforms, guns pointed. Hog-tied, blindfolded, dragged out. Arrested. Suddenly panicking, she calls Hayat back.

"Did you tell them it was a mistake? Did you tell them he was just a doctor?" she asks.

"Please be calm," Hayat answers. "Inshallah, this will be over as soon they realize . . ." His voice trails off.

"Can you talk to the Americans?" she croaks. *"What did they say?"*

"I don't know," he replies. *"They didn't tell us anything. We will straighten this out, show them it's a mistake."*

Waheeda clutches the receiver long after the call is over. Her eyes fill with tears, and she whispers a prayer. *"Bismi'Allah—God protect him."*

The children have climbed out of bed and come into the room. She dries her face quickly.

Eleven-year-old Kumail asks what's wrong.

"The Americans came and asked Baba to come with them," she says. *"But it's just to ask a few questions. It's nothing to worry about. They made a mistake and once they find out that they have the wrong person, everything will be okay."*

"When are they going to let him go?" asks fifteen-year-old Abu-Zar. His gaze lingers on her tear-stained face.

"Inshallah, very soon, bachai—*my child,"* Waheeda says and tells them to pray hard for their father. *"Allah listens to children's prayers."*

"But Baba fought against the Russians a long time ago, not the Americans. Why would the Americans take him?" Abu-Zar asks. Waheeda is silent, holding Hajar tight. The little girl twists around to look up at her big brothers. She is the youngest and her father's favorite. Then, she jerks her head back around and shoves it into her mother's chest, wailing.

"Hajar-jaan, Baba will be home soon. It's just a mistake," Waheeda says. But Hajar keeps weeping, muffling her cries in her mother's shirt.

CHAPTER ONE

SECRET CLEARANCE

It was Google that got me to Gitmo.

In 2005, I was in law school at the University of Miami. We
were studying the federal torture statutes in my international
law class and how policy makers had cleverly circumvented legal
principles in creating the military detention camp at Guantánamo Bay, Cuba, where prisoners in the "war on terror" could
be held indefinitely without being charged with any crime.

I don't remember when I first heard about the detention
center, but by then, it was something everyone knew about, a
daily issue in the news. When people said "Guantánamo," you
knew instantly what they were talking about, and it wasn't
just the military base that the United States has maintained in
Cuba since the Cold War.

As a law student and a daughter of immigrants, I thought
the prison camp's very existence was a blatant affront to what
America stands for. How could our government create legal

1

loopholes to deny prisoners the right to a fair hearing? I didn't know whether the men at Guantánamo were innocent or guilty—how could anyone know if there was no investigative process or trial?—but I believed that they should be entitled to the same justice that even a rapist or a murderer gets in the United States.

I was young and idealistic. But so were the framers of our constitution when they tried to establish the rights and responsibilities of a young nation. All my life, I'd been taught that the United States guarantees everyone certain inalienable rights. My parents had left their home in another country to come to the United States so that their children could grow up with all those rights and with the freedoms that exist here for everyone, no matter a person's background or socioeconomic status.

"Now is not the time to be complacent," my mother often said when I was growing up. She believed in political and civic engagement, and I got my passion for it, and a persistent streak, from her. Almost from the first time I heard about the "war on terror" prison, my mother's words echoed in my mind. It was hard to be complacent.

Some of my passion had to do with my own Afghan-Pashtun heritage. As an American, I felt the pain of September 11, and I understood the need to invade Afghanistan and destroy the Taliban and al-Qaeda. But I also felt the suffering of the Afghans as their country was bombed. And when hundreds of men were rounded up and thrust into a black hole of detention, many apparently with no proof that they had any terrorist connections, I felt that my own country had taken a wrong turn.

They were people like me and my relatives. I couldn't help thinking of my own family; how would my aunts or cousins feel if their husbands and sons and brothers were swept up and deported to Cuba? How many mothers and wives and children were waiting at home in Kabul, or Gardez, or other Afghan cities, waiting for men who couldn't know when, if ever, they might return home?

Why, I thought, should the luckless Afghans, among others, be deprived of a shot at proving their innocence?

One day, after launching into another tirade about the injustice of Guantánamo Bay, my fiancé got tired of listening to my seemingly never-ending rant. "Why don't you stop complaining and get yourself involved if you feel so strongly about it?" he asked.

So, I turned on my computer and Googled the names of the attorneys on the landmark Supreme Court case *Rasul v. Bush*, a habeas corpus case brought in 2004 by two Guantánamo prisoners who challenged the U.S. government's practice of holding prisoners indefinitely without giving them access to lawyers, the right to a trial, or the right to know the charges against them. In late June 2004, the Supreme Court ruled that the prisoners at Guantánamo Bay had to be allowed access to U.S. courts to challenge their imprisonment.

One of the names that kept popping up on my Google search was Michael Ratner, a lawyer who worked for the Center for Constitutional Rights (CCR) in New York. I started bombarding him, his secretary, and his colleagues with calls and e-mails saying that I wanted to help in their work on behalf of Gitmo prisoners.

They asked me to send a resume. It took a few weeks to figure out exactly how best I could help. Eventually, the attorneys I contacted at CCR put me in touch with Peter Ryan at Dechert, a Philadelphia-headquartered law firm that was representing fifteen Afghan detainees. I quickly realized that they had no one with a security clearance who spoke Pashto, which meant that none of the attorneys had been able to meet his or her Afghan clients yet.

I'm the daughter of Afghan immigrants. My parents met in medical school in Peshawar, a city in northwest Pakistan on the Afghan border. They came to America in 1977. They had just gotten married, and Mumma sold some of her wedding jewelry so that they could make it to America. Mumma was twenty-six and Baba-jaan was twenty-seven when they arrived in Baltimore and enrolled at Johns Hopkins University to complete their medical training. I was born a year later, and my brother Hassan came two years after that. My older brother, Ali, was born in Iran, where my parents had lived for a brief time.

When they first came to America, Baba-jaan and Mumma were desperately homesick. Mumma used to write long let-

Baba-jaan.

ters to her parents because the international calls were too expensive. Initially, they were somewhat let down by their new country. They didn't like the big supermarkets that sold cold pita bread packaged in plastic bags. They missed the fluffy hot naan that street-side bakers made in brick ovens and the spicy *chapli* kebobs wrapped in newspaper to soak up the

oil. And they saw a lonely side to
America, where people call before
they visit. They were used to an
endless stream of guests ringing the
doorbell unannounced. Baba-jaan
often reminisced about how he
would come home from school, put
his things down, and walk from
house to house visiting friends and
relatives.

Mumma.

They decided early on that they
would leave America after they fin-
ished their residencies. But when the time came to pack up
their little apartment, they changed their minds. They felt it
was their duty to give their children the best opportunities.
And so they stayed, working late nights at the hospital so that
they could afford to send six-year-old Ali to private school,
where the tuition was half their salary at the time.

Over the years, my parents grew to admire and love America, and they gradually called it home. Soon enough, they
were living the American dream. Baba-jaan became a successful cardiologist. Mumma became the director of neonatology
at her hospital close to West Bloomfield, Michigan, where we
settled. She was also active politically. Members of Congress
attended fund-raisers at our house.

And yet, they were deeply concerned that we children not
lose touch with our heritage. They would overcompensate for
their decision to come to America. Some aspects of American
culture made my father especially anxious about the example,
or lack thereof, that it provided me. He wanted me to have a

successful career, but he was adamant about raising a good, conservative Pashtun girl with traditional Eastern values. That literally meant no MTV, no short skirts, no tight jeans. No drinking. No prom and definitely no boyfriends. Ever. "You take the good from this culture and leave the bad," they would say.

For some time, they insisted that I wear traditional clothes, *kameez-partoog*, to school. *Kameez-partoog* consists of a long tunic of varying length and loosely fitted matching pants underneath. For women, they are often mirrored or embroidered and come in an assortment of colors and fabric. Now I think they are beautiful, but for a fourth grader, this was a nightmare. I wanted only to look and dress like everybody else. Once, on picture day in elementary school, Mumma picked out a blue tunic with red pants. I grudgingly put it on. I remember standing in line in my colorful *kameez-partoog*, wishing I could find a hole to crawl into. My outfit made the girl behind me in line curious. I've forgotten her name, but I remember she had long blond hair, and *her* mother dressed her in a skirt and blouse.

"Why are you wearing pajamas?" she asked.

I was wildly embarrassed. At that age, everyone just wants to blend in. I took to changing my clothes once I arrived at school. It was a small school, so many of my friends and some of the teachers were in on the changing routine. Mumma and Baba-jaan never found out.

As I got older, my life was sheltered and laden with restrictions to keep out the influence of American sex, drugs, and rock 'n' roll. I felt stifled. As a teenager, I didn't really care for the funny food and clothes, and it drove me mad when my parents spoke to me in Pashto in front of my friends. Thanksgiving at our house was different too. We didn't have gravy, stuffing, or cranberry sauce, and our turkey was marinated in spices like cumin, coriander, and *tandoori masala*. Whatever was left over, Mumma turned into turkey kebobs. I never asked them to do anything differently because I knew it was just as challenging for them as it was for me. The idea of heritage was so central to them; besides, Mumma thought the American way of making Turkey was too bland, and she couldn't fathom how meat and cranberry sauce went together.

"I'm American," I remember saying to my grandmother. "I was born in America, and I've lived my whole life in America."

"No, you're not," she would object in Pashto. "You're a Pashtun girl, and, above all, you are a Muslim girl."

By the time I entered college, I felt suffocated by the expectation to uphold traditions I was unfamiliar with. When I moved into my all-girls dorm room at the University of Michigan, I was by all standards a very good Eastern girl. I had never tasted alcohol or had a boyfriend. Latently, though, I struggled with the prospect of balancing two very distinct cultures. I distracted myself with campus life. I wrote for the *Michigan Daily*, joined the Fencing Club, took part in student demonstrations, and made friends from around the world. I soaked up everything, inside and outside the classroom. But I made a point to stay away from the Muslim Student Association, and I didn't go out of my way to befriend people of Eastern backgrounds.

By my early twenties, I felt unsatisfied. Sometimes, when I came home after an absence, Baba-jaan would test me: "Have you found what you are looking for?" he would ask.

I never knew how to answer him. Gradually, I came to appreciate two things: I was not a comfortable, plain, macaroni-and-cheese American, and, more importantly, being American didn't require me to abandon the Pashtun influences. America is uniquely generous: it finds room for all heritages and traditions, many more complicated than mine. By the time I moved to Miami and enrolled in law school, I had begun to learn how to cook traditional meals: *kabali pillau, mantu,* samosas. I developed a liking for green tea and *chai*. I downloaded Pashto music and began collecting embroidered pashminas and went on Myspace.com to meet Afghan Americans who were in the same boat as I was.

And now, I wanted to put the fruits of my upbringing, as well as my parents' insistence that I hold on to where I came from, to use.

Dechert agreed to take me on as an interpreter. My intention was eventually to try to get involved with the legal end of the cases in the hopes of requesting an Afghan detainee as a client of my own once the attorneys got to know me better. This was precisely the sort of legal work I'd always been interested in.

The first step was to apply for secret-level security clearance from the Department of Defense since I would presumably be exposed to classified information. I didn't know what I was letting myself in for. The background check took six months. The Federal Bureau of Investigation (FBI) contacted my former landlords, employers, and numerous friends and neighbors going back ten years. Between high school, college, and law school, I must have moved a dozen times, so the check involved agents all over the country.

Agents contacted my former professors at the University of Michigan and my law school professors. I wondered whether my scandalous attendance record in commercial law might affect my security clearance. I don't know what I'd been thinking when I signed up for that class. Whenever I did manage to drag myself in to the two-hour lecture, I ended up either falling asleep while the professor ranted about Article 9 of the Uniform Commercial Code (trust me, you don't want to know) or checking e-mail on my laptop. Maybe I'd have made a greater effort if I'd known that one day the FBI would be pulling my transcripts and meeting my deans.

The agents asked random friends and neighbors whether I had ever been involved in any plots to overthrow the U.S. government. That was funny. I had a hard enough time remembering to feed my pet ferret and my Chihuahua Sofie, much less contriving a plan to overthrow the government.

They wanted to know whether I had an alcohol or drug problem or ties to any terrorist groups or organizations. They drove around my fiancé's neighborhood and visited him at work. And they consistently asked everyone whether I had any financial difficulties or spending issues. The concern, apparently, was whether I could be bribed to reveal classified information. A friend in Boston called me after her FBI session and jokingly asked whether my winter-collection Chloé handbag and boots qualified as evidence of a spending problem.

I assumed that I wouldn't get the clearance when the agents started pulling my credit history. As a freshman in college, I'd been taken in by the credit card guys on campus who gave away random toys and T-shirts if you filled out an application. And foolishly, I'd always ended up activating the cards when they came in the mail. I maxed out three credit cards in a few months on clothes. By sophomore year, creditors had started calling my apartment. Like so many nineteen-year-olds, I still had a pretty adolescent sense of responsibility and thought of myself as quite clever, so I told the callers that this "Mahvish" person they were trying to reach had moved permanently to Egypt. Eventually, the creditors got hold of my parents, who were furious but paid off my debt.

I figured that between commercial law and my past credit indiscretions, the Department of Defense would not consider me to be in any position to handle classified information.

But in December 2005, I got a call from an FBI agent who asked me to come to the Broward County office for an interview. I lived on South Beach and rarely ventured outside Miami Beach except to go to campus, so I ended up lost and stuck in traffic on my way to the appointment. I called the agent and asked him to meet me on South Beach another day. In a rare attack of scholarly conscience, I told him that traffic was terrible and that I would never make it back in time for my commercial law class. Instead, he told me to stay where I was and that he would come to me. I pulled into the parking lot of an Einstein's Bagels and waited.

About fifteen minutes later, a man in dark shades and a frumpy suit, looking like an *X-Files* wannabe, pulled up. I asked him for identification. I was disappointed when he didn't pull out the kind of gold shield that I'd seen so many times on TV.

He proceeded to ask me a series of questions, never bothering to take off his sunglasses. "Is it part of your MO to wear dark shades even when you're not in the sun?" I asked him sweetly. He took the glasses off and glanced at me briefly. Satisfied, I gave him a grin. He asked me whether I had met any foreign nationals on my recent trip to Italy.

I managed not to be flippant about meeting Italians in Italy. "Other than shopkeepers and people who worked at the hotels, no," I said.

I must have satisfied him in return because eventually I received my clearance. I got a phone call from the Defense Department and was briefed on the "protective order" governing classified information related to Guantánamo Bay. I was instructed that I could only discuss classified information with others on a "need-to-know basis." Classified information could not be discussed via e-mail or over nonsecure telephone lines. If I needed to discuss classified information with anyone, it had to be with the blinds closed—to prevent lip reading. Classified documents could only be photocopied at the Defense Department's secured facility using special photocopiers. Blank copies were to be run afterwards to clear the copier's memory.

I felt like James Bond, and "need-to-know" quickly became the buzz phrase among my friends and me. After the briefing, I took off on my first trip to the base on January 29, 2006.

CHAPTER TWO

THE PEDIATRICIAN

The sailor at the entrance to Camp Echo peered through the
gate as Peter Ryan and I held up our laminated brown-and-
white photo ID cards. "HC," they read, for habeas counsel.
"Escort Required." He waved us through, searched our bags
for recording devices, then issued safety instructions—dial
2431 on the wall phone in the room—in case anything should
happen during our meeting with prisoner No. 1154.

The gravel crunched beneath our shoes as we walked behind another young soldier toward a tall gate in a fence covered with green tarp.[1] "North side. We have traffic," he said
into a walkie-talkie before pulling out a big brass key and un-
locking the gate. He ushered us in, then closed and locked the
gate behind him. We walked a few more paces, and he unlocked another gate with another big brass key.[2]

We were in a dusty courtyard with gravel laid out in odd
patterns that our guide warned us not to step on. A series of

13

numbered doors lined the square, which was surrounded by a twenty-foot fence covered in the same green tarp and topped with razor and barbed wire.[3] We followed the soldier to a painted brown door. I quickly arranged the shawl I'd brought over my head and arms. I was nervous. Peter was too. I think we were both expecting a violent foreigner, even a member of the Taliban, the kind of man who'd want me stoned to death for walking around with Peter, a man I'm neither married nor related to. Peter motioned for me to enter the room first.

I turned the steel knob and walked in.

The prisoner was standing at the far end of the room behind a long table. His leg was chained to the floor beside a seven-by-eight-foot cage.[4] He looked wary as the door opened, but as our eyes met and he saw me in my traditional embroidered shawl, a smile broke across his weathered features. I smiled back and gave him the universal Islamic greeting:

"As-salaam alaikum—May peace be upon you."

"Walaikum as-salaam—May peace also be upon you," he responded.

With that, I shook hands with my first "terrorist."

He was a handsome, soft-spoken man with a short, neatly groomed beard. His once-dark hair was heavily flecked with gray. He was dressed in an oversized white prison uniform. I thought he looked much older than his forty-six years—closer to sixty or seventy.

I introduced myself and Peter as I removed the lid from the Starbucks chai I'd brought along. I handed it to No. 1154, explaining that it was the closest thing to Afghan tea that I could find on the military base. We opened boxes of baklava, cookies, and pizza, but the prisoner didn't reach for anything. Instead, in true Afghan fashion, he nervously encouraged us to share the food we had brought for him. I smiled to myself when he did that. It was such a familiar gesture.

His name was Ali Shah Mousovi. He was a pediatrician and the son of a prominent Afghan family from the city of Gardez, where he'd been arrested by U.S. troops more than three years earlier. He had returned to Afghanistan in August 2003 after twelve years of exile in Iran, he told us, to help rebuild his *wathan*, his homeland.

Peter had become involved in Mousovi's case two years earlier. After reading the Supreme Court decision in *Rasul v. Bush*, he (like me) had called the Center for Constitutional Rights in New York and asked how Dechert could do pro bono work with Gitmo detainees. Through the Afghan Embassy in Washington, D.C., he found a petition that had been signed by the family and friends of Dr. Ali Shah Mousovi in Washington and Virginia.

Our courts recognize the difficulty of filing a habeas corpus petition from jail. Many detainees did not speak English or understand our laws. In such cases, the courts will allow a "next-friend petition," in which a father, brother, mother, or friend may act as an agent for the prisoner. That's how many Guantánamo detainees got lawyers.

Laws don't get much more fundamental than habeas corpus. It's an old safeguard preventing imprisonment without charge and a right embedded in the U.S. Constitution. "Habeas corpus" is a Latin phrase meaning "You have the body." Bringing a habeas petition forces the captor to provide justification for holding his captive.

There was a ceiling camera in the cage to the right of our table, into which Mousovi was put before and after our meetings and at lunchtime. We'd been told that the camera was there for our protection. I wondered what could happen to us in a room with a prisoner who was shackled to the floor.

Attorney-client meetings at Guantánamo are supposed to be privileged and confidential, and the base captain had told us that morning that because the camera was located inside the cage, it couldn't pick up images of the legal papers laid on the table. He also told us that the camera wasn't recording us and didn't have audio, so we shouldn't worry about the military listening in on our conversations. I wondered about that.

But I leaned across the table and, to put us all at ease, told the prisoner a little bit about myself: How I'd learned Pashto growing up from my parents and grandparents. That like him, my parents were physicians. That, also like him, they had lived briefly in Iran. I told him about Peter and his family. When I said that Peter and his wife were expecting a baby in a few months, he smiled for the second time. He told me later that I'd triggered his first smile when I'd entered the room in my headscarf because he'd mistaken me for his younger sister.

As I translated from Pashto, Mousovi hesitantly described his life since his arrest. He had gone back to Gardez in August 2003 and remembered the small crowd of well-wishers who came out to greet his car as it jostled down the rocky mountain road into town. Sixty or eighty people, maybe more, rushed to meet him. They threw their arms around him, grateful for the return of professionals to Afghanistan.

In the coming days, he, his brother Ismail, and his cousin Reza, who were also physicians, planned to open their clinic. Once it was up and running, the men would fetch their families from Iran. Instead, on his second night in Gardez, American soldiers broke down the door to Mousovi's family guesthouse and took him away. He was accused of associating with the Taliban and of funneling money to anticoalition insurgents.

After his arrest, he spent twenty-two days in a makeshift outdoor jail in Gardez under constant interrogation and without the opportunity to shower or bathe. Then, he had been transported by helicopter to Bagram Air Force Base in Afghanistan. There, he was thrown into a tiny three-and-a-half-by-seven-foot shed—face down, blindfolded, hooded, and gagged. Lying like this, he said, he was kicked in the head repeatedly.

At some point, his jailers cut the clothes off his body, and he squirmed, trying to cover himself. "This is American soil," he was told. "This is not your soil. You will obey us." He had become a stranger in his own land: the soil had changed beneath his feet. Twenty miles from Kabul, he was apparently no longer in Afghanistan.

Obeying, he had quickly learned, meant not resisting.

He described how he was beaten regularly by Americans in civilian clothing. More painful than the bruises and wounds that covered his body were the unbroken days and nights without sleep. Tape recordings of screeching sirens blared through the speakers that soldiers placed by his ears. His head throbbed. Whenever he managed, mercifully, to doze off, he'd be startled awake by wooden clubs striking loud blows against the wall. He recalled the sting as he was repeatedly doused with ice water. He said he was not allowed to sit down for two weeks straight. At some point his legs felt like wet noodles; when they gave out, he was beaten and forced to stand back up. He couldn't remember how many times this happened.

In rotating shifts, U.S. soldiers periodically kicked and beat him and the other prisoners. Some yelled things about September 11. Others spat on him. Many cursed his mother, sisters, and other family members. They cursed his nationality and religion. He wanted to stand up for his loved ones and for himself as the young soldiers swore obscenities at him, but he could only groan as the hard boots slammed into his throbbing head.

"Many of the Afghans did not understand the terrible things they were saying," he told us, "but I understood." He used to understand English well, he said, but years of abuse and sleep deprivation had taken a toll on his memory.

Peter scribbled notes furiously as the doctor spoke, describing how soldiers had tied a rope around him and dragged him around through dirt and gravel. He said he was subjected to extreme temperatures of heat and cold. Sometimes he was kept in complete darkness for hours and then made to stare into intense bright light. He was made to stand endless hours of the night in uncomfortable positions. He was punished if he looked to his right or to his left. Each moment, he believed, could be his last.

And with every blow, he would repeat to himself, "La-illaha-illa-Allah—There is no God but God."

These words are the first words a Muslim hears upon his birth and often the last words spoken before he dies. When a baby is born, the doctor or the father utters this prayer into the crying infant's ear. On the threshold of death, a doctor or family member often urges the dying person to speak these final parting words. And afterward, the family will echo this prayer as the deceased is laid to rest.

"La-illaha-illa-Allah, Mohammad-an-rasul Allah—There is no god but God, and Mohammad is his messenger."

Mousovi said he didn't sleep for an entire month. Then, a uniformed soldier made him take drugs, he said. To his consternation, the names of the pills evaded him, try as he did to remember them. "A doctor remembers the names of medications the way he remembers the names of his sons," he said, shaking his head in dismay.

There was one last item on his tally of torture. He shifted his eyes away from me and looked at the wooden table as he spoke of the *sharam*—the shame—he had endured at Bagram. "They made us take all our clothes off. We were naked . . . a lot of prisoners. They tied us together and herded us around like sheep," he said as quickly as he could get the words out.

I felt a bit like a voyeur and couldn't meet his eyes.

"Peter may not understand why this is so humiliating for our people," Mousovi said to me. "But you are a Pashtun. You understand why." I nodded awkwardly.

Afghan culture is much more puritanical and guarded in these matters than the West. For example, in America, men can change or shower in front of other men in a locker room—and it's no big deal. But Afghan or Arab men would not dream of it.

Mousovi said he didn't know why he'd been brought to Guantánamo Bay. He believed that someone had sold him to U.S. forces to collect a reward of up to $25,000 for anyone who gave up a Taliban or al-Qaeda member. Perhaps his political opponents had given false reports to the Americans to prevent him from running for parliament. He could only speculate. He insisted that he was simply a doctor who wanted to help rebuild his country.

He spent more than a year and a half in detention before he was told that he would be given a hearing before a combatant status review tribunal (CSRT). The hearing would theoretically allow him to challenge his designation as an "enemy combatant."

At last, he had hope. A trial would be an opportunity to show his captors that his arrest had been a mistake. Asked whether he wanted to call witnesses, he drew up a list of eight names. Three of the men were in Afghanistan. Three were in Iran. Two were Guantánamo Bay detainees.

I read the transcript of the hearing later.

On January 15, 2005, guards led him from Camp Delta to a small room for the hearing. The Bush administration designed the CSRT in response to the U.S. Supreme Court ruling that Guantánamo detainees should be allowed to challenge their detention before an impartial judge, who would be a military officer. The hearing is supposed to determine whether a detainee is an enemy combatant and therefore not entitled to normal legal rights. But in most cases, the CSRTs are little more than dog and pony shows. They admit hearsay and evidence obtained through torture and coercion. They don't allow prisoners lawyers, witnesses, or even the right to see the alleged evidence against them. CSRTs are a sham, designed to confirm a decision that has already been made.

Mousovi's hands were cuffed and his feet shackled to a thick steel bolt in the floor. A panel of three military officers sat behind a long table to his right. Also present were a court reporter to transcribe the hearing, an interpreter, and an appointed military "personal representative."

Always respectful, Mousovi stood up from the white plastic lawn chair provided for him and waited quietly for the officers to begin the proceedings.

When he stood, the panel of officers glanced at each other and then back at the prisoner. Finally, the interpreter turned to him and explained that he should be seated. The chains rattled as he resumed his seat.

The tribunal president read the hearing instructions. Ali Shah indicated that he understood, then turned and faced the panel of military officers.

"Mr. President and respectable tribunal members, with utmost respect to all of you, I am delighted that after about one and a half years, I am for the first time witnessing a tribunal, which apparently looks like a court system," he said nervously through the interpreter.

But this court, it appeared, wasn't going to allow him to bring forth any witnesses. Because the United States doesn't have diplomatic relations with Iran, there had been problems processing the request to find his witnesses there. The Afghan Embassy, meanwhile, had simply never responded to a request to locate the witnesses in Afghanistan. But the panel told him that one of the Guantánamo detainees would be allowed to testify on his behalf. The other would be allowed to submit something in writing.

Mousovi's mind raced, he told me later. How could he prove his innocence without witnesses? He tried to persuade the panel that, at the very least, he needed the second Guantánamo detainee witness to be present to answer specific questions. This was a man from his hometown who could offer valuable evidence and testimony. "He was a security chief of Paktia province, so he knows about my case very well," he pleaded.

But his requests were quickly denied. Seeing his disappointment, the tribunal president reassured him that this would not be held against him in any way.

The panel's first accusation: "The detainee is associated with the Taliban and/or al-Qaeda."

"Not only do I have nothing in common with the radical Taliban or extremist al-Qaeda, I am completely against their

ideology!" Mousovi responded. He had been a refugee in Iran
during the entire Taliban rule, he said. He had refused to set
foot in his country for even a day to tend to his personal prop-
erty while the Taliban held his homeland hostage and looted
his home and estates.

In Iran, Mousovi had been forced to work as a taxi driver, a
tailor, and a tutor to feed his family. But he hadn't even
thought about taking his family back to Afghanistan.

"I am a Shiite Muslim," he said, "and they looked at Shiites
as infidels. As enemies. They butchered my people. The Shiites were an endangered minority with no political voice under the Taliban. If I had associations with them, why wouldn't
I have returned to my country?"

Far from associating with the Taliban, Mousovi insisted that
he was a zealous supporter of Afghan democracy. After coalition forces ousted the Taliban, he returned to his country in
April 2002 and worked with the United Nations to help increase support for a new democratic Afghanistan. In June of
that year, he also attended the first *loya jirga*, an internation-
ally backed assembly of leaders who met in Kabul to select
Hamid Karzai as the country's post-Taliban head of state.

But the military panel accused him of going to Afghanistan
to funnel money to anticoalition insurgents.

"Please. Tell me, which money?" he asked. "This is imagi-
nary, invisible and psychic money. I was in Gardez for just two
days, so what happened with this money?"

The tribunal president said that the evidence concerning
the money was classified. The panel proceeded to accuse
Mousovi of distributing money, food, and Kalashnikov rifles
to al-Qaeda fighters preparing to fight the United States, al-

legedly before the Taliban was defeated, even though Mousovi was in Iran at the time.

Finally, he was accused of fighting in the U.S.-backed war against the Soviet invasion of Afghanistan in the 1980s. This was something that the United States had wanted and encouraged Afghans to do. Now, Mousovi was being forced to respond to this allegation as if it were a crime.

He didn't deny his support of the mujahideen during their fight against the Russians. He had been a medic helping wounded resistance fighters. There were still bullet fragments lodged in the muscles of his neck, where he had been shot twenty-eight years before by a Russian soldier.

Mousovi had hoped for some clarity. He had hoped that the tribunal would see that there had been a mistake. Instead, his day in court left him confused.

"It's still not clear to me what I am being charged with," he said. "Is it my fault, or is it my sin, that I fought against the Russians? That I fought against communism? Or was it my sin that I didn't associate with the Taliban? Or maybe it is my fault that after the establishment of democracy, I returned to my country to serve my people and help my people and our national security with the *loya jirga*? Or maybe it was my fault because my people love me and thought of me as a good servant."

The panel sat in silence.

Mousovi spoke again. "By our friends and by our enemies we are punished," he said. "The bullet, the Russian bullet is still in my neck. That is a gift from the Russians, and I consider Russia our enemy. These handcuffs and this uniform is a gift from our friends, from you."

Finally, the tribunal president spoke. "Very well, thank you for your testimony," he said. And that was all.

Mousovi went back to Camp Delta that afternoon. Several days later, he received notice that the military panel had declared him an enemy combatant.

Peter stepped out to speak with the guards, and the doctor leaned closer to me and asked about my family. He told me how happy it had made him to see me walk through the door.

"I had no idea that there were Pashtun girls like you in America," he said with a laugh. I told him that I had no idea there were men like him at Guantánamo, that he was just like any member of my family, and that I was shocked to see him there.

It was amazing to me how quickly I'd come to feel comfortable in the presence of this man. It wasn't hard to pinpoint why. He was articulate, just like my father, and extremely hospitable, like any of my uncles or aunts. He looked like them too and was immediately affectionate toward me. But I warmed up to him quickly also because he is probably one of the most gentle individuals I've ever met. Almost immediately, I knew he was good, someone I could relate easily to and trust.

He asked me what I was studying and said that my parents must be proud that I was in my final year of law school. We talked briefly about the life he missed. More than anyone, he missed his daughter, Hajar. His memory may have been impaired, but there was one moment with her that he remembered as though it had happened just the day before. Hajar had run to him in her ruffled dress and thrown her little arms around his neck, pulling his face down to hers. He'd lifted the eight-year-old onto his lap and asked what kind of gifts she wanted from Afghanistan. "She told me, 'I want you to come back quickly, Baba-jaan,'" he recalled, and his voice broke.

Mousovi fiddled with the label on the Coke bottle he was holding. When he looked up, I didn't know what to say to him. I just sat there. Luckily, Peter came back into the room.

Ali Shah Mousovi, a.k.a. detainee No. 1154, with his family before his arrest. *Courtesy of Dr. Ali Shah's family.*

In his third year of detention, Mousovi looked for solace in God. Five times a day, he would perform his Muslim duties when he heard the prerecorded Arabic call to prayer played over camp loudspeakers.

"*Allahu Akbar, Allahu Akbar*—God is the Greatest, God is the Greatest. *Hayya 'ala-s-Salah, Hayya 'ala-s-Salah*—Come to prayer, come to prayer."

He would wash, align his prayer rug to the East, and stand shoulder to shoulder with a few of the other detainees in Camp 4. They would pray together and pray for one another.

The doctor interacted as much he could with the other prisoners. He preferred to be detained in predominantly Afghan blocks. Guantánamo has eight camps. Each is subdivided into several blocks with military-style alphabetical names: Alpha, Bravo, Charley, Delta, Echo, and so forth.[5] Detainees not in solitary confinement are moved every few months so that they are never in one place long enough to form friendships with the prisoners in adjacent cages.

It was difficult for Mousovi when he was held for a time in a predominantly Arab block, where some of the Arabs, who looked down upon Afghans, treated him badly. It didn't help that he didn't speak Arabic.

But he also felt like an outsider among some of the other Afghans. Unlike him, many of his fellow prisoners were farmers, butchers, and laborers. Many of them had multiple wives and herds of children. Mousovi had been committed to the same woman since the day they met. He had only three children, not ten.

He tried to stay busy. He wrote poetry and kept a record of his experiences. Once a week, a soldier would push a book cart through the camp. But Mousovi and the other detainees were all tired of reading *Harry Potter* in Pashto. Some of the detainees were so bored that they tried memorizing it because it gave them something to do. The doctor told us that he wished he could keep up his studies and asked us to bring him a *Physicians' Desk Reference* and give it to the military for clearing. We were sure, however, that the military would never allow such a book in the camp library for fear that some detainees would figure out how to create lethal concoctions of drugs to commit suicide.

So, Mousovi spent a lot of time with the one book he was allowed, the Qu'ran. American imprisonment would help him become a better Muslim. And he wrote letters home and read and reread the letters written to him and delivered by the International Red Cross. They were his only window onto what his life had once been.

A letter from Hajar:

May 10, 2006

I am sending the biggest and warmest greetings to my Baba-jaan—sweet father.

I hope you are in good health and all right. We are all doing fine here—other than longing for the presence of a badly missed kind father. But I am certain that with the grace of God, we will have you here again very soon. My dear sweet Baba, I miss you very much. I hope and pray that your innocence is proven and that you are released very soon.

Everyone is sending you their salaams and greetings. Abi-jaan, sweet aunty and her family, Grandma, and everyone else sends their love. Dear father, Abi-jaan is doing fine. She is taking her medications and is waiting for you to come home.

Dear father, this year you missed my birthday again, but I hope you will be here for Abu-Zar's birthday so we can throw him a big party.

Dearest sweet father, the space on this paper is running out, but my words are always unfinished. I am hoping and praying to tell you everything else I have to say, when I see you in person. Kind sweet Baba—by the way Abi-jaan has a message for you too: [along the edges of the page] Bachai-jaan—my dear child—salaam. I am doing well. The kids are studying hard, and I am with them. You are an innocent man without blame, and I am waiting here for you. Khuda hafiz—May God's peace be with you.

Well, Baba-jaan—sweet father—if I could, I would kiss your gentle dear hands from far away.

Khuda hafiz—*May God's Peace be with you.*

With love from your daughter,
Hajar
[To be handed to my innocent father]

The doctor often stared for hours at the neat handwriting of his little girl. This letter was a gift; it made it though the censors in good shape. He ran his fingers across the folds and creases of the small pages. The sentences filled the margins vertically, not wasting any precious space. He was unable to read much of many of his daughter's letters because they were redacted by the military, forcing him to imagine what was written beneath those thick blocks of black ink where something had been marked out. What could a ten-year-old child have written to her father that could pose a threat to U.S. national security?

One Arab detainee complained to his attorneys that his daughter's letters were also being constantly censored. The lawyers, curious as to what the military found so sensitive in a little girl's messages, called the detainee's family and found out. Knowing that the detainee's children were his weak spot, the censors were blacking out every "I love you" or "I miss you" that the child had written.

Once in a while, Mousovi would look at the photographs his family sent. Family photographs are gold at Guantánamo Bay, but they, too, must go through a process of military review and clearance. The military checks for encoded messages. Once the photos are cleared, they are stamped and given to the detainees.

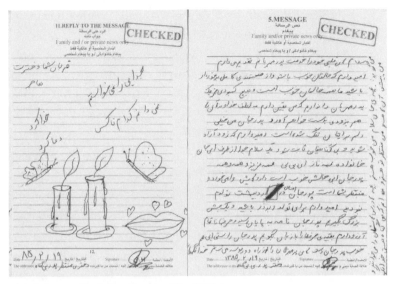

Hajar's letter to her father. *Courtesy of Dr. Ali Shah.*

Family pictures, though, made the doctor sad. Despite the family's reassurances that all were doing fine, that there was nothing to worry about, he grew listless over the years, worrying about his wife and about his children growing up without a father. Every time he received another picture, the children looked different. And he worried about living to see his seventy-nine-year-old mother again. Sometimes he wondered whether she was alive or dead.

Peter, Mousovi, and I discussed various strategies that could help his case. We talked about contacting witnesses in Afghanistan and collecting evidence to support his defense.

Then, Mousovi asked about news from Afghanistan. Was it peaceful? Was there fighting? Were the Taliban gone for good? Who had been elected to the Afghan parliament?

Military rules allowed lawyers to discuss political news with their clients only if it was somehow related to their cases. So, Peter could only respond with some vague answers about what the U.S. media were reporting about the political climate in Afghanistan. Mousovi seemed a bit disappointed, but he didn't press.

Just then, a guard knocked on the door, signaling that our time was up. The doctor quickly signed a document agreeing to have Peter represent him in filing a petition for habeas corpus before U.S. civilian courts. He asked us to return soon and to write and keep him updated on his case. But he remained hopeful that he would be freed before we would have a chance to visit him again. If, "Inshallah—God willing" that happened, he said, his door would always be open to us, and we would have to visit him in Afghanistan, where we would be his honored guests.

"I pray to Allah," he said, holding his open palms together, "for *sabar*—patience." "Please remember me in your prayers, my sister, and ask your mother to pray for me too." He stood up, a gesture of respect, as Peter and I said goodbye. When I glanced back after we walked out, he was still standing, gazing after us.

I don't know exactly what I had expected coming to Guantánamo Bay, but it certainly wasn't that weary, sorrowful man.

As our guard led us out of Camp Echo, I pulled the heavy shawl off my head and thought about everything he had told us and of the long years he had spent in confinement without ever being charged. "I've been duped," I thought. "My government has duped me."

CHAPTER THREE

GETTING THERE

The journey to Guantánamo begins at the commuter terminal of the Ft. Lauderdale/Hollywood International Airport. With the exception of one corporate law firm that always makes a grand entrance in a chartered private jet, the attorneys doing habeas work at Gitmo fly one of two commercial airlines, Air Lynx or Air Sunshine.

At the counter, you're asked to show clearance documentation provided by the Department of Defense. Then, you hop onto the luggage scale because seating on the tiny puddle jumper prop planes is determined by body weight. The ten-seat cabin is so small that it's impossible to stand fully upright. Before boarding, everyone hits the bathroom because there aren't any lavatories on board. Some people bring earplugs or large headphones in a futile attempt to drown out the noise of the engines.

Surprisingly, we don't have to go through any kind of security procedures before boarding. There are no metal detectors to walk through and no X-ray machines to scan our baggage. Nor does anyone bother to open our checked luggage.

"Why don't you guys look through our bags?" I asked one of the Air Sunshine workers on an early trip.

They used to, he replied, "but sometimes people pack dirty laundry, and I don't want to touch that stuff."

In preparation for takeoff, the copilot stands with his neck craned sideways to avoid hitting his head against the cabin roof while giving safety instructions. "Ladies and gentlemen, welcome aboard Air Sunshine, nonstop to Guantánamo Bay," he says. "Life vests are under your seats. Help yourselves to plenty of drinks." He points at a red plastic cooler in the middle of the aisle filled with an obscure grape-flavored soda called Faygo.

On my first trip, I started looking around for my life jacket and frantically told Peter that I couldn't find it. He laughed.

"Don't worry. If this plane goes down, your life vest isn't going to do you any good," he said.

That was reassuring.

The flying experience itself is a little dodgy, and there's almost always some sort of drama. On one flight, we had no copilot, and I prayed all the way down that the pilot didn't have any history of heart disease in his family. Once, a big brown cockroach joined us on the flight and crawled up an attorney's leg. She screamed. So did I. When the bug started flying around the cabin, I think the weight distribution was definitely altered.

The lack of lavatories on the planes often leads to some dicey situations. Even though Cuba is only ninety miles from the mainland, the flight takes three hours because the plane has to go all the way around the island to avoid Cuban airspace. Air Lynx used to carry bags of sand for passengers to use for relief but eventually stopped because none of the passengers seemed to know what they were for. Occasionally, some attorneys use an empty Coke bottle if they're desperate.

That's not a terrible arrangement for a man, but it doesn't work quite so well for a woman. On one trip back to Florida, a female paralegal tapped my shoulder just forty minutes into the flight.

"What do I do if I need to go to the bathroom?" she asked with a look of discomfort on her face.

"You hold it," I advised.

"Well, what about in the case of an emergency?" she asked.

I tried to think creatively because she looked really uncomfortable, and a Coke bottle wasn't going to do the trick.

"You could use the drink cooler," I suggested seriously. I could tell that she was starting to panic.

"Do they ever land the plane early?" she asked.

"There's nowhere to land. We're over the middle of the ocean."

She hobbled back to her seat, but ten minutes later she was hovering above me again. She stuck her head past the curtain that separated the cockpit from the cabin and told the pilot, a woman, about her dilemma.

Without a word, the pilot handed her an empty Snapple bottle and asked the passengers at the rear of the plane to move forward.

"I'm so embarrassed," the paralegal said, turning crimson.

The pilot, though, was unfazed. "Don't worry about it," she said. "Once someone went No. 2 in the middle of the aisle." She held up two fingers.

The paralegal looked horrified. "What did you do?" she asked.

"I put on my oxygen mask and flew the plane."

We feel lucky when the flights are uneventful because no one likes incidents on airplanes. One time, all the passengers were pulled off the plane because the engine wouldn't start. We sat around on the Gitmo tarmac for a half-hour waiting for a jump start. It's also not uncommon for an overweight passenger to break one of the twenty-year-old seats, forcing us back out onto the tarmac while a spare is brought in. Once, during a stormy night flight, the plane dropped several hundred feet. Screaming passengers hit their heads on the low cabin ceilings, and belongings went flying.

The worst thing, though, is when the plane leaves early from Cuba. On a few occasions, the Iranian Air Sunshine pilots—there are three who rotate, Farshad, "John," and Mohammad—have decided to leave Guantánamo Bay before the scheduled departure time. They are a lovely bunch, but why they think this is okay, I don't know. Lawyers have arrived on time only to see their plane disappearing off down the runway.

Upon arrival, we're greeted by armed U.S. Army personnel who direct us to customs, which consists of a couple of brown tables where more Army boys rifle through our bags.

The base is divided into two areas, the leeward side and the windward side, by the two-and-a-half-mile-wide Guantánamo Bay. The main base is on the windward side, which is where the detention camps are built. There are nine camps (of which we are presently aware) named 1, 2, 3, 4, 5, 6, 7, Echo, and Iguana. Each numbered camp is subdivided into several blocks with alphabetical names: Alpha, Bravo, Charley, Delta, Echo. There's also India, Tango, Romeo, Whiskey, Foxtrot, and Zulu.[1]

Camps 1, 2, and 3 consist of rows of adjacent steel-mesh cages with one man per cage. Camp 4 is a medium-security prison for "compliant" detainees and houses up to ten men per room. They are allowed to watch nature films, sports, or prescreened movies once a week. Camp 4 prisoners are also allowed to pray and eat communally, and they have greater access to reading material, an exercise bike, and a soccer ball. Many show up to attorney meetings with broken or injured toes because they play soccer in flip-flops.[2]

Once Camps 5 and 6 were built—these contain solitary-confinement cells—many prisoners were transferred there from Camps 1, 2, and 3. Camp 7 holds the fifteen high-value detainees and is run by a special military unit, code-named Task Force Platinum. I have met mostly Afghans in Camp Echo, which is used for habeas meetings (and other classified activities). Sometimes meetings also take place in Camps 5 and 6 and Iguana.[3]

Habeas counsel are lodged on the leeward side at the Combined Bachelors Quarters (CBQ) for $20 a day. It provides cable TV, a phone, dial-up Internet, a small kitchen, and maid service. Strangely, each room has four twin beds. On my first trip, I debated whether to sleep in a different bed each night.

For several months, some rooms were under renovation, so the attorneys were lodged two and three together. That led to some gossip about whose snoring sounded most like that of a dying animal.

In the early summer months, it rains, and that caused another problem. Hundreds of orange crabs would take cover in our rooms. I freaked when I saw the creatures rushing under my door. I ran out immediately to ask for a room on the second floor. Attorney Carolyn Welshhans of Dechert's Washington, D.C., office was more valiant. She took to smashing the ugly things with a metal trash can.

Gitmo is a strange place, but you find yourself conforming quickly to its clockwork military rhythm. Every day begins at 7:30 AM. It's almost always bright and sunny. The Jamaican gardener, William Bartley, holds the garden hose with one hand and waves at visitors with the other, laughing and addressing us at the top of his lungs with the Jamaican term of endearment, "Hello, my Dods!"

We smile and wave back.

"Hi, Bartley!"

Everyone at Gitmo seems to have a story. Sometimes, when I had downtime in the evenings, I would wander off to the Clipper Club, the local greasy spoon, and chat up the Jamaicans who made me pizza and deep-fried hot dogs and chicken strips. The place was usually dead, and the guy behind the counter would happily chat away while intermittently commenting on the *American Idol* contestants. He had five children with five different women. At one point, one of the women was threatening to tell his wife about their child. She was blackmailing him for gifts and money. I was amused but tried to give him advice as I ate his fried chicken fingers, fried cheese sticks, or something else equally deep-fried.

The CBQ desk workers were exceedingly polite Filipinos who wore Hawaiian shirts, as if we were checking into a Maui resort. All of them earned well below minimum wage, but they said it was still better than the jobs back home. At night, they would log into their accounts on Myspace.com and chat with friends in the Philippines or watch TV in the lobby.

In the morning, we all meet at the concrete circular tables at the front of the CBQ to wait for the bus, which leaves at exactly 7:41 AM. It pulls up to the dock at 7:51 AM, just as the ferry that will take us to the windward side is arriving.

At exactly 8:20 AM, we're dropped off on the other side, where a military escort greets us and hands out our habeas badges. Next stop is Starbucks and the food court to have breakfast and pick up food for the detainees. Then, on to Camp Echo, where meetings with detainees are held.

The only part of the Gitmo experience that doesn't run with military precision is the counsel meetings themselves. More often than not, there's a delay in bringing the prisoners over to Camp Echo. Once, we had to wait five hours on the bus. Naturally, this frustrates the attorneys, considering the time, money, and weeks of work they've spent preparing. And the ice cream we've brought turns to soup.

At the end of our visit with Ali Shah Mousovi, our military escort drove Peter and me and another group of attorneys to the Navy Exchange. Adjacent to this large supermarket are a Subway, a gift shop, and ATM machines. Across the street are a KFC and a McDonald's. At the exchange, we picked up a stack of porterhouse steaks, charcoal, potatoes, chips, lots of beer, and assorted wines. Everyone barbecues for dinner because, unless you head for the Clipper Club, there's nowhere and nothing to eat on the leeward side.

Over a steak dinner that night, I commented on how nice our military escorts were, that they joked and laughed with us. One of them had given me pointers on pool in the CBQ lobby. Everyone brought them beer and cigarettes. I had expected them to be more aloof, even hostile.

But Tom Wilner, a partner with the Washington, D.C., office of Shearman and Sterling, was having none of it. "Yeah, they're nice," he retorted. "But this whole place is evil."

His words hit me hard. Tom was one of the most passionate lawyers working at Guantánamo. He would get angry talking about the conditions under which the detainees lived, reminding us that most of them were held in isolation in metal cells, separated by thick steel mesh or concrete walls. Each cell was fifty-six square feet. Many of the lawyers compared it to something slightly larger than a king-size mattress. That tiny space held a concrete bed and a steel toilet.

And in the cells, every man ate every meal alone. Sometimes prisoners were allowed out just two or three times a week for about fifteen minutes to exercise, often in the middle of the night. Many never saw sunlight for months at a time.

"It's naïve for us to think that evil is committed only by people who appear like monsters or ogres," Tom said. "Guantánamo is evil. It's a place where men have been imprisoned for more than five years without charge and without any sort of fair hearing on the basis of only the flimsiest of allegations."

Tom and his firm took on the representation of twelve Kuwaiti detainees in March 2002, after a group of families contacted him. At first, like most of the lawyers, Tom took the cases because of the legal principle at stake. But when he was finally allowed to meet his detainee-clients in January 2005, his attitude changed.

"I was no longer fighting just for disembodied legal principles but for real people who had suffered," he said. "The case changed for me, from one purely of principle to one of human suffering, with individuals counting on me to protect them and give them a fair chance to show their innocence."

He said he didn't know whether any of his twelve clients were guilty or innocent, only that they were entitled to a fair hearing. "When I got to meet them, and after talking with them, I realized that most of these guys were totally innocent and had been swept up simply by mistake."

I thought of Ali Shah Mousovi when he said that. Even the presiding officer at Mousovi's hearing had declared that he found it "difficult to believe" that the United States had imprisoned Mousovi and flown him "all the way to Cuba." He had spent so much time away from his family and country. Was it because he had been swept up simply by mistake?

One of the things Tom hated most was having to tell his clients that a close relative had died while they were detained. But he'd had to do it countless times: Fouad al-Rabiah's father and brother had died; Omar Amin's father had died; Nasser al-Mutairi's father had died; Saad al-Azmi's father had died; Khaled al-Mutairi's father had died; Fawzi al-Odah's grandmother had died.

"I can't describe how difficult it is to convey that news," he said. "The way they've been treated and what they've had to suffer makes me ashamed. It brings shame on our country."

The attorneys took their frustration out on the iguanas on the base—those "bastard" lizards. The U.S. government claimed that because Guantánamo detainees were foreigners outside of U.S. jurisdiction, they could be denied rights under U.S. law. But the lawyers quickly discovered that even the iguanas in Guantánamo were protected by a U.S. law, the Endangered Species Act. An iguana that wandered off the base into Cuba was soon eaten, but the iguanas at Guantánamo were protected. Anyone, including any federal official, who hurts an iguana can be prosecuted. The prisoners at Guantánamo are entitled to fewer protections than an iguana. This annoyed the lawyers so much that Tom brought it to the attention of the U.S. Supreme Court, and at oral argument, Justice David Souter pointed it out in response to the government's arguments.

That first night I was in Guantánamo, Tom was impassioned, going on about the face of evil, how normal it looks, how so many of the men who perpetrated some of the worst crimes in history—Hitler, Stalin, Pol Pot—had been men who appeared perfectly ordinary, who were kind to children and dogs.

CHAPTER FOUR

THE OLD MAN

Haji Nusrat Khan, detainee No. 1009, is Guantánamo Bay's oldest prisoner. Except he's not sure exactly how old he is: no one recorded births back when he was born. "I do not know the year," he told me. "But I am eighty. Or perhaps I am seventy-eight." Who knows?

When I first met him at Camp Echo, I found it hard to imagine how this old man could be a threat to U.S. national security or a global terrorist. A stroke fifteen years earlier had left him paralyzed and bedridden; he was still unable to stand up without assistance. When he needed to go to the bathroom, he hobbled slowly, leaning heavily on a walker.

His hugely swollen legs and feet were tightly cuffed and shackled to the floor. He told me that his shoes were too tight, and he needed new ones. He couldn't see well either, but the eyeglasses he'd been given didn't really help much; they were the wrong prescription. He'd asked for medical attention for the inflammation in his legs, as well as a list of other ailments, but he had yet to be taken to a hospital.

In our first meeting with him, as I tried to introduce myself and Peter, he interrupted me often, like a grumpy old uncle. He craned his neck and peered at me. *"Bachai,"* he said. "My child. I can't hear you over this fan." I jumped up and turned it off.

As I sat back down, I took the lids off the cups we'd brought and handed him one. "It's chai," I said.

"Does it have milk in it?" he asked. "My stomach isn't good with milk."

"I think it's soy milk," I replied.

"What is that?" he asked.

"It means it's not milk from a cow; it's made from beans, a plant," I said. "So, it should be okay on your stomach." I found myself talking louder and louder.

"I cannot hear you, *bachai,*" he said, suddenly deaf again. "Turn off this machine, this air-conditioning. It's making too much noise." He waved his hand in the air.

I turned the air off, and we went back to the chai issue. He seemed confused by the concept of soy milk.

"Well, I'll drink it since you brought it," he said, looking into the cup and taking a sip. The chai seemed to pass muster.

I introduced Peter and explained that he was a lawyer who had come to help him. Nusrat interrupted to ask whether Peter worked for the U.S. government. Before Peter could respond, he added that he couldn't afford a lawyer.

"I am a poor man," Nusrat said. "We Afghans, we are not like the Arabs here who have money."

Peter Ryan was the first lawyer to visit an Afghan detainee. The attorneys for Arab detainees at Guantánamo had been visiting their clients for an entire year before any of the Afghans got representation. This was partly because the families of wealthy Arab prisoners immediately sought out American lawyers when their sons and brothers went missing. A lot of the Afghan detainees had also learned that the families of Kuwaiti prisoners had been paying Shearman and Sterling's hefty legal bills instead of accepting pro bono representation. While the Kuwaiti families insisted on paying so that they could feel more in control of legal decisions, it created confusion among the Afghans. Many of the prisoners who came from less affluent families speculated that lawyers only helped the rich.

"I don't want my family to go into debt paying for a fancy American lawyer because of me," Nusrat grumbled. "I thought only Arabs got lawyers because they have money, and the *ghareeb*—poor prisoners—don't get lawyers."

Peter explained that Dechert was a private corporate law firm with no ties to the U.S. government and that he was working pro bono. There was no need to worry about legal fees.

Nusrat had a long, straggly white beard and grayish brown eyes that drifted from Peter's face to mine as we spoke about the legal issues and tried to explain what a habeas corpus petition was. He interrupted Peter mid-sentence to turn to me.

"*Bachai*," he said. "Why are you sitting on the edge of the chair like this? Sit back in your chair."

I realized that I looked tense, so I leaned back in my plastic chair. He smiled and gestured for us to drink our tea. Then, he told me that I needed to spend time in the mountains of Afghanistan to improve my dialect. I should go live with his family for a few months, he insisted. Then, he asked me whether my parents were still living and how many brothers and sisters I had.

Every now and then during the meeting, Nusrat would catch me adjusting my shawl. I wanted to make sure that I was covered properly since I assumed that he was used to seeing only very conservatively dressed women in Afghanistan. He squinted at me.

"You are like a daughter to me, and I want you to look at me like a father or grandfather," he said, nodding his head. "Don't worry so much, and relax, *bachai*."

"*Dera manana*, Baba—Thank you very much, Father. That's kind of you," I replied. While it's typical of Afghans to familiarize with each other quickly, I also sensed that he was particularly trying to reach out to me.

Haji Nusrat Khan was from a small mountainous village in Sarobi, forty-five miles east of Kabul. He could neither read nor write. He had ten children and didn't know whether his wife was still alive; he hadn't received any letters from home. During our meeting, his emotions swung erratically between frustration and fear, amusement and despair. At times, he seemed resigned to his predicament, and at others he unleashed sudden tirades against the injustice of his captivity. Sometimes he laughed, and at other times he was obviously irritated that no one would listen to his story.

"*Bachai*, look at my white beard," he said to me. "They have brought me here with a white beard. I have done nothing at all. I have not said a single word against the Americans."

Nusrat had insisted on his innocence from the beginning. But I could sense that his hopes for release had faded over the years. He didn't want to die in prison, he sighed, for a crime he had not committed.

Nusrat's troubles began in early 2003, a few days after he went to the U.S. authorities to complain about the arrest of his son Izatullah (who was also detained at Guantánamo Bay). The Americans had accused his son of having ties to al-Qaeda and for harboring a cache of weapons. When Nusrat complained that his son had done nothing wrong and should be released, U.S. soldiers paid a visit to his home. They told him that he should come with them; they needed to speak to him, and they would bring him back home that evening.

Instead, they tied him up, blindfolded him, and drove him to Bagram Air Force Base. There, he said, he suffered countless humiliations. He found it hard to talk about the abuse. The Americans took away his crutches and pushed him to the toilet in a cart, he said. Once, he was forced to take off all his clothes in front of a female soldier as an interpreter explained that he was to bathe while she stood guard. He hesitated before telling us about his beatings at the hands of the Americans. During one beating, he fell to the floor and injured his arm. He was frequently ordered to hold out his arms for great lengths of time. When he couldn't hold them up any longer, his captors found other ways to bring him discomfort. U.S. soldiers tied him tightly to a wooden plank, which they used as a means of transporting him. One time, he said, two soldiers tied him to the board and left him lying on the ground for some time. One of the soldiers finally glanced down at him from a chair and asked how he was doing. When the interpreter translated, Nusrat began to laugh.

"You must be an idiot to ask me this," he said. "I am a paralyzed old man, and you have tied me like a dog. I'm lying on the floor, and you are sitting in a chair. Look at me. How do you think I am doing? Why are you even asking me this?"

It was hard to keep track of time at Bagram. He was regularly blindfolded and couldn't tell whether it was day or night.

He thought he had spent about forty days at the airbase before he was tied up again, forced to wear special black goggles to prevent him from seeing, and flown to Guantánamo Bay.

When Peter asked for additional details about his torture, Nusrat shook his head. It was a humiliating episode, he said. He had already said enough.

After I met with other detainees, I realized that many are reluctant to talk about torture. Most of them believe that the military eavesdrops on attorney-client meetings, so they're afraid to speak about their captors. But I know that many, like Haji Nusrat, are reluctant to give details because it's uncomfortable to remember being stripped naked, beaten, and tortured. It forces the men to relive the shame and humiliation.

One detainee, who was released in November 2006, said that U.S. soldiers at Guantánamo "put their fingers inside" him. His eyes welled when he talked about it. It wasn't for a medical reason or to see whether he was hiding something, he said, because they did it at least fifteen or sixteen times, maybe more. "There was no purpose for this," he said, "other than to degrade Muslim men."

This detainee said he endured multiple full cavity searches and was forced to strip while female soldiers watched him.

Some of the lawyers told me they believed it was something that happened to all the prisoners at Guantánamo Bay but most were too ashamed to admit it.

But Haji Nusrat said that being at Guantánamo beat Bagram by a long shot.

"Bagram was very, very bad," he said. "The soldiers here, maybe they have a shred of humanity."

Nusrat was happy to be reunited at Gitmo with his son Izatullah. For a time, father and son were together at Camp 4. But Nusrat was upset when soldiers came unexpectedly one day and took Izatullah off to Camp 5, the maximum-security prison that he says is notorious for prisoner abuse. We do not know why he was taken there. "Men go insane there—crazy," he told us.

Nusrat waited daily for the soldiers to bring Izatullah back, but it was ten long months before he saw his son. And when Izatullah returned, he wasn't well. He'd been kept alone in the dark for almost a year. The old man gestured toward his head and said that his son was suffering from mental problems because of the prolonged isolation at Camp 5.

"They gave him medicine for his brain, so he can find peace," he said.

The details of the U.S. case against the old man remained murky even at his 2004 combatant status review tribunal hearing. Like Dr. Ali Shah Mousovi, Haji Nusrat was pleased that he was finally going to have a trial. But unlike Mousovi, Nusrat, an illiterate old man from the mountains of Afghanistan, didn't try to articulate points or show respect for the officers at his hearing. As soon as he was shackled into his plastic chair and the instructions for the proceeding were read to him, he interrupted to say that he wanted to make a few comments. Then, he plunged ahead before the tribunal could object or agree.

"We asked our Great God and finally there is a tribunal!" he boomed, looking through milky eyes at the military officers seated before him. "You are smart people. You know that I have been paralyzed for the past seventeen or eighteen years. I could not even stand up, but you brought me here as an enemy combatant. You should think to yourselves, how could I be an enemy combatant if I cannot stand up?"

"We have some administrative issues to go through here," the tribunal president said, cutting him off. "There will be a place in the hearing for more comments."

"Okay. I will not interfere again," Nusrat grumbled, "but all I wanted to say is that we were not against the government of Afghanistan, and we were not against the government of America."

The panel ignored his statements and asked whether he wanted to swear an oath to tell the truth.

"Lying is against my religion," he retorted. "I am very close to my grave at this age. I will not lie to you in any matter."

The panel accused Nusrat of supporting a terrorist organization in Afghanistan called Hezb-Islami-Gulbadin (HIG), which is alleged to have ties to Osama bin Laden. He was also accused of possessing a cache of weapons.

Izatullah, who testified as a witness at the hearing, maintained that the weapons were in a storehouse set up by the Afghan defense ministry that he had been paid to guard and maintain. The ten-year Soviet occupation of Afghanistan had left behind large amounts of uncollected heavy armaments, Izatullah explained. Following the ouster of the Russians, tribal feuds and civil strife were rampant. After the Taliban fell, the United Nations launched the Afghanistan New Beginnings Program to help President Hamid Karzai's defense ministry implement nationwide disarmament. Under this arms collection program, weapons were gathered from the people and placed in warehouses for storage. It was one of these storehouses that the Karzai government paid him to guard, Izatullah insisted.

Nusrat swore by Allah and "my gray beard" that this was the truth. If anyone could prove otherwise, he said, "I will allow you to sacrifice all of my children."

The panel, apparently unimpressed, read off another charge: Nusrat was "a primary coordinator" for the HIG in Sarobi, and the HIG leadership had plotted to kidnap coalition force members and use them as hostages to be exchanged for Nusrat.

Nusrat demanded to face his accusers, but the panel informed him that their names were classified and could not be revealed.

The weapons cache was brought up again, and Nusrat went into a frustrated tirade. "Yes, I had these weapons in my possession, but I told you that they belonged to the Afghan government, and I had all the numbers," he fumed. "To ensure the security of these weapons, the government of Afghanistan gave my son fifty men to guard the weapons, with salary and meals."

"How can I be a *dushman jangee*—an enemy combatant?" Nusrat demanded, reminding the panel of his paralysis. Finally, he insisted that it was the United States that had betrayed the Afghans.

"While we defeated the Russians, you didn't help us," he asserted. "You turned your backs on us and left. The people of Afghanistan are like your children. You don't leave your children and turn away from them. You are our leaders."

Nusrat insisted that all the accusations against him had probably been brought by some "shameless" Afghan enemy who had sold him to the Americans for a large bounty. He maintained that he and his family had fully supported the Americans and the Karzai administration and had hoped that the United States would bring peace and help rebuild his country.

While he languished in Guantánamo, he said, another son, Abdul Wahid, was fully embracing America's democracy initiative in Afghanistan. The twenty-seven-year-old had been elected a parliamentary representative in the 2005 United Nations–backed National Assembly and Provincial Council elections, Afghanistan's first democratic voting in decades.

Not long after his hearing, Nusrat was classified an enemy combatant.

Peter and I had brought the old man some lunch—pizza, pistachios, baklava. He was grateful, but he was tired of the bland American way of cooking. He wanted meat or fish. He asked us to bring him something with spices. I promised to make him some *kabali pillau*, a popular rice-and-lamb dish, and lamb chops if he was still there when we came back.

I cracked open some pistachios and handed them to him as we discussed his case. He took a few sips of the chai and told me that he preferred his tea with crushed *lachi*, or cardamom.

Every now and then, he would look at me and say, "*Bachai*, you should come spend time in the mountains of Afghanistan so your Pashto dialect improves."

This quickly became a running joke between us. Sometimes he would get frustrated with me for not knowing enough about the history of Afghanistan.

"What kind of Pashtun girl are you? How can you not know about Bacha Khan; he was the leader of the Pashtuns," he snapped, raising his bushy gray eyebrows. "You need to spend time in Afghanistan with my family. We will fix you."

He grinned broadly when I promised to visit Afghanistan as soon as he was released.

Some off-duty guards at the Clipper Club told me their pet name for Nusrat: they called him "Speedy" because he hobbled at such a snail's pace with his walker.

When Peter asked him about his health, it opened a Pandora's box.

Nusrat had become very ill two years earlier, while in Camp 4. His legs started deteriorating badly, and although a military doctor treated him, the elderly man was not satisfied with his medical care.

"He gave me just six pills, and I asked for more," he said. "They never give enough medicine to heal, only enough so I don't die," he said. "They diagnose your problem but never make it better."

He also had digestive problems and complained of constant swelling in his legs. He was given pain killers, but the medicine upset his stomach, so he only took it when he couldn't stand the pain.

As Peter took notes and asked questions about his hearings, the elderly man extended his trembling hands, offering us some of the pistachios and almonds we had brought for him.

As the meeting wound down, Nusrat seemed tired. We couldn't engage him on legal issues. He asked why no journalists had been allowed to come to Guantánamo. He wanted the world to know his story. Then, he asked me what I was studying in school. When I said I was in my last year of law school, he smiled and nodded. "Inshallah—God willing—you will be a lawyer," he said.

Then, he asked about my marital status. When I told him I was single, he seemed to find it incomprehensible. "Bachai, why aren't you married? Don't ruin yourself," he said. I smiled when he said that. While my parents rarely pushed the issue, it was something I was familiar with. There's a preoccupation with marriage in the East, particularly in rural areas and particularly for girls, whose social and economic well-being is linked to finding a husband. Most Afghan women don't work, and marriage is their only ticket to a life outside of their father's home. They marry very young too—sometimes in their mid-teens. So, as I was in my late twenties, Haji Nusrat likely thought I was an old maid and worried that I was destined for a childless life of celibacy.

Peter turned the subject to filing petitions and the length of time court proceedings might take. Nusrat's mood changed again, this time to one of despair. He stopped eating pistachios and gazed at Peter's face as he spoke.

"Allah has made you a very handsome man," he said to Peter. "You are also a great man. May Allah make you even greater." Then, he promised he'd make Peter a famous lawyer and bring him endless business if he helped him get home. "Everyone in Afghanistan will know your name," he pleaded.

As I translated, I felt a lump growing in my throat. Suddenly, I couldn't speak. Peter and Nusrat watched as the tears dripped onto my shawl.

The old man looked at me. "You are a daughter to me," he said. "Think of me as a father and pray for me, *bachai*." I nodded, aligning and realigning pistachio shells on the table as I translated.

As the meeting ended, it was obvious that the old man was in pain. His legs hurt, and he tried to stand and stretch them. He pushed hard against the tabletop with his palms, trying to lift his weight. I leapt to his side and helped him stand. He gripped the edge of the table for balance and exhaled deeply.

A few moments later, I helped him sit back down. As we started collecting our things to go, I turned back to Nusrat, who was watching us gather up the pizza boxes and pistachio shells and unfinished baklava. The military didn't allow any food to be left with the detainee, so we had to take any leftovers with us.

"*Bachai*, tell your mother and your father that an old man with a white beard sends his salaams," he said.

I responded with the customary reply: "*Walaikum assalaam*—And may peace also be upon you."

I adjusted my shawl one last time and glanced at him. He was quiet for a moment. Then, he opened his heavy arms to me, and I embraced him. He pushed my head into his white prison uniform and for several moments prayed for me as Peter watched: "Inshallah—God willing—you will find a home that makes you happy. Inshallah, you will be a mother one day. Inshallah, you will always have a family that will protect you. Inshallah, you will finish law school and continue to help us. Inshallah, you will make the world proud."

Then, he patted my back. "You are a great woman, and may Allah make you greater," he said.

Finally, he let me go and asked me to say *du'a*—prayers—for him.

"Of course," I promised. "Every day."

And until the next time I saw him, I did.

CHAPTER FIVE

BIG BOUNTIES

Before I got involved with Guantánamo, I had no opinion about whether the detainees there were guilty or innocent; I just thought they all deserved a fair hearing and due process. But after I met some and talked to them, and after I read their files, I came to believe that many, perhaps even most, were, as Tom Wilner had put it, innocent men who'd been swept up by mistake.

I really became convinced when I found out about the bounties.

Many of the men I met insisted that they'd been sold to the United States. During the war after September 11, the U.S. military air-dropped thousands of leaflets across Afghanistan, promising between $5,000 and $25,000 to anyone who would turn in members of the Taliban and al-Qaeda. Considering that the per capita income in Afghanistan in 2006 was $300, or 82 cents a day, that's like hitting the jackpot. The median income for each American household was $26,036 in 2006.¹ If a bounty system of equal proportions were offered to Americans, it would be worth $2.17 million. The average American and the average Afghan would have to work for eighty-three years to make that kind of money. One particularly disingenuous leaflet offered Afghan locals up to a whopping $5 million.

Of course, offering large sums as bounty doesn't violate any international laws. But when the result is a pattern of hundreds of men being randomly sold into captivity and then held without due process on the basis of flimsy allegations made by people who benefited financially, it's at the very least cause for concern—and a second look.

The Department of Defense (DOD) has said it was unaware of any sort of bounty being paid for prisoners. Here are two of the leaflets:

GET WEALTH AND
POWER BEYOND
YOUR DREAMS ·
HELP THE ANTI-
TALIBAN FORCE
RID AFGHANISTAN
OF MURDERERS
AND TERRORISTS

FRONT

"Get wealth and power beyond your dreams.
Help the Anti-Taliban Gorces rid Afghanistan
of murderers and terrorists"

YOU CAN RECEIVE MILLIONS OF DOLLARS
FOR HELPING THE ANTI-TAILBAN FORCE
CATCH AL-QAIDA AND TALIBAN MURDERERS
THIS IS ENOUGH MONEY TO TAKE CARE OF
YOUR FAMILY, YOUR VILLAGE, YOUR TRIBE
FOR THE REST OF YOUR LIFE ·
PAY FOR LIVESTOCK AND DOCTORS
AND SCHOOL BOOKS AND HOUSING FOR
ALL YOUR PEOPLE

Bounty leaflet 1 in English.

Bounty leaflet 2, front and backside, in Pashto and Dari. (English translation: Up to $5 million will be awarded for providing information about the whereabouts and/or capture of Taliban and al-Qaeda leaders.)

Then defense secretary Donald Rumsfeld told reporters in late 2001 that leaflets were dropping across Afghanistan "like snowflakes in December in Chicago."

Afghanistan has been a country of deep-seated, relentless conflict for generations. Here, in the United States, with our rule of law and live-and-let-live traditions, we can't understand the complex animosities, based on tribal affiliation and religious, ideological, and political differences, that might lead one Afghan to turn another in. Territorial feuds over land are common. Throw large monetary rewards into the mix, and the result could easily be a lot of false reports—and wrongful detentions.

Afghan warlords and locals went for the bait. But they weren't the only ones. The hefty bounties also created an extensive black market for abductions in Pakistan. That's where many detainees' road to Guantánamo began—specifically with Pakistan's notoriously unscrupulous Inter-Services Intelligence.

When the United States began bombing in late 2001, thousands of Afghans fled to neighboring Pakistan. The Pakistani police, border guards, and locals, all eager to get their hands on large sums of cash, seized hundreds of men. It was big business. Pakistani president Pervez Musharraf even bragged about it in his memoir, *In the Line of Fire*.

"We have earned bounties totaling millions of dollars," he wrote, admitting that his agents had handed over 369 men to the U.S. military in exchange for Central Intelligence Agency (CIA) "prize money." When he got a lot of flak for his published admissions, Musharraf quickly backtracked. Subsequent editions of his book have dropped this mention of the 369 men and CIA prize money.

According to Amnesty International reports, two-thirds of the men who landed in Guantánamo were picked up in

Pakistan, where many were "groomed" in local jails to grow out their beards and look more like Taliban before being sold to the U.S. military.

Arabs in particular became a valuable commodity and an opportunity for profit. They stood out and were easily rounded up. Tom Wilner told me that none of the Kuwaitis at Guantánamo had been captured on any battlefield; they weren't even accused of engaging in any hostilities against the United States. His clients told him that they had been sold by Pakistanis or Afghan warlords.

Several Chinese Muslim detainees, known as Uighurs, told their attorney, Sabin Willett of Bingham and McCutchen, that they had been betrayed by Pakistanis. They had gone to Afghanistan for military training so that they could fight for independence from China. When U.S. warplanes started bombing Afghanistan, they, along with many others, fled to the Pakistani border, where locals welcomed them.

"They killed a sheep and cooked the meat and we ate," Adel Abdul-Hakim told Willett. Then, that night, Hakim said, they were driven to a local prison and, from there, handed over to the U.S. military.

Theoretically, a bounty program for terrorism suspects could be effective—if there were an actual investigation to determine who was al-Qaeda and who had been swept up inadvertently. But the U.S. military conducted no investigations.

"America is a strong, powerful country," Haji Nusrat Khan told me. "I know that my own people turned me in for money, but the Americans can find anything out. They should have investigated these wrongly made accusations about me."

I don't believe that the military arrested and detained innocent men maliciously. I know that September 11 sparked great fear and that the military is charged with protecting U.S. national security. But in pursuit of that goal, the U.S. government abandoned the most fundamental legal principles and failed to conduct the most basic inquiries. Supreme Court Justice Louis Brandeis once said that the most insidious threats to liberty come from well-meaning people of zeal who act without understanding. There was a lot of zeal after September 11. In keeping Guantánamo Bay in operation, the DOD has dismissed the notion that innocent men may have been sold and brought there. Rumsfeld called the Guantánamo detainees there "the worst of the worst." White House officials echoed his sentiments and said that the detainees had been trained to lie based on al-Qaeda manuals.

But in response to an Associated Press lawsuit brought in March 2006 under the Freedom of Information Act, the Pentagon was forced to declassify information pertaining to the detainees. The numbers tell another story. A statistical analysis of DOD documents relating to 517 current and former Guantánamo detainees shows that only 5 percent of the detainees had been captured as a result of U.S. intelligence work. The report, by Seton Hall law professor Mark Denbeaux and his son, attorney Joshua Denbeaux, also shows that 86 percent of the prisoners at Guantánamo were captured not by American forces but by Pakistani police and Afghan warlords at a time when the U.S. military was passing out cash rewards for turning over al-Qaeda and Taliban suspects.

Some of the detainees were accused and seized because they owned a Kalashnikov. That's actually fairly common in

Afghanistan. The report also found that detainees were commonly held because they stayed at guesthouses in Afghanistan or wore Casio watches, which were thought to be used by al-Qaeda to detonate bombs.

Afghan detainee Abdul Matin was a science teacher who was arrested wearing a Casio watch. Matin thought someone was having a good laugh as they wrote up reasons to hold him. At his combatant status review tribunal, the military asked him to explain his "possession of the infamous Casio watch."

Matin admitted that he had one—just as women, children, and old men in Afghanistan and elsewhere do. But he argued that wearing an ordinary black plastic watch didn't make him a terrorist. Many of the guards at Guantánamo wore the same watch.

The Denbeaux study concluded that the vast majority of detainees aren't connected to al-Qaeda, and most aren't even accused of engaging in hostilities against the United States. When I read it, I thought about many of the men I had met. No doubt there are some terrorists at Gitmo. But it's just as likely that there are good and innocent people. They've all been swept together without due process. Because there were no investigations, most of Guantánamo's men are being held in a stateless black hole, an eerie Neverland where American laws and justice don't exist. They've been presumed guilty without having a fair shot at proving their innocence. They're numbered and kept away from journalists, while the Bush administration touts them collectively to the media as treacherous monsters and bomb makers.

I've encountered a few individuals who believe that, given the political climate, this is not the time to adhere to legal principles. We're engaged in a war on terrorism, and the United States has been threatened by an unconventional enemy. For these reasons, they say, constitutional laws shouldn't apply to Guantánamo detainees.

But the idea that due process and fair hearings go out the window when we are afraid of something or feel threatened erodes the essence of constitutional safeguards. Yet, such an erosion has stained U.S. history before. In times of war, threats to national security become the basis for abandoning the cornerstone principles enshrined in our constitution.

During World War II, which generated its share of fear and hysteria, more than one hundred thousand Japanese Americans suspected of espionage were taken from their homes, fired from their jobs, and detained in what President Franklin Roosevelt then called concentration camps. Not a single Japanese American was ever charged with or convicted of spying or committing any act of hostility toward the United States.

When Japanese American Fred Korematsu refused to relocate to one of Roosevelt's detention centers, he was arrested by the Federal Bureau of Investigation and subsequently convicted in federal court. In *Korematsu v. United States*, Korematsu took his case challenging the legality of the president's wartime policy to the Supreme Court. In a sharply divided 6–3 decision, the Court upheld Korematsu's conviction in late 1944. The majority opinion, written by Justice Hugo Black, rejected Korematsu's discrimination argument and upheld the government's right to put Japanese American citizens in detention camps due to the wartime emergency. The Court's reasoning echoes the rhetoric the Bush administration uses to justify its actions today: We are at war with an enemy who threatens our national security.

Today, the *Korematsu* case is viewed as a sad blemish on the history of the U.S. Supreme Court. I was taught that it represented everything the high court should not do: allow pressure and fear to strip people of their legal and human rights.

But history repeats itself. Many of the Guantánamo detainees were taken from their families and homelands, many from their own beds at night, brought halfway around the world, tortured, and held in secret, without charge or trial. The Guantánamo cases raise lasting and fundamental questions about America's willingness to abide by its principles and adhere to the rule of law, especially when under threat. Not long before he died in March 2005, Fred Korematsu filed another brief before the U.S. Supreme Court, this time on behalf of hundreds of Muslims being held at Guantánamo Bay, Cuba.

I wrote about my first trip to Guantánamo, and my feelings of shame when I met a pediatrician and an eighty-year-old paraplegic who asked me why the United States hid him from the world and from journalists, in an article for the *Washington Post* that was reprinted in newspapers around the world. I received an outpouring of e-mails from readers. Of nine hundred messages, about twenty were hate mail. One reader suggested that I might be working for "the enemy." Another told me that I was being duped by al-Qaeda manual-reading terrorists. But the vast majority of responses were from regular Americans who felt just as deceived by our country's actions as I did.

Shortly after the story ran, I received an unpleasant phone call from the Pentagon telling me that I was being banned from the base. I was upset. I'd been extremely careful only to publish information that had been reviewed and declassified by the government. I'd also been careful not to violate the protective order of military base rules governing Guantánamo Bay, which I'd been required to sign. I knew I hadn't done anything wrong, but I wasn't sure how to handle the situation.

I received a flurry of e-mails from various habeas attorneys advising me to do different things. Many suggested that I hire an independent attorney and file a lawsuit. I decided not to fan the flames and instead to call the Pentagon official back and ask him why I had been banned. I got a voicemail the first time and left a message asking for an explanation. Then, I decided it would be better to have a written record, so I e-mailed and called again.

Essentially, I was told that my base privileges had been revoked because my *Washington Post* article had created a security and safety threat to the base, as well as to the individuals who worked and lived there. I was told that I was in violation of the protective order I had signed because I had published a photograph of the sun rising over the hills in Guantánamo and because I had printed the name and photograph of a military escort.

I knew there was no protective order violation; several attorneys had helped me comb through the entire document. Furthermore, my photograph of the Guantánamo landscape could not have been any more of a security threat than any of the real-time Internet satellite and aerial photos of the base. I think DOD officials were just looking for a reason to ban me because of the negative publicity the article generated.

This began a two-month-long back-and-forth of negotiations via e-mail and telephone. Once, I tried joking with the DOD guys, telling them that in the spirit of the giving season (it was Christmas), they should reconsider their position. I'm not sure what finally convinced them, but eventually, I was instructed to write and sign a statement saying that I would not photograph the base or military personnel. I also apologized profusely for creating a security threat by publishing a Gitmo soldier's photo. And I promised never to bring a camera onto the base. I said whatever I had to get my privileges back. But I also pointed out a recent article in a scuba diving magazine that included lots of photos of some of the camp's X-ray guards, complete with their full names in the captions.

On June 8, 2006, base commander Adm. Harry Harris wrote me a long letter. It was on DOD letterhead, and it was harsh. It scared me. But at the same time, I felt that it was a kind of honor to have been reprimanded by the Gitmo base commander. I knew I hadn't violated the protective order as they claimed, but I'm thankful that I hadn't been accused of wearing a Casio watch or staying in a guesthouse.

I had the letter framed and hung it in my bathroom, right above the toilet.

CHAPTER SIX

THE GOATHERD

I know it's not good to play favorites, but I couldn't help it. Of all the detainees we worked with, I most looked forward to the meetings with Taj Mohammad. Taj, No. 902, was a twenty-seven-year-old goatherd from Kunar, Afghanistan, who formed crushes on his female interrogators and had taught himself perfect English in his four years at Guantánamo.

It's not that I liked Taj better than the other detainees. They're all different. But he was easy to talk to, and he made me laugh. I felt sorry for Haji Nusrat, who was old and sick, and for Ali Shah Mousovi because he was so polite. But Taj was my age and loaded with personality. Unlike the others, he rarely came across as vulnerable. He was highly opinionated and very sarcastic. Even his misogyny was somehow comical. I'm sure he would have gotten on my nerves if I'd spent more time listening to his sarcastic wisecracks, but in our limited contact he was pure entertainment.

In our meetings with Paul Rashkind of the Miami Federal Defenders, Taj's attention was always drawn to written English. He would sound out the lettering on coffee cups and napkins, and when legal papers were put on the table, he would immediately start reading under his breath.

He asked us repeatedly to bring him a Pashto-English dictionary so that he could improve his English. Over several months, he had compiled and memorized a list of almost one thousand English words. But during a routine search, the guards had found and confiscated his neatly written glossary.

When Paul told him it was unlikely that he'd be given permission to bring him a book, Taj looked unhappy.

"If you can't bring me a book, how do you plan on getting me out of here?" he said. "Even the interrogators give us magazines."

I asked what kind of magazines.

"*Playboy*," he said.

I'd heard the same from guards at the Clipper Club, who said that lots of detainees made associations between American women based on what they saw in the soft-core men's magazine *Maxim*.

Sometimes the guards helped that along, it seemed.

At the beginning of my second meeting with Taj, he pulled out a small piece of creased white paper and handed it to me. "I told the guards that the girl who speaks Pashto is coming, and I asked them to make a list of words so you could translate them for me," he said.

My jaw dropped as I scanned the list. "What does it say?" Taj asked. "Tell me."

The first word on the list was "bestiality." The second was "pedophile," the third was "intercourse," and the fourth was "horny."

"I think those soldiers have played a little trick on you and me," I smirked.

"Tell me," he persisted. "What did they write?"

"I don't know how to say these words in Pashto," I responded. "I learned Pashto from my parents."

Taj's eyes widened. "Okay, just tell me one of the words," he insisted.

"I don't know them," I said.

"Then, tell me what it means."

I scanned the words again.

"Bestiality means showing *meena*—affection or love—to one of those goats you tend," I said smiling. "But it's not a good sort of *meena*."

Taj let out a laugh. He got the picture. He grabbed a pen from the table and scribbled something in Pashto next to "bestiality." That's when I realized that he had probably known the nature of his vocabulary lessons all along.

Taj's command of English was amazing. When I later saw a May 24, 2006, letter he'd written to Paul, I thought he had to be a goat-herding genius. Or at least a highly educated goatherd. He sounded very American. His grammar and punctuation were perfect. He indented properly and started each sentence with a capital letter. He even underlined for emphasis.

Of course, I suppose it's also possible that one of the government interpreters helped him write the letter. Taj said he'd learned a lot of English from Abdul Salam Zaeef, an ambassador to the Taliban, when he was held in Camp 4. And he also practiced as much as he could with the guards.

Taj sent me a letter at one point, with a drawing of flowers and a poem. I'd share it, but the DOD wouldn't declassify any poetry or art for fear that it might contain coded messages for terrorists. The Pentagon did, however, allow one poem that Taj wrote in a letter to Paul to slip through.

> *The grass is green,*
> *My love is clean.*
> *The sky is blue,*
> *My love is true.*

The first time Paul and I met with Taj, he was sitting behind a long table. One leg was extended, and he was dressed in white, which meant that he was being held in Camp 4. He had longer hair than the other detainees and pushed it behind his ears to keep it out of his face.

He casually asked who paid Paul's salary and whether he was employed by the U.S. government. This is a tricky subject for federal public defenders to address. They must truthfully convey that although they work for the government, their decisions remain independent. Naturally, many detainees have a hard time accepting that someone can act in their best interests when they're being paid by the same government that's imprisoning them.

Paul worded his answer carefully, explaining what kind of law he practiced, who his regular clients were, and, above all, that he was in no way influenced by the U.S. government.

How are you my lawyer! I'm doing great and I hope you are too. looking Forward into meeting you. I have never met a paul before. When you receive this letter please let me know. Do you remember us talking about the book <u>Please</u> make sure you bring it with you. It's vital that I have this book please do not forget May God bless you my freind. and please give my regards to the interpreter girl. I made you flowers, but I don't have the girls flowers. cause I don't have her address.

Sincerely, Mr. Taji Muhammad

24 MAY 2006

THE grass is green
MY LOVE Is CLEAN
THE SKY IS BLUE
MY LOVE IS TRUE.

THANK
YOU,
PAUL

UNCLASSIFIED

Taj Mohammad's letter to Paul.

"I work for you," he said to Taj with a smile.

"What benefit is it for you to help me?" Taj asked suspiciously. "What do you get out of it?"

Paul explained that not all Americans agreed with the actions of their government and said that he wanted to help Taj receive a fair hearing and get him released one day.

Taj was having none of it. "You're really here because you want people to see you as a big lawyer who represented the famous Guantánamo detainees, right?" he said.

This back-and-forth continued for a while. It was difficult for Taj to conceive of why an American whose government had declared Guantánamo detainees a threat to U.S. national security would want to get involved.

"Is this going to help your business when you tell people you freed a man from Guantánamo?" he challenged Paul again.

Taj's quick wit and efforts to shock amused me. He didn't bother trying to be polite, like the other Afghans, and he didn't sugarcoat anything.

"I don't think a lawyer can get me out of here," he declared. "A lot of detainees have been released without the help of any attorney."

But he listened as Paul explained why it was beneficial to have an attorney. Without one, he would be hidden from the world, subject only to the U.S. military. "An attorney is like chicken soup," Paul said, looking for a metaphor. "It can help you to have one, and it's definitely not going to hurt you."

Finally, Taj relented and began to ask questions about his habeas petition.

"Is the judge on my case a man or a woman?"

"Your judge is a man."

Taj held two thumbs up and broke into a smile.

"What do you have against women?" I blurted. In spite of myself, I felt annoyed at his display of glee over not having a female judge.

"Nothing," he said. "I like women, but no one listens to a woman." And he gave me a grin.

Taj had been arrested in late 2002. Although he hadn't been formally charged, the U.S. military accused him of associating with the Taliban and al-Qaeda and of taking money to attack a U.S. base. Taj maintained that it was all nonsense. He was a goatherd on a mountain, and watching his goats took up all his time, he said.

Taj didn't believe that he'd been sold to the U.S. military by bounty hunters or political opponents. The real reason he was arrested and brought to Guantánamo, he said, was simple: he had a temper.

He told us his story. The houses in his village didn't have access to running water, and the U.S. military was trying to help out. His cousin, Ismael, was employed by the Americans and was responsible for setting up the waterlines.

"He gave every house in the village a water pipe, except mine," Taj said.

It was Ramadan, the month of fasting, and he had just returned from a short trip out of town. When his mother told him what had happened, Taj went to confront his cousin, whom he found smoking a cigarette. When he inquired about the water, Ismael curtly told him to ask the Americans about it.

The two started arguing and soon began fighting.

"I got a stick, and I beat him over head," Taj said. "His head started bleeding."

Villagers pulled the two men apart. Ismael shouted at his cousin, saying that he would have him reported to the Americans.

"He said he was going to make sure I was sent to Guantánamo," Taj told us. "Everyone heard him."

After the brawl, Taj walked home, not thinking much about Ismael's threats. But four days later, a group of Americans with Afghan interpreters came to his house late at night and woke him up. They questioned him about attacking his cousin. Then, they searched his house, tied his hands, and took him to the nearby military base, where he was put in a room for the night.

"I slipped my hands out of the cuffs and went to sleep," Taj said, smiling.

He figured Ismael would get over his anger and tell the U.S. soldiers to let him go the next day. When he woke up in the morning, he heard his cousin speaking with the Americans. He quickly slipped the cuffs back on and waited, expecting to be released.

Instead, he was taken to Bagram Air Force Base. From there, he was flown to Guantánamo. It was his first flight in an airplane.

"It was so bumpy, I felt more like I was riding on a donkey," he said jokingly.

Over the years, Taj told us, even Ismael had come to feel badly about Taj's ending up at Guantánamo. His cousin wrote to tell him that he regretted what had happened and that he wished Taj were home. Taj looked sad for a moment, telling us that.

We asked about his interrogations. He said that he was asked the same questions over and over. He described not being allowed to sleep for long periods. "You have no idea what it feels like not to sleep for over a week," he said, shaking his head. One soldier, though, felt badly about his sleep deprivation. "When it was her shift, she let me sleep the whole time," Taj said.

There was one interrogator at Guantánamo whom he particularly liked. Her name was Susie, he said, but he hadn't seen her in a while. "She left, I think. Now it's a girl named Mi-shal," he said.

"Michelle?" I asked.

"Yes, Mi-shal. She dances well."

I looked at him in confusion. "The guards had some music playing, and I saw her dance," he said. I never quite understood what that was all about.

Personally, I never bought into the goatherd story. Taj always came across as much more sophisticated than I'd imagined a goatherd to be. That said, I didn't think it mattered whether Taj was or wasn't a simple goatherd. The more important fact was that there was no evidence suggesting that he was al-Qaeda.

At a military hearing in 2003, he was accused of firing rocket-propelled grenades at the U.S. military base in Kunar in exchange for a pair of tennis shoes. Taj admitted that he owned a pair of tennis shoes, but he said he'd purchased them himself. In a separate charge, he stood accused of attacking the military base in exchange for twenty thousand kaldars, about $400.

The military also accused him of working with Afghan warlord Hekymatyar Gulbadin, of associating with the Taliban and al-Qaeda, and of being a member of Lashkar-i-Tayyiba, an organization reportedly based in Pakistan that trains insurgents to fight against the Indian army in the disputed Kashmir territory.

And he was further accused of being connected to the smuggling of explosives from Pakistan into Afghanistan and to attacks using improvised explosive devices on a U.S. air base.

But Taj insisted that he was only a goatherd.

"I am a nomad taking care of animals. That is all I do," he told the military panel. "I come from generations of animal caretakers. My father and grandfather did the same."

When the accusations were exhausted, the presiding officer turned to the subject of Taj's small skull cap—these are given to many of the detainees.

"Most detainees wear white hats," the officer said. "Is there some significance to your black hat? Does it mean that you are higher up in the organization?"

"No. I look nice in it. I have darker skin, and it matches the hat," Taj replied.

Finally, the panel asked him what he planned to do if he were released. He replied that he had initially planned on working for the Americans as an interpreter, but over the years in detention, he had changed his mind because the Americans had caused him too much grief.

"I will go back to my own way of living and keep my goats," he said.

"And stay away from your cousin," the presiding officer admonished.

Paul left the room briefly during our first meeting, and Taj immediately confronted me. "Why are you working with the Americans?" he asked.

I was shocked. I had thought the meeting was going well and that we had established a decent level of trust and rapport. At the same time, the detainees often confronted me about something whenever the lawyers I was with left the room. I suppose that because I spoke Pashto, they thought of me as an Afghan just like them, one of the tribe, so to speak. So, they wanted to talk to me about things they didn't always bring up with lawyers sitting in front of them. But I was struck by Taj's "us versus them" attitude and his inability to place me on either side. Or perhaps he had placed me on both.

"What are you talking about?" I replied. "He doesn't work for the military, and he's not an interrogator."

Taj looked at me with suspicion.

"There are people in America who think all of this is very wrong," I informed him. "He's a lawyer. Trust me, I wouldn't lie to you."

He thought for a minute. "Well, is he a good lawyer, or are there better lawyers I could have?" he asked finally.

"He's a good lawyer."

Taj was satisfied. Then, he asked me the question that I'd come to expect from all the detainees: "Are you married?"

Afghans are far more inquisitive about personal matters than Americans are. And the Afghans at Gitmo, or a few of them anyway, are shamelessly so. They'll ask lawyers their salaries, how much they have in savings, why they don't accept Islam, or whether they slept with their wives before marriage. Usually, when they directed personal questions at me, they asked me for permission to do so first, afraid that I might be offended. It's not proper to ask a girl in Afghanistan anything personal without her consent. Most of the detainees immediately asked about my family, where I was brought up, whether my parents were alive, and what they did for a living. They also often had an opinion about all of it.

When I said I wasn't married, Taj had the typical reaction. "Well, why not?" he asked. "I know someone just right for you in Kunar."

I rolled my eyes.

His wife, he told me, was fourteen when they got married.

"That's an eighth grader!" I exclaimed. "How old were you at the time?"

"Eighteen."

"That's very young," I said. He asked me how old I was.

"Twenty-seven."

"You'd better get married while you're young," he said. "If you wait till you're old, what good is that?"

At least he thought I was still young.

At 4:25 PM, a short young woman in tan fatigues and desert boots knocked on the door and stuck her head in. Her hair was pulled tight under her hat.

"You have five minutes remaining," she said in a high-pitched voice.

As soon as she closed the door, Taj started mimicking her in English.

"You have five minutes re-maii-ning," he said. "What has the world come to? In Afghanistan, I didn't listen to anyone. No one could tell me what to do. Now I have to take orders from a woman." He shook his head.

By our third meeting, however, he had softened his views a bit.

"I've decided that I want to marry an American woman," he said. "I want you to find me the right one."

"I have some cute friends," I said, going along.

"No, I'm serious, and I don't care about cute. Good looks are not as important as intelligence. I want a smart woman."

"One of my good friends is a lawyer and cute," I said, smiling.

"That's the type of woman I need," he said.

"What is she going to do while you're on the mountain looking after goats?"

"I'm serious. When I get out, you find me an American woman I can marry."

I wondered what he would say to his wife if I did.

When I saw Taj two months later, he was wearing tan, the color indicating noncompliance. After some prodding, he sheepishly said that a female medic had accused him of trying to touch her lips. He denied it, of course.

A few weeks before, on June 10, 2006, the Department of Defense had reported that three detainees had committed suicide by hanging themselves in their Camp 1 cells using clothing and bedsheets. Each had also reportedly left a suicide note in Arabic.

These were the first suicides at Guantánamo since detainees had been brought to the camp in 2002, and the drama raised questions among the detainees. Taj wanted to know where the men were buried and whether they had really committed suicide.

Not knowing the details of the autopsies at that time, we told him that the government was calling it suicide. Taj was glad to know that all three men had been flown home to their countries for burial.

Then, he told us that it would be impossible for one person, let alone three, to commit suicide by hanging given the strict rules and continuous surveillance at Gitmo. There was simply nothing to hang yourself from, he said. Many people had attempted suicide over the years, and it couldn't be done. "I tried to hang myself several times, and I'm alive," he told us. "I think the Americans killed those men."

"I don't know," Paul replied. "But why did you try to kill yourself? What happened?"

It was when he was being held among Arab detainees, Taj said. He couldn't communicate with anyone for months. The others didn't speak Pashto, and he didn't speak Arabic. It was a difficult time. Then, one day he got a letter from his mother. He hadn't learned to read or write yet, and there was no one in the adjacent cells who knew Pashto. So, he just stared at the letter and grew depressed. That's when he tried to hang himself. But the guards saw him on the security camera and came running immediately.

Taj was questioned about the suicide attempt the next day. The interrogator told him that if he began to feel suicidal again, he should contact him through the guards.

"But the next day, I called the bastard and said I was suicidal, but he never came." Taj burst into laughter.

Taj remembered the book he'd asked for. Paul told him that he had in fact found one, but it had to stay in his bag.

"If you can't give me the book, what good is it to me?" Taj demanded.

"I just wanted to show you that I brought this book for you, but I can't give it to you."

Taj was not amused. "How can you possibly help me get out of Guantánamo if you can't even give me a book?"

"You can read the book in Afghanistan," Paul said calmly. "I'll send it to you when you go home."

"I don't need your book when I go home. When I go home, I can buy my own book."

Taj seemed resentful, so to appease him, we spent the afternoon helping him with his English vocabulary. We asked him about the Gitmo "library" we'd heard rumors of.

"The library is a goddamn woman with a cardboard box of books on her head," he said dismissively. He said he'd looked the books over a long time ago, but recently he'd gotten into an argument with the book lady, so his privileges had been suspended.

"Who needs her books anyway," he said. "They are filled with pictures of dumb dogs."

Taj surprised me with a question out of nowhere. He wanted to know whether I was Muslim.

"Yes," I said.

"Do you eat pork?"

"No."

"Do you pray?"

"Yes."

"Five times daily?" he asked.

"No, but I pray sometimes," I said.

Taj wasn't convinced that I could be Muslim, having grown up in the United States, so he demanded that I recite a sura from the Qu'ran.

I started reciting Sura Fatiha, an easy one. It's the first sura they teach you in Sunday school at the mosque, and you can't pray without knowing it. I started zipping through it in Arabic.

"*Al-Hamdu lillahi Rabbil-Allah amin*—Praise be to God, lord of the worlds. The beneficent, the merciful."

"No, stop. Even a child knows that one," Taj interrupted. "Pick one that's not in the daily prayers at all."

That was hard. I'd had to memorize a lot in Sunday school, but that was more than ten years ago. I tried a short one and surprised myself by making it through a few verses. Taj nodded and corrected me as I went.

Then, he asked about my relationship with Paul.

"You're here with this man. Where do you sleep at night? In the same room, right?"

"No, no. I have my own room," I said.

He seemed mollified.

Paul brought along another attorney to our third meeting, and it seemed to unsettle Taj. He sized the newcomer up and summed up his feelings to me in Pashto under his breath.

"*Da yo harami dhey,*" he said.

The new lawyer asked what he'd said.

"He said, 'This one is a bastard,'" I translated, smiling.

The new attorney decided to see whether the goatherd story held water. He began to cross-examine Taj, who didn't like it one bit. How many goats did he have? What colors were they? What did they eat? Who watched them at night?

Taj responded but protested that he was being interrogated.

The lawyer ignored him and continued. Did he have any other animals?

"Yes, two dogs. And chickens."

"Chickens? Well, who watched the chickens while you were watching the goats?" the lawyer demanded.

"Who do you think watched the chickens?" Taj retorted, annoyed. "The women! Men don't watch chickens. What kind of questions are these?"

Paul and I just watched in astonishment as Taj turned the questioning on the lawyer.

"Are you married?" he demanded.

"Yes," the lawyer replied.

"How many children do you have?"

"We don't have any."

"Why not?"

The lawyer shifted in his seat. "Well, we tried, but we don't have any," he finally said.

"What do you do every night, just go straight to sleep? Your poor wife."

"I'm up working on your case," the lawyer said.

"No, you just started on my case. What have you been doing for the past fifteen years?"

There was no response.

"If I wasn't in here, I'd have twelve kids by now!" Taj exclaimed.

I don't think the two men really liked each other after that.

CHAPTER SEVEN

THE LAWYERS

I met as many lawyers as detainees at Guantánamo in similar rainbow assortment. The detainees all wore white, or if they were "noncompliant," tan or orange, but the attorneys sported even more colorful wardrobes, especially when the female lawyers donned headscarves.

Even in the 85-degree Caribbean sun, some of the male lawyers wore suits and ties to meet with their bearded Afghan or Arab clients. That's what they wore for all their other clients, these attorneys said; they believed that the Guantánamo detainees should be offered the same respect. The detainees knew what suits and ties signified; even the farmers and shopkeepers knew that those formal outfits were the uniform of important men who work in offices.

But most of the lawyers weren't so formal. Some wore T-shirts and zippered cargo pants. Most dressed business-casual in khakis and polo shirts. I developed my own uniform: a long skirt or pants with a white cotton wife-beater, all covered with a big shawl. The shawl was really just symbolic modesty because you could still see locks of hair that slipped out when I'd be balancing baklava, *kabali pillau*, and Pepsi in my arms.

There were more than five hundred habeas attorneys from assorted law practices representing Guantánamo Bay prisoners pro bono. They came from all over the United States and even a few from England. Almost 80 percent were with large firms such as Shearman and Sterling, Wilmer Hale, and Covington and Burling. When lawyers from these firms weren't at Gitmo, they were busy representing people and companies like Giorgio Armani, Morgan Stanley, Harley Davidson, Halliburton, IBM, and Microsoft, as well as tobacco and pharmacy giants.

When Pentagon official Cully Stimson publicly suggested in January 2007 that corporate clients sever their business ties with these top firms because they were representing terrorists, the lawyers, American Bar Association leaders, and legal scholars all denounced his comments, and as far as we know, no major corporate clients defected from any of the firms.

In addition to corporate lawyers, there were about fifty to sixty U.S. federal public defenders working on behalf of Gitmo prisoners, as well as several law professors from Northwestern, Georgetown, Fordham, and other universities.

A small number of solo practitioners paid out of their own pockets to represent Gitmo detainees. Richard "Dicky" Grigg was a tall, sixty-year-old personal injury lawyer from Austin, Texas, and a great favorite among the lawyers and interpreters on the base.

"I was tired of bitchin' and moanin' about George W," he told me in his Southern drawl, explaining his reasons for getting involved at Gitmo. "This was a chance to put my money where my mouth was."

Dicky was never shy about telling you what he thought. When I told him once that I had brought roses for Afghan prisoner Chaman Gul, he did a double take and said, "What in the shit would a man want with roses?"

During some of the intense meetings with prisoners, Dicky would moderate, making sure to throw in a few laughs. All of the prisoners wanted to know what was going on in the world because it helped distract them for a little while and gave them something to talk about. Dicky's client was pressing for news too. So, Dicky asked me with a straight face, "Now, do you think we ought to tell him about Paris Hilton? She's been big in the news." I started laughing, and the prisoner naturally wanted to know what was so funny. I explained, "There's this American woman called Paris Hilton. She comes from a wealthy family and became famous by getting caught on tape having sex with her boyfriend. She is a high school dropout, and no one knows why she's famous, but America is fascinated with her because she's rich and hot. So, lately, she's been in the news because she was drinking and driving and ended up in jail for a month."

The detainee gave me a confused look, as if to say, *"That's* big news in America?"

Many of the detainees would vent and unload onto their lawyers because they had no one else to talk to. Sometimes it would go on for several intense hours and often ended in a series of unanswerable questions: Why I am still here? It's unfair. Why this injustice? Why?

Dicky had tried to placate his client many times during one meeting, then decided to tell him what he really believed.

"It's because George Bush is an asshole."

I turned to the young Afghan detainee, who didn't look at me much, and said, "He says it's because George Bush is a son of a bitch."

The detainee tried to control his laughter.

Dicky turned to me. "How'd that one translate?" he asked.

"George Bush is a son of bitch," I said.

"Asshole. Son of a bitch. Close enough." Dicky grinned.

Over the years, the lawyers formed various kinds of relationships with the prisoners. A few were fired early on because their clients didn't trust them or didn't have faith that they had any ability to influence a release. But others were greeted with bear hugs and ongoing gratitude. A few formed such a rapport with the prisoners that once the legal issues were dealt with, they spent the rest of the time talking about cricket or sharing photos of their wives and children. Some attorneys and clients told jokes, played cards, or took turns quizzing each other about their respective cultures.

Some of the American lawyers were fascinated by their Afghan clients' multiple wives. One federal defender formed a particularly close friendship with his Afghan client, a tall, gray-eyed former mujahideen commander with two wives.

The lawyer barraged the Afghan with questions: Did the two women have their own rooms? How did he decide whom to go to on which night? Didn't they get jealous? Did he like one more than the other? Was his first wife upset when he decided to marry a second time?

The commander smiled, cracked a few pistachio shells, leaned across the table, and began explaining. More conservative Afghans wouldn't even tell you their wives' names, much less allow you to see photographs of them. But in the vacuum of the prison meeting room, away from other prisoners' prying eyes and judgments, he answered his lawyer's personal queries.

When the lawyer asked whether the commander had ever had both wives in bed with him at the same time, I thought the questioning had gone a bit too far and suggested that we change the subject. I knew how quickly word traveled through the camp. The men at Gitmo had nothing to do all day but think about their imprisonment, reread a letter for the seven hundredth time, or gossip with other prisoners. Even in the solitary cells of Camp 6, it was common for a prisoner to lie down next to his cell door and shout through the crack at the bottom to other prisoners, then quickly put his ear to the narrow gap waiting for a response. Word also traveled from one camp to another as prisoners caught a glimpse of each other at the hospital or when they were moved for interrogations. They shouted whatever news they'd heard at the top of their lungs. I knew it wouldn't be good if it ever got out that I had participated in a conversation about a ménage à trois. So, we steered the conversation to something not quite so risqué.

Just as the lawyers were curious about mysterious tribal mores, the Middle Eastern men were curious about similarly baffling American customs. Some of the detainees didn't understand why Westerners exchange simple rings during their wedding ceremonies as opposed to the heavy gold jewelry and clothing given to an Afghan girl on her big day. Others were fascinated by certain societies' tolerance of children born out of wedlock or with the American habit of getting drunk to the point of impaired judgment.

Some found it inexplicable that Americans sometimes meet their husbands or wives on the Internet or often wait until they are thirty-five or older to get married. They concluded that Americans would marry at sixteen, eighteen, or twenty if they too had to maintain their virginity until marriage. Some prisoners wanted to confirm the myth that American men could only marry one woman.

Aminullah, a farmer said, "I had heard this, but I didn't believe it. Even the poorest man in Afghanistan has more than one wife. Having one wife is like wearing just one pair of clothes over and over."

Aminullah was a kind and gracious old man who had been cleared by the Department of Defense to be transferred back to Afghanistan, but the way he compared a woman to a pair of clothes was striking. I know that men all over the world have extramarital affairs, but in the United States, men don't marry a second wife. They sometimes divorce the first one and remarry, often a younger woman, but to hear a woman being compared to clothing that can be changed and discarded made me cringe. I silently thanked my lucky stars once again that I'd had the good fortune to grow up in a country where those kinds of views had been discredited and discarded long ago.

The attorneys all had different ways of explaining legal issues to the prisoners. Some talked a lot about case law and crammed a year of constitutional law into a thirty-minute lecture. Some dominated the meetings by discussing congressional legislation. A partner at a large New York corporate law firm attempted to explain the implications of the Detainee Treatment Act, a 2005 congressional statute, to an illiterate prisoner from rural Afghanistan. The lecture put the lawyer's associate to sleep, and the prisoner started to doze off too.

Other times, prisoners like Taj Mohammad, Nabi Omari, or Haji Rohullah dominated the meetings. They would tell their attorneys what they thought of U.S. foreign policy and how the United States' image as a symbol of justice had crumbled. Many of the prisoners were very sophisticated and quickly grasped cornerstone constitutional concepts such as the separation of powers, checks and balances, and the U.S. federal court system. Others passively told their attorneys that they didn't understand anything and that the attorneys should simply act in their best interest. Some attorneys didn't bother to explain what the Geneva Conventions were all about before going off on a convoluted tangent about Article 3's provisions on the treatment of prisoners, which would frustrate some prisoners, while others would politely pretend to understand.

There were some talented poets among the habeas team— as there were among the prisoners. Portland federal defender Chris Schatz wrote this poem to his friend and client Chaman Gul, in which he imagines Chaman's Gitmo experience:

I am a prisoner in a foreign land,

the circumference of my life reduced to a cage not fit for a
     dog,

a prisoner of despair that is not of my own making—
     for I was betrayed.

When the soldiers from the West first brought me to this
     maze of tombs

my heart was still young,

now my beard is gray and the rose of my life is withering,

day after day my captors try me with their questions,

insisting that I be other than what I am,

when I answer, the voice I hear is no longer my own,

my soul has become a wisp of smoke, my heart—a stone.

In the lunar landscape of my solitary room

I walk in silence with fear following hard upon my every
     step,

fear not only that I will be forgotten, but that in time I will
     myself

forget the rhythm of life and death,

the touch of my aged mother's hand,

the warmth of home and marriage bed,

until my memories are as if fallen into a dry well—
     buried in sand.

Only when the gentle face of my sister hovers in the air
     before me,

comforting me with her tears, do I remember that I still love.

From my cell I cannot see the sea though she is near,

her dark eyes haunt my dreams

and when I pray I hear her song of freedom—
     wave upon wave.

Someday the sea will cast herself against these walls
and break them down,
and I will float away upon her breast
under the blue sky of day and the star-pocked void of
    night
until I am at last returned to the mountains and valleys of
    my own land,
to Afghanistan, where my two dear wives
and my brave children will greet me with shy smiles and
    tender kisses,
and I will be a man again and free.

Many attorneys readily admitted that the court process wasn't going to be the magic bullet that would send their clients home. At a barbecue one night, a few lawyers said that the media and the global pressure on the administration to restore America's tarnished image would make the difference. While lawyers helped keep Gitmo in the world's eye via lawsuits, many of the habeas brigade felt helpless as they waged a seemingly fruitless legal battle.

Sometimes, it even seemed as though to the clients, legal counsel was beside the point. One lawyer told me that he often felt like a glorified waiter and social worker. Some of the Arab clients gave their attorneys grocery lists. One of the Kuwaitis once asked his lawyers to bring him two large pizzas, three McDonald's fish filet sandwiches, ice cream, ten Hershey's chocolate bars, eight KitKat bars, a package of Oreo cookies, and a half-gallon of chocolate milk. The attorneys brought it all and stared at the young Arab man as he devoured the food later that afternoon. His interpreter told me only half a cup of chocolate milk and some cookies were left. The detainee ended up with a bad stomach ache.

Then, there were the odd and even comical situations that attorneys had to deal with. I think the prize in this category has to go to Clive Stafford Smith for his exchange with the military regarding contraband lingerie and bathing suits.

On August 12, 2007, Smith received this communication from the military regarding two of his firm's clients, Shaker Aamer and Muhammed Hamid al-Qareni:

Dear Mr. Stafford Smith:

Your client, Shaker Aamer, detainee ISN 239, was recently discovered to be wearing Under Armor briefs and a Speedo bathing suit. Neither item was issued to the detainee by JTF-Guantánamo personnel, nor did they enter the camp through regular mail. Coincidentally, Muhammed al-Qareni, detainee ISN 269, who is represented by Mr. Katznelson of Reprieve, was also recently discovered to be wearing Under Armor briefs. . . .

We are investigating this matter to determine the origins of the above contraband and ensure that parties who may have been involved understand the seriousness of this transgression. As I am sure you understand, we cannot tolerate contraband being surreptitiously brought into the camp. Such activities threaten the safety of the JTF-Guantánamo staff, the detainees, and visiting counsel.

In furtherance of our investigation, we would like to know whether the contraband material, or any portion thereof, was provided by you, or anyone else on your legal team, or anyone associated with Reprieve. We are compelled to ask these questions in light of the coincidence that two detainees represented by counsel associated with Reprieve were found wearing the same contraband underwear.

Thank you as always for your cooperation and assistance,

Sincerely,
[Name redacted] Commander, JAGC,
US Navy Staff Judge Advocate

Clive responded at length on August 29:

Dear Cmdr. [redacted]:

Thank you very much for your letter dated August 12, 2007. . . . I will confess that I have never received such an extraordinary letter in my entire career. . . . I take accusations that I may have committed a criminal act very seriously. In this case, I hope you understand how patently absurd it is, and how easily it could be disproven by the records in your possession. I also hope you understand my frustration at yet another unfounded accusation against lawyers who are simply trying to do their job—a job that involves legal briefs, not the other sort.

Let me briefly respond: First, neither I, nor Mr. Katznelson, nor anyone else associated with us has had anything to do with

smuggling "unmentionables" in to these men, nor would we ever
do so. Second, the idea that we could smuggle in underwear is far-
fetched. As you know, anything we take in is searched and there is
a camera in the room when we visit the client. Does someone
seriously suggest that Mr. Katznelson or I have been stripping off
to deliver underwear to our clients?

Third, your own records prove that nobody associated with my
office has seen Mr. Aamer for a full year. Thus, it is physically
impossible for us to have delivered anything to him that recently
surfaced on his person. Surely you do not suggest that in your
maximum security prison, where Mr. Aamer has been held in
solitary confinement almost continuously since September 24,
2005, and where he has been more closely monitored than virtually
any prisoner on the base, your staff have missed the fact that he
has been wearing both Speedos and "Under Armor" for 12
months? Since your records independently establish that neither I
nor Mr. Katznelson could have been the one who delivered such
undergarments to Mr. Aamer, this eliminates any "coincidence" in
the parallel underwear sported by Mr. el-Gharani. Your letter
implies, however, that Mr. Katznelson might have something to do
with Mr. el-Gharani's underthings. Mr. Katznelson has not seen
Mr. el-Gharani for four months. As you know, Mr. el-Gharani has
been forced to strip naked in front of a number of military
personnel on more than one occasion, and presumably someone
would have noticed his apparel then. . . .

It seems obvious that the same people delivered these items to both
men, and it does not take Sherlock Holmes to figure out that
members of your staff (either the military or the interrogators) did

it. Getting to the bottom of this would help ensure that in future there is no shadow of suspicion cast on the lawyers who are simply trying to do their job, so I have done a little research to help you in your investigations. I had never heard of "Under Armor briefs" until you mentioned them, and my Internet research has advanced my knowledge in two ways—first, Under Armour apparently sports a "U" in its name, which is significant only because it helps with the research.

Second, and rather more importantly, this line of underpants is very popular among the military. One article referred to the fact that "A specialty clothing maker is winning over soldiers and cashing in on war." . . . There must be other clues as to the provenance of these underpants. Perhaps you might check the label to see whether these are "tactical" underwear, as this is apparently something Under Armour has created specially for the military.

Under Armour has a line of apparel called Tactical that's modified for soldiers. It features the same styles as civilian tops and bottoms. . . . But Tactical items are offered in army brown, olive drab, midnight navy, and traditional black and white. Also, the Tactical section of the Under Armour Web site features military models, not athletes. In one image, a soldier poised on one knee wears a LooseGear shirt, looking as if he'd just as soon take a hill as take off on a run. His muscular arms protrude from the tight, olive-colored fabric. He's a picture of soldierliness. And he's totally dry.

I don't know the color of the underpants sported by Messrs. Aamer and el-Gharani, but that might give you a few tips. Indeed,

I feel sure your staff would be able to give you better information on this than I could (though I have done my best) as this Under Armour stuff apparently provokes rave reviews from your colleagues:

Soldier testimonials are effusive. On Amazon.com, a convenient place to buy Under Armour online, a customer who calls himself Spc. Sublett says he's stationed in Afghanistan. Although his identity cannot be verified, Sublett does note the Tactical line's less apparent benefits. "Sometimes I have to go long times in hot weather without showers. Under Armour prevents some of the nasty side effects of these extreme conditions. All of my buddies out here use the same thing. They're soldier-essential equipment. The only thing that would make them better is if the Army would issue them."

I don't mean to say that it is an open-and-shut case proving that your military provided the underwear, as I understand that other people use Under Armour. One group I noticed on the Web were the amateur weight lifters . . . However, in the grand scheme of things, I would like to think we can all agree that the interrogators or military officers are more likely to have access to Messrs. Aamer and el-Gharani than the U.S. Amateur Power Lifting Association.

On the issue of the Speedo swimming trunks, my research really does not help very much. I cannot imagine who would want to give my client Speedos, or why. Mr. Aamer is hardly in a position to go swimming, since the only available water is the toilet in his cell. . . .

Please assure me that you are satisfied that neither I nor my colleagues had anything to do with this. In light of the fact that

you felt it necessary to question whether we had violated the rules,
I look forward to hearing the conclusion of your investigation.

All the best.

Yours sincerely,
Clive A. Stafford Smith

The last I heard, the military hadn't replied to Clive's letter.

CHAPTER EIGHT

THE BUSINESSMAN

Wali Mohammad was standing to shake our hands when his attention was drawn to my right ear. I handed him the flower I had tucked there, along with a bouquet of red hibiscus that I'd picked outside the Navy Exchange supermarket that morning.

He held up the flowers and smelled them. They left yellow pollen residue on the tip of his nose, which stayed there for the rest of the meeting. "They are so red," he said, holding the flowers and touching the petals. It was the first time he'd seen flowers in five years.

We sat down, and I opened a box of Klondike bars. Mohammad hadn't had much of a chance to indulge his weakness for ice cream in years either. "I like ice cream, and this is really good ice cream," he said, laughing in between mouthfuls.

He nudged the cardboard box toward Peter and me.

"Eat with me," he said. But we ended up nibbling on pistachio nuts and left the ice cream for him.

It was our third meeting with Wali Mohammad. Over the months, he had slowly let his guard down, allowing himself to believe that Peter was not an agent for the U.S. government. He was beginning to treat us more like friends.

During this meeting, he was also in particularly good spirits. Instead of the usual Camp Echo meeting room, we were in Camp Iguana. It was a far cry from the solitary-confinement setting of Camp 6, where Mohammad spent his days and nights. We met with Mohammad there once. Claustrophobia overtook me as we were led through a narrow passageway to a tiny soundproof meeting room. The walls in the hallway were bare cement. I felt as though I was in a dank dungeon (I was in fact) and was relieved to get out of there once the meeting was over. Mohammad didn't complain about the conditions, but I felt badly about leaving him behind. When prisoners were held in those solitary conditions, their mental decline became apparent from visit to visit. One Afghan told Dechert lawyer Rebecca Dick that the military had shot rays into his head. Moments later, the absurdity of his statement dawned on him. He looked at her and said, "I am fighting for my sanity."

By contrast, Iguana was Gitmo's version of the Four Seasons Hotel. When prisoners were escorted to the bathroom there, they could peer through the high fences and see the endless Caribbean Sea.[1] Sometimes, if they were lucky, they might even spy a ship sailing in the distance.

Prisoners meeting their lawyers in Camp Iguana sat on sofas in a large room with wood floors, instead of on white plastic lawn chairs. There were no holding cells in the meeting rooms, and we could sit close to the prisoner on an adjacent couch without the barrier of a long table between us. These small things made the meetings go better.

When I sat next to the prisoners, they often wanted to see my rings and asked who had given them to me. They noticed when I wore a new one or when I wasn't sporting an elastic hair tie around my wrist the way I had four months before. Once I arm-wrestled an Afghan prisoner. He won and gave me a toothy grin, as if to say, don't be fooled by my old age and graying beard, lady.

The camp was also teeming with wildlife. True to its name, it hosted iguana families that scurried around the camouflage-clad guards or sunbathed in front of the meeting rooms. Sometimes during our meetings, woodpeckers hammered relentlessly at the walls. It made the prisoners laugh to see lawyers and interpreters beat their fists against the walls in a vain attempt to shut Mr. Woodpecker up.

Mohammad, No. 560, as the military referred to him, was a complex man who hid his emotions behind an abundance of hearty, animated laughter. Sitting beside him, I told him that I was planning to go to Afghanistan to collect evidence on behalf of some of the detainees represented by the lawyers I was working with. He looked at me sharply, his attention distracted from his fourth Klondike bar.

"Are you really? Will you be going to Peshawar?" he asked.

"For a few days, yes."

He got very excited, and after some back-and-forth, I realized that my grandmother's house was three blocks from his.

"You must go to my house!" he declared. "You must tell my family that you saw me and sat with me here. Tell them I looked good, I was healthy, and not to worry. Tell them that I'll be home soon, *inshallah.*"

Finally devouring the fourth Klondike, he quipped, "Also tell them that you brought me ice cream and that I ate all of it."

I smiled.

"If you go, you'll see my twin girls Sara and Amina. They are the most beauutttiiful girls in the world," he said. "I want to show the other prisoners here their photographs. When they see my girls, they will know that God is great!"

He paused to unwrap Klondike bar number five. Then, he remembered something: "When you see my wives, don't tell them that I have any white in my beard. They'll be upset if they know I've grown old here. Tell them that I look young and that my hair is still black."

In 2002, when their father was seized by Pakistani police and turned over to the U.S. military, which accused him of having associations with the Taliban and al-Qaeda and brought him to Gitmo, Sara and Amina were only two years old. At the time of this meeting, they were nearly eight.

Mohammad told us that he was a just a businessman in Taliban-run Afghanistan who was turned in by a former business partner who wanted to avoid repaying a large loan. At the time, Mohammad said, he was a currency and gold trader on the foreign exchange market. He used to travel back and forth between Peshawar, Kabul, and Dubai to exchange currencies for profit. He became well known and had developed a good relationship with the Bank of Afghanistan, which would lend him large amounts in dollars for his investments and trade. Since Islamic banking systems do not allow interest, the bank made money by keeping 75 percent of Mohammad's profits.

A typical transaction meant that Mohammad would take out a large dollar loan from the Bank of Afghanistan, drive across the border to Pakistan, and exchange his dollars for kaldars, the Pakistani currency. With the cash in his briefcase, he would fly Afghan-run Ariana Airlines to Dubai, where he would exchange the money for dollars at a profit since dollars sold more cheaply in Dubai than in Kabul.

Then, he would go to the local Dubai gold dealers and buy several pounds of gold bars. Dubai's gold markets, or souks, are notorious for their inexpensive, high-quality twenty-two- and twenty-four-karat gold, which is about as close to pure gold as you can get. He would take his gold bars and hefty profits, return to Pakistan, and sell the gold to local jewelers at much higher rates.

This trade of turning cash into gold and gold into cash was big business, and most of the time, Mohammad lived well. He had a beautiful two-story house decorated with imported furniture and Persian rugs and bought his family whatever they needed. But then, during one of his transactions, he took out a loan in the amount of $1.5 million. He borrowed in dollars and converted to kaldars.

The problems began when the value of the dollar suddenly skyrocketed and devalued the kaldars that Mohammad had just purchased. To make matters worse, the value of gold also dropped before he could sell. Within a short period, he lost about $500,000. And the Bank of Afghanistan, the government bank run by the Taliban regime, wasn't happy.

The Taliban arrested Mohammad and ordered him to pay back the sum in dollars. He agreed and borrowed from his family and friends to pay off the huge debt. His business partner, Assef, owed him a large amount of money, and Mohammad started demanding repayment. But Assef had no intention of paying. The two were about to go before a tribal court, or *jirga*, of village elders to settle the matter.

But the night before the big meeting, the Inter-Services Intelligence (ISI), the Pakistani secret police, came to Mohammad's home and tried to extort $100,000. Mohammad owned a large house, and the ISI agents suggested that he sell it and pay them off to avoid arrest. This sort of extortion is something I've heard many wealthy Afghans allege.

Mohammad was furious and started shouting at the police. He cursed at them and told them to get out. Instead, they arrested him and took him away. Then, he was accused of having ties to the Taliban and turned over to the U.S. military.

The Department of Defense accused Mohammad of taking money from the Taliban. In his combatant status review tribunal (CSRT), the presiding officers accused him of associating with al-Qaeda and other terrorist organizations and of having links to Osama bin Laden. As for his gold sales to Pakistani jewelers, the presiding officer accused him of "smuggling gold for al-Qaeda."

Mohammad had explained his case over and over to military interrogators, to the tribunal, and to us.

"I took loans from the Bank of Afghanistan, which happened to be controlled by the Taliban government at the time," he said. "I didn't take money from the Taliban, but from my country's bank. I was a businessman taking a loan from a bank."

That bank, he said, had been around for decades and had been controlled by various governments: the Communist-backed Najibullah regime, the Northern Alliance, the Taliban, and now the American-backed government of Hamid Karzai.

He maintained that he had never had anything to do with the Taliban's politics and that he was in business long before the Taliban came to power. The allegations against him were roughly comparable to accusing an American with a Bank of America loan of taking money from the Bush administration and being in cahoots with its war policies.

"This has no logic at all," Mohammad told the panel at his CSRT. But like most of the other detainees, he was declared an enemy combatant.

Each year, after his initial appearance before the CSRT panel, Mohammad went before another panel to determine whether he was an ongoing threat to the United States. And every year, the panel came up with outlandish new allegations. In 2007, he told us, the panel accused him of working with Osama bin Laden in 1996. But he was in Peshawar in 1996, he said. And while he admitted having heard the name Osama, he said it wasn't until he got to Guantánamo Bay that he learned that Osama was an Arab. The whole military court system, he said, was a big joke.

"It's drama! These hearings are a big game they're playing," he said, bursting into laughter and shaking his head. "The lies they accuse us of are crazy! They aren't small lies; they reach the sky!"

He pulled out a piece of folded white paper. It was the result of his latest hearing, once again declaring him an ongoing threat to the United States. He shrugged. "These decisions are meaningless," he said. "It's just a stupid game they play."

We asked Mohammad about hunger strikes, and it was then that he told us that some of the prisoners had found a way to get a little revenge for what they had endured. While he had never gone on hunger strike himself, he told us how many of the prisoners on strike were dragged away and force fed. "They wait sometimes twenty days, until the prisoner has lost a lot of weight and withers away, and then they take you away," he said. "They treat the hunger strikers with no dignity. They throw them in isolation as soon as they start refusing their meals."

Some of the Camp 6 prisoners protested the treatment handed out to the hunger strikers.

"Some of the guys gave the guards a gift," Mohammad said with a mischievous smile.

"A gift?" I asked.

"What sort of gift?" Peter asked, glancing up from his notes, a puzzled look on his face.

Mohammad laughed out loud, and the corners of his eyes crinkled.

"Number two," he said finally.

Peter looked confused.

"Some of the prisoners gave the guards number two."

Peter and I looked at each other.

"Well, the problem is that there is no gift shop at Guantánamo, and so we give the very bad guards a nice gift," Mohammad said. "The ones who are particularly cruel."

"Ooohh," Peter said with a smile, finally getting it. The guards had told us that sometimes prisoners threw urine or excrement out of paper cups at them, so they'd had to start wearing plastic protective shields over their faces.

"Once a guard got twelve gifts," Mohammad said, cracking up again. "Everyone in the block was counting, and this Afghan who was transferred out of Camp 6 told us about it," he said, explaining that the incidents had occurred several months prior to his transfer to Camp 6.

Peter and I were amused by his animated laughter.

"Twelve nice gifts," he said, squealing. "We ended up giving her a name."

"Wait, it was a woman?" I asked, horrified. "They did that to a female guard?"

"No, no, no! It wasn't a woman, but those guys gave the guard a woman's name," Mohammad said.

"What name?"

"Who was that lady who ruined her reputation by having an affair with Clinton?" he asked, racking his brain.

"Monica Lewinsky?" I offered.

"Yes!" He laughed again. "That's what they named him. But everyone pronounced it Moonica, and that's what they called him."

After the laughter, Mohammad grew serious, and his tone softened. He told me that he'd had a dream about his first wife. "Maybe the dream means I will see her soon."

He asked me to call her—or even better to see her in Peshawar and tell her that she was in all his prayers. When we left the meeting, he reminded us to remember him in our prayers and repeated once again that he would like photos of his daughters.

"I'll do my best," I told him.

CHAPTER NINE

AFGHANISTAN

I'd always wanted to go to Afghanistan, but as it played host to the Soviets, the Taliban, the war lords, and instability over the past several decades, there was never a good time. My family warned against traveling there. "It's not the place it used to be," Baba-jaan, my father, would say. "You could be killed." My grandmother and aunts in Peshawar concurred.

Instead, I romanticized the country of my ancestry, wondering when it would once again be celebrated for its poetry, philosophy, and art. The repeated destruction of Afghanistan has made it a land of Shakespearean tragedy. The Afghans are passionate, charming, and incredibly hospitable people—and perpetually devastated by conflict and calamity.

Afghanistan lies at a crossroads between the East and West, a centuries-old hub for commerce and migration. It's also a strategic link between the Middle East and southern and central Asia. Controlling Afghanistan is pivotal to controlling the rest of the region and its natural resources. This is why Afghans have been caught in so many power struggles and fought numerous invaders and conquerors over its long history.

This land was invaded in 330 BC by Alexander the Great. Later, the Mongols took a stab at ruling the Afghans, and then in the nineteenth century, the British invaded, twice, and were defeated both times. In 1979, the Soviet Red Army marched in to Afghanistan hoping for an easy takeover. Instead, the invasion kicked off the mujahideen resistance, a U.S.-backed and -financed movement made up of Islamic freedom fighters. When the Russians finally retreated in 1989, 1 million Afghans were dead, 5.5 million had been displaced, and Afghanistan was littered with an estimated 10 million land mines. From this sprung another deadly wave of civil war between various tribes and warlords. And then came the oppressive Taliban movement. Finally, in 2001, Afghanistan cycled around and was again at odds with the West, America.

The summer after my first year in law school, Afghanistan, cleansed of the Taliban, was preparing for its 2004 presidential elections, the first democratic vote in decades. I wanted to be a part of it, so I got a job with Human Rights Watch in New York to research election security and voter intimidation by warlords. The data was to be presented at the North Atlantic Treaty Organization's Istanbul Summit to push for more election peacekeepers and for basic things, such as money for ballot boxes and guards.

It was hard to get a real grasp of the situation from an office in New York City, so after some discussion, I made plans to go to Afghanistan to investigate what the rural warlords were really up to. On my itinerary were Jalalabad, Kandahar, and

Ghazni, places where locals had reportedly been killed for possessing voter registration cards.

When I told my family about the trip, they thought I'd lost my mind. My aunts and grandmother were up in arms.

"*Sama laywanai yeh*—You're insane," my maternal grandmother, Amiji, said to me angrily. "What is this going-to-Afghanistan business? Does your life mean nothing to you?"

She told me that I had an obligation to obey her. "If you go to Afghanistan, you're not my granddaughter anymore," she threatened.

It was impossible to argue with Amiji. She wouldn't listen to my reasoning, and anytime I mentioned Afghanistan, she'd start to pray. She and my aunt pressed my parents to forbid me to go. But my parents knew my stubborn side. Their dissuasion technique was to frighten me into changing my plans by e-mailing me statistics about violence against international workers.

Those stats did make me uneasy, but I tried to ignore them. Then, a few weeks before my scheduled trip, five Doctors without Borders aid workers were ambushed and shot in northwestern Afghanistan. The incident gave me cold feet, and I wondered how to tell the people I worked with at Human Rights Watch that I was scared. Fortunately, when I brought it up, it turned out that my coworkers felt the same way. The trip was canceled. I was relieved and disappointed at the same time.

I didn't think much about Afghanistan again until I went to Guantánamo Bay. Having met some detainees, I knew they'd be helped if evidence in their cases could be gathered in Afghanistan. I urged some of the attorneys to plan a trip. Most wanted to go, but their firms considered travel to Afghanistan still too dangerous.

I decided to go alone and collect evidence for the clients of two lawyers in Dechert's Washington, D.C., office. I made arrangements to meet with the prisoners' families, to locate employment records showing where they had worked, to collect affidavits and photographs of their former places of employment—anything to corroborate their stories.

I planned a winter trip to Kabul, trying to ignore my family's vehement pleas. Even some of the habeas lawyers were concerned because of a spike in suicide bombings. I tried to calm my nerves by asking some of the prisoners what they thought about my solo trip.

Abdullah Wazir Zadran, a young Afghan from Khost, told me that I'd be kidnapped if I ventured outside Kabul.

"Do you think I could be killed?" I asked.

"No. Kidnappers just want money; they'll make you call your family for ransom," he said.

I began to have second thoughts and called my friend Rahman, a journalist in Kabul. He dismissed my fears and said that the media had a tendency to exaggerate everything.

"It's peaceful here. There's nothing to worry about," he told me. "You'll have a great time." Some foreigners based in Kabul whom I knew echoed Rahman's sentiment.

So, I called my travel agent and booked flights, scheduling a stopover in Peshawar to see my relatives and have some traditional clothes made before flying into Kabul. Once I'd ordered my tickets, my grandmother began to pray nonstop, and

Baba-jaan started giving me tips. He even told me what to do if I were taken hostage.

"Say your prayers out loud," he advised. "Maybe they'll feel badly about killing a Muslim girl."

He told me to call every older man *kaka* or *kaka-jaan*, a term that translates roughly as "uncle," as a way of showing respect and indicating that I viewed the individual I was addressing as family. My family insisted that I leave my jeans and other Western garb behind. They instructed me to wear traditional clothes, to cover myself properly, and never to leave Kabul. My father told me not to wear big sunglasses—or any sunglasses, for that matter.

"Sunglasses are very Western," he said. "You want to blend in as much as you can."

When Mumma suggested that I wear a burka, I cringed at the thought. At a minimum, I should veil my face, she told me. I decided to take my cues from the local women and dress accordingly.

As the day of my trip approached, my father's torrent of tips continued: Don't go out after dark. Never spend the night at anyone's house. Trust no one. If they can sell each other to the U.S. military for bounty money, what makes you any different? Don't travel alone. Don't take a taxi anywhere by yourself. Get a cell phone immediately. Give me the numbers for everyone you're meeting and call me every day from every location.

"Okay, okay," I said, wishing they had a little more faith in my judgment. But the only one who did was my younger brother Hassan. When he heard about my family's concerns that I might get killed, he called me, laughing.

"Take out a big life insurance policy and put it in my name," he quipped. He reassured me that I'd be fine.

On my way to the airport in mid-November 2006, I stopped at a Best Buy to pick up a Sony camcorder. I wanted to make video affidavits and home videos of the prisoners' families and bring them back to Gitmo.

I tore the camera out of the box and shoved it into my carry-on along with my laptop and my Dictaphone. A few hours later, I was on a long British Airways flight, excitedly watching the LCD display as we got closer to Peshawar, an ethnically Pashtun city teeming with Afghan refugees, exiled warlords, and smugglers.

After twenty-two hours of flying, I was excited to be there at last, but my relatives still weren't happy about my impending trip into Afghanistan. I spent three days with them, and each day I got an earful about what not to wear in Kabul.

One afternoon, I came home from Peshawar's Saddar bazaar and changed into a pair of sweatpants and a T-shirt. My grandmother took one wide-eyed look at me and started cursing at my clothing.

"*Ya Allah—towba!*" she said, eyeing me. There's no direct equivalent in English, but it roughly means, "Oh God—repentance!" The pants were too low-rise for her liking.

"I'm just sitting around the house, Amiji," I said, defending myself.

"*Jamai dhey rookshee*—May your clothes get lost," she retorted. She's deeply conservative; it even irks her when I walk out of the bathroom wearing a towel.

"Bay-sharamay—without shame!" she muttered as she sat down to read the Qu'ran, as she did every afternoon. I started unloading my shopping bags. I'd spent the morning buying hand-embroidered pashminas and mirrored throw pillows. I showed them to my grandmother while she recited the Arabic verses out loud. I've always liked the sound of the Qu'ran; it's like rhythmic singing. She glanced over the top of her reading glasses briefly to see what I'd bought and then went back to the Arabic.

I never bother to read the Qu'ran in Arabic because I don't understand Arabic—and neither does my grandmother. I've read portions of interest in English, but I've always been skeptical because many translations are written by Arab men. I have a Lebanese friend who, like me, has a very feminist spin on Islam, and I like hearing her translate the Arabic for me. All the nonsense about women covering their heads isn't in the Qu'ran. Neither is the notion that women mustn't work or drive a car—as is the law in Saudi Arabia—but somehow men have transposed their culture onto the religion. At least that's her take on it.

I tried to tell my grandmother that there was nothing to repent for about my clothing.

"All the Qu'ran stresses is modesty, for both men and women," I said. "And modesty is interpreted differently in different times and places."

"There is nothing modest about your clothing," she insisted. "You should cover yourself properly."

And she started reciting verses again. I just smiled to myself. I was used to the clashing cultures by now.

When I'd arrived in Peshawar, I'd called Wali Mohammad's son Ismail and went to his house the following afternoon. Unlike many of the mud houses described by Gitmo prisoners,

Mohammad owned a spacious two-story house with sprawl-ing wraparound balconies, a gated driveway, and marble inlay. The yard was surrounded by a six-foot wall.

I rang the door bell and was greeted by Mohammad's nephew, a tall man in his late twenties with strong features. Next to him stood Mohammad's twenty-year-old son, Moham-mad Ismail, who had just arrived from Kabul minutes before.

Ismail was soft-spoken, thin, and much older than his years. He invited me in. I noticed that he was careful not to maintain eye contact with me for too long since I'm a woman and local etiquette dictates that he shouldn't stare at or ogle women to whom he is not related. He was somewhat reserved in my presence, but he slowly relaxed, and his father's playful nature crept out, as did his quick wit and intelligence.

As I walked into the gated complex toward the house, my attention was drawn to two irresistible little girls who ran out into the grass barefoot. They had short brown hair and were wearing matching outfits. I knew at once that these were Mo-hammad's daughters. They were gorgeous children, with their father's big brown eyes and magnetism. I forgot about Is-mail and went over to them.

"So, which one of you is Sara and which one is Amina?" I asked.

"I'm Amina," one of the little girls said shyly.

"I'm Sara," said the other. Just as Mohammad had said, I couldn't tell them apart. I pulled out my camera, and the girls started to giggle but ran over to stand by a plant for the cam-era. Their brown eyes followed the camera lens.

The girls followed me into the house where I met Moham-mad's first wife, Hidaya, a good-looking lady wearing a green chiffon outfit. The daughters looked a lot like her. She kissed me on both cheeks and motioned for me to sit down with her on the cushions and colorful pillows that lined the wall. Then, I met the other daughters: Pahlwahsha, Farishta, Asiya, and Kubra. Their eyes were all on me, but I felt oddly comfortable in their home.

I liked the girls' names. Pahlwahsha was one of Mohammad's teenage daughters. She looked like a young Sandra Bullock and sat on her knees next to me. Like the other daughters, she was shy and didn't speak a lot. She wore yellow and had stack of silver bangles on her right wrist. I told her they were pretty.

She immediately took the bangles off her wrist and extended them to me. "No, no, they look good on you," I said.

She insisted that I take them, but I felt badly about it, so we compromised: I took three, and she kept three. I slid them on my wrist. It seemed like a simple exchange of the moment, but I didn't know how it would grow in meaning once I returned to Guantánamo Bay.

The family gathered around me with questions.

"Did you see my father?" Ismail asked.

"Yes, a few times," I said. "I'll be going again in January to show him the video."

Dechert had hired a local aid worker to make a home video of Wali Mohammad's family. The video would be cleared by the Department of Defense so that we could show it to Mohammad on our next trip. Lawyers were often granted permission to show their clients home videos because they are essential tools in establishing trust.

"How was he doing? What did he look like?" Ismail asked.

I told them about his sense of humor, his good health, the way he laughed, and his overall positive demeanor. "And he told me to tell you that he ate all of the ice cream I brought him," I said. Ismail, his sisters, and his mom looked on intently as I spoke.

"We heard from a few of the prisoners that were released that he had some white in his beard," he quipped. "My mom's not happy about that!"

"He told me not to mention the gray hairs," I said, smiling.

I also told them that Mohammad missed them all and talked a lot about Sara and Amina, who were sitting by their mother, playing around and stealing shy glances at the adults. Hidaya explained that the twins had no memory of their father. They knew him only through photographs and discussions.

I had imagined that Mohammad was wealthy and that he had a nice family, but the reality of his life far exceeded my expectations, and my perspective on him changed profoundly. I realized that his daughters, sons, wives, and neighbors missed him deeply. They recalled his little pranks and his love of cricket. Meeting his family in his home allowed me to see the life he had been a part of.

A few days later, my aunt, Aunty-gul, drove me to the airport. She'd packed me a lunch: kebabs wrapped in naan.

My friend Rahman would be waiting for me at Kabul International Airport. But when I went to check in for my flight, I learned that it had been cancelled for "operational reasons." There wouldn't be another flight for a week. I wanted to scream. It seemed as though something was always holding me back from getting to Afghanistan.

As we left the airport, I told Aunty-gul that I couldn't wait for another week. I would drive to Kabul the next day. Aunty-gul looked as though her eyes would pop out of her head. The drive from Peshawar to Kabul takes about five hours and goes through the Khyber Pass into Torkham and through Jalalabad. It's a mountainous road frequently traveled by coalition convoys and armored vehicles, making it a target for bandits and bombs.

"I am responsible for you now, and if something should happen, what would your parents say to me?" Aunty-gul asked. "You cannot go without informing your parents first."

There was no way I was going to tell my parents that I would be driving through the tribal areas and rural Afghanistan to Kabul. They would have had a panic attack. I began to reason with my aunt.

"They can't possibly gauge the situation in Afghanistan from Michigan," I said. "Telling them will accomplish nothing except to worry them. Please trust my decision. I've spoken to people who take that road."

"*Bas*—enough!" she said, raising her voice. She looked panicked by the decision she knew I'd already made. "I am not letting you drive to Kabul. There is no way. Do you hear?"

That evening I strategized with Rahman. He called my aunt and reassured her that I would be safe. To put everyone at ease, he arranged for his friend Munir to accompany me on the drive to Kabul. Munir was a journalist who worked part-time for USAID in Kabul. He had been visiting his family in Peshawar and was heading back to Afghanistan. After several long talks with Rahman, Aunty-gul finally gave in.

Munir arrived at 8:20 the next morning. Wearing a leather jacket over his Afghan clothes and carrying a backpack, he looked like a green-eyed version of my older brother. My aunt asked him whether I should be dressed more conservatively.

I was wearing traditional clothes like all the locals, but I'd given the tailor very specific instructions. There has been a resurgence of 1970s fashion in Peshawar, so I wanted my clothes tailored to look the way my mom's did in photos from that decade. My shirt was a brown floral print, very formfitting, with cap sleeves. But I planned to wear a big shawl to cover it all.

Munir smiled.

"It might be okay," he said diplomatically, "but something longer and looser might be better."

My aunt gave me an *abaya*, a big, black, robelike garment to wear over my clothes. It fell to my ankles and had long, loose, flowing sleeves. On top of this, I had to wear another big piece of fabric to cover my hair. My aunt instructed me to practice veiling my face with it too. The fabric kept falling, but when I got it right, you could only see my eyes.

I worked on veiling my face in front of the mirror while my aunt spoke to Munir about the drive. I'd never veiled before, but I thought the look was intriguing, and it didn't stifle my individuality as definitively as a burka would have. I think veils have an element of mystery. I'd seen a veiled woman in the bazaar a few days before—only her arched eyebrows and dark eyes were visible. You could tell she had high cheek bones and delicate features underneath, but it left me wondering what her face looked like. Instead of deflecting attention, I think veils hypersexualize women.

I pulled out my dark eye shadow, pencil, and mascara and gave myself dark, smoky eyes. Perfect.

My aunt took one look at me and shook her head.

"*Bilkul laywanay yeh*—You're absolutely crazy," she said. "You're not driving around Miami with your American friends; you're going through the tribal areas and driving to Afghanistan. What is this makeup business?"

"You're just jealous because I look hot in a veil," I told her, laughing.

"Jealous your head!" she said, trying not to smile.

She did have a point. I softened the smoky eyes a bit.

Aunty-gul drove us to the taxi stand, where Munir got out to make arrangements with a cab driver. She grabbed a pen from her purse and scribbled down the license plate number of the white Toyota Corolla taxi that would take me across the border.

"Just in case something happens, and I don't hear from you," she said. "I'll know how to track you down."

I threw my arms around her and planted a kiss on her face. "Don't worry so much. I'll call you all along the way. I'll be fine."

She forced a pursed smile.

I got into the back seat of the taxi with Munir and waved to my aunt as she slowly drove away. There was another passenger in the front seat, chain-smoking out the window. We waited for a fourth guy to get in. Each person would pay 160 kaldars, about $2.60, to be driven across the border into Torkham.

I sat by the window, and Munir took the middle seat next to me. I didn't sit in the middle because it would be improper for me to sit so close to a man unrelated to me. As far as everyone else was concerned, Munir was my brother or a cousin. The fourth passenger finally arrived, and the adventure began.

Whatever nervousness I had about the trip was suddenly re-placed by excitement. Kristin Wilhelm, a partner at the At-lanta offices of Sutherland, Asbill, and Brennan, had told me this would happen. She had gone to Yemen to meet the fami-lies of her clients and said she stopped worrying once she ar-rived in Sanaa.

There was so much to absorb that I didn't have time to worry or to fear the unknown. But I did remain cautious and tried to stay as inconspicuous as possible while we drove along, even though I was itching to pull out my camera. The other passengers made some small talk, and the guy in the front just kept smoking out the window. Finally, I turned to Munir and asked him quietly whether I could take pictures. I wanted to be sure I was behaving in a culturally appropriate way. I was also hesitant to let anyone hear me speak Pashto because I have an obvious American accent and didn't want to draw attention to myself.

"Sure, go ahead," Munir said.

I snapped away. The driver was playing some loud Pashto music and wove in and out of traffic. We drove quickly through Peshawar's bustling Hayatabad market into the Northwest Frontier Province tribal areas, a loosely adminis-tered territory straddling the Afghanistan-Pakistan border, just minutes from my grandmother's house. For the Pashtuns who live here, it's a state of anarchy, a land of convoluted tribal loyalties and ferocious feuds, of gun-running, drug traf-ficking, and the occasional kidnapping. The only legal system in this modern-day Wild West is Pashtunwali, the unwritten tribal statutes and their complicated fabric of revenge, hospitality, and honor. The tribal area is also the rumored home of Osama bin Laden and al-Qaeda training camps.

I cranked down the window and snapped pictures of mud houses, children playing cricket, and unpaved village streets. I also got a good shot of a sign that read, "No foreigners allowed." Another sign in red lettering read in English, "Attention, Entry of Foreigners Is Prohibited beyond This Point." It seemed like something the current occupant of the Oval Office might want to put up along U.S. borders.

I was careful to avoid photographing women, even though the few I saw were covered head to toe in burkas.

As our car passed through a crowded market, Munir politely asked me to veil the lower part of my face. As I pulled my shawl over my nose and lips, it occurred to me that Munir adhered fairly strictly to Pashtun tribal law. Since I was passing him off as a cousin or brother, he in turn was expecting me to try to behave appropriately. In Pashtun culture, honor is often more important than one's life. A woman's chastity is often directly tied to the honor of her father, husband, brother, or other male family members, and her behavior reflects immediately upon the honor of the men in her life. Even though Munir wasn't my cousin, I veiled myself whenever we drove through a crowded market.

About ten minutes before we reached the fabled Khyber Pass that would take us into Afghanistan, we hit a roadblock—right in the middle of the tribal areas. Our car could not move, and there was commotion in the street around us. A big crowd had formed right in the middle of the road. Suddenly, I was in the thick of it—and very scared. I felt vulnerable. I grabbed my pashmina and veiled my face tightly, avoiding eye contact with anyone in the street. We weren't moving, and the driver leaned out of the window to see what was going on. The front seat passenger seemed indifferent and merely rolled his window down to have another cigarette.

"What's going on up there?" our driver shouted out to the locals who had gathered around.

"Some people were shot up the road," a guy on the street replied. "Some idiot shot five people because they didn't put electricity in his house."

I turned to Munir.

"This is insane," I said.

He smiled. "These are the tribal areas."

I had a hard time believing that someone would get killed over electricity, but then I remembered Taj Mohammad, who'd beaten up his cousin over water and ended up at Gitmo.

"So, what's the justice system over here?" I asked Munir.

"Tribal justice. They hold a *jirga*—a gathering of elders—to decide what to do."

"Is it effective?"

"Fairly, yes."

"This is crazy," I said, still shocked by the crowd that had formed and the casual discussion of the gunman turning on five people.

"People don't think. They're very hotheaded here," Munir said.

Finally, the bodies were removed, and the crowds thinned out enough for traffic to start moving again. I started snapping pictures, which drew a few curious glances.

"Do you think someone might shoot at the car if they see me taking pictures?" I asked Munir.

"No, you can photograph as much as you like. No one will ever say a word to you," he said. "They have great respect for women and will go to lengths to protect them here. Women are sacred to the Pashtun."

Sacred's not exactly the right word, since the Pashtun are also known to kill women who dishonor their families. According to the codes of Pashtunwali, custom often compels a father, husband, brother, or son to kill a female relative who has shamed her family by having an affair, premarital or extramarital, or is even rumored to have had one. In extreme cases, even rape victims have been killed. It happens mostly in very rural areas, but it's barbarism all the same.

We drove on into the Hindu Kush mountains, and in typical Afghan fashion, no one said anything about the men who'd been shot on the road behind us. No one gave death another thought. It reminded me of the time when Carolyn Welshhans, an attorney in the Washington, D.C., office of Dechert, told one of her clients that she was sorry to hear that his father had died, even though it had happened years before. His response spoke volumes about the impact that war had had on his generation.

"For Afghans, death is a part of life," he said. "We are used to it."

And so, the driver pushed a tape into the cassette deck and rewound to a particular song. I hadn't heard the sound of a tape whirring in ages and wondered whether anyone there knew what an iPod was.

As we crossed the Khyber Pass, the driver reduced his speed, and my imagination took off, unfolding pages of history. This is the same gateway that Alexander the Great marched his armies across in 330 BC. The Persians, Mongols, and Tartars plowed through this mountain passage too. Centuries later, the Pashtuns demonstrated their freedom-or-death style of fighting to the British army here. Ancient merchants and traders also traveled through the Khyber Pass in huge camel caravans.

I pulled out my camera and clicked away, photographing both sides of the gateway where ancient villages lie and local Pashtun tribesmen shop in the vegetable markets, toting AK-47s over their shoulders. As we moved through the mountain passage, the driver slapped the steering wheel in rhythm to the sultry sounds coming through the car speakers of an Afghan woman singing about her beloved. He glanced into the rearview mirror occasionally and saw me snapping away with my digital Elph. I snapped photos of fruit markets, children, animals, and shopkeepers.

I kept elbowing Munir to get a better look at the awesome Hindu Kush mountains. I had a similar sense of awe the first time I saw Vatican Square and the Great Wall of China, but this mix of beauty and history had greater personal impact. Munir had traveled this way a thousand times before and was amused by me.

"I didn't think an American would feel so tied to her roots," he said as I gawked out the window.

When we reached Torkham, Munir asked me whether I wanted to go to the passport office to get my passport stamped. I didn't know I'd have a choice; I'd assumed that there would be multiple checkpoints, border guards, and at least one customs and immigration search. But there was nothing. You can simply drive into Afghanistan without a visa.

I decided to get the stamp in case I was questioned about my point of entry on my return to the United States. And besides, I wanted the stamp in my passport. At the border, someone piled my bags into a wooden cart and pushed them all the way to the passport office.

I ran inside and joined a line of waiting men. A bearded, middle-aged man immediately waved me to the front of the line. The men in front stepped aside to let me pass. Without a word, the counter clerk looked over my visa, stamped my passport, smiled, and handed it back.

"*Manana*—Thank you," he said. I nodded and was on my way.

I saw such preferential treatment for women over and over during my stay in Afghanistan. Anywhere there was a line for service, women or women accompanied by men were immediately brought to the front and assisted first. On buses, men in the forward seats immediately vacated them for female passengers. Once, at a security checkpoint outside Bagram, a guard flagged down Munir's car. As we slowed to a stop, he saw me in the front seat, made an apologetic gesture toward Munir, and immediately waved us through. On a later Ariana Airlines flight to Dubai, women boarded first, and when I got up to go to the lavatory, the flight attendant motioned for all the waiting men to be seated so that I could go first.

"They try as much as possible to help women and not to burden them," Munir explained to me.

But I had a feeling that it was also because in Afghan society, women aren't supposed to gather in places with unrelated men. So, the men help them get in and out as quickly as possible. Still, I also sensed that the men around me, friends or strangers, were trying to protect me in simple ways. Afghanistan is unquestionably a male-dominated society. Men are viewed as almost godly by the women who depend on them for everything. Women, in turn, are perceived as fragile creatures who must be protected.

When I came out of the passport office, Munir and I crossed the Torkham border on foot into Afghanistan. I noticed gradual changes. The guards' uniforms went from the camouflage print worn in Pakistan to forest green. The faces varied too. There were freckles, olive skin, dark skin, and blond, red, and black hair. Some had piercing blue eyes; others had brown, green, or hazel. The languages spoken were Farsi, Pashto, and Dari.

I saw many women with unveiled faces; others wore sky blue or white embroidered burkas. Vendors on the border sold bananas, sugarcane, and nuts. Small children ran up to travelers trying to sell Chiclets chewing gum.

The history of this land was peculiarly etched on all the faces around me. They emanated a rugged, wary pride and seemed somehow hardened by all that their country has endured. Even the younger faces looked older than they were.

Munir glanced over and read my mind.

"We are in Afghanistan now," he said, nodding at the first red, green, and black flag. I remembered Farah, an Afghan

American friend who lives in San Francisco. "You are going to be on the soil that I miss the most in the world," she wrote me once. "When you're there you'll know what I mean, and when you leave, you'll miss it the way I do."

Finally, I understood.

It's not that I felt differently about the United States. I love America, and I'm proud to be American. I feel incredibly indebted to my country for everything I have. I feel at home and most in my element in America, and I would defend it if it were truly threatened. Sometimes, I even get teary when "The Star Spangled Banner" is sung. I'm especially grateful for having the freedom and the right to speak out against U.S. policies; it's part of what makes America great.

Yet, stepping into Afghanistan, I felt a tremendous connection, a genuine homecoming.

We found a cab and climbed in. The windshield had a big crack across it, and like the first car, this one too needed a good wash. An older Afghan man wearing Western garb and spectacles got into the front seat. I learned later that he was a physician from Germany visiting family in Kabul. Another guy got in the back next to Munir.

As we drove toward Kabul, the air grew gradually colder.

"You're going to freeze in Kabul," Munir said when I told him that I hadn't brought a coat.

I was struck by Afghanistan's incredible beauty. All I'd ever seen on the news were barren, dry landscapes. But now I saw that there were flowing rivers, turquoise lakes, flowers, trees, and, in the distance, staggering snow-covered mountains that made Aspen seem like a collection of bunny hills. If not for the political unrest and economic instability, Afghanistan would be an amazing tourist destination.

When we drove through downtown Jalalabad, Munir pointed to the U.S. military base. It instantly evoked images of secret prisons, renditions, and torture. But at the same time, I felt grateful that the United States had rid Afghanistan of the terrible Taliban.

Moments later, the driver jerked our car over onto the right shoulder and stopped. All the other cars in our lane did the same. Passing by at full speed was a convoy of U.S. vehicles. I instinctively pulled out my camera and took a few quick shots. I got one photo of a soldier looking at me. Munir was mortified.

My biggest threat, he told me, was not from Afghans but from American soldiers. He explained that we had pulled off the road so that the soldiers wouldn't open fire on motorists whom they feared might be suicide bombers. I would soon realize that the U.S. military is a hard-to-ignore presence in Afghanistan. The country is speckled with U.S. soldiers, military bases, convoys, and jails. There are constant references to Bagram and Guantánamo Bay. I asked Munir what Afghans think of the U.S. presence.

"We are grateful that the Taliban are gone and happy for the reconstruction, but this is Afghanistan," he said. "A foreign military cannot overstay its welcome. Eventually, they will have to leave."

With each mile, the air grew colder. When we passed through Sarobi, the mountains were white with snow. Beautiful lakes filled the valleys, and locals sold fresh fish and pomegranates on the side of the road. I lowered the window and let the cold air whip against my face.

During this drive, I rarely saw a woman. And when I did, she swam in the head-to-toe fabric of a burka. I wondered who those women were, what their faces looked like, what their names were, whether they were young girls or grandmothers. I also wondered whether their husbands kept them happy or life had dealt them a crueler hand. They were invisible, ghostlike creatures passing through without personality or expression. But under that wall of fabric, they were girls with names, stories, feelings, and dreams.

Burkas and veils are hard for Westerners to understand. Many associate democratization with women throwing off their burkas. But my father described Afghanistan before the Soviet invasion and before the Taliban era as a peaceful place where women with stylish haircuts wearing miniskirts strode in the streets alongside other women in burkas. It's inaccurate for the media to portray burkas as simply a new, Taliban-era edict. The Taliban may have forced all women to wear them, but there have always been Afghan women who choose to wear them on their own. My paternal grandmother was one. Nobody forced her to don the burka, neither her husband nor any other male relative. My dad, in fact, used to try to persuade her to wear a shawl instead. But everyone says she preferred the burka.

We had been driving for several hours, and my camera was being passed around the car so that everyone could help get the best angles for various photographs. But the other passengers were still reserved and didn't speak directly to me. I drew curious glances, though, when they heard my accented Pashto.

"Her Pashto sounds as though she has spent time outside," the man next to Munir finally said. Munir explained who I was and what I was doing. The Afghan from Germany turned around to face me.

"God keep you. I am very happy you have come," he said, nodding his head. He reminded me somehow of Dr. Ali Shah Mousovi.

In the Sarobi mountains, we came to another roadblock. Fortunately, this time there was no shooting. A Chinese road crew was rebuilding the road, which had been barely drivable for years. It was bombed heavily during the U.S. invasion and was largely unmaintained during the Taliban era. But with the help of international workers, it is being rebuilt to allow for easy commerce between Peshawar and Kabul.

Half an hour later, the road crew let us through to the Afghan capital.

CHAPTER TEN

KABUL

I checked into Ariana guesthouse in downtown Kabul, a large house with gardens and a friendly staff. I was surprised to find the room charge to be $50 a night; that's cheap for the United States but a lot for Afghanistan. The cost of living in Kabul had skyrocketed after the fall of the Taliban because of the rise in foreign aid workers from organizations such as the Red Cross, the United Nations, and various international businesses and nongovernmental organizations (NGOs). In fact, Kabul's posh downtown commercial and high-end residential Wazir Akbar Khan district is now more expensive than many U.S. cities.

At first glance, my room seemed comfortable. The two-man hotel crew dragged in a big heater, but they told me to turn it off at night so that I wouldn't die of carbon monoxide poisoning. I wanted to take a shower, but the water was icy. The crew came in (after knocking and asking for *ijaazat,* or permission to enter) and turned the water heater on, but it wouldn't work.

The hotel staff boiled some water on the kitchen stove and brought it to my room in a big red plastic bucket. It was scalding hot, so I mixed it with cold water in an empty Coke bottle, then "showered" by pouring the water from the bottle over my head. Afterward, I realized that there weren't any towels; I drip-dried in front of the carbon monoxide gas heater.

To add to the Third World experience, the electricity kept going in and out. I was freezing but afraid of the poisonous gas coming from my heater. I figured it was better to freeze than to be gassed in my sleep, so I turned the heater off. The next morning, I woke up early. I knew I wasn't being fussy when I exhaled and saw my breath.

I had an interview set up with Abdul Salam Zaeef, a former Taliban ambassador and Guantánamo detainee. Once again, I was looking forward to a hot shower, but the water was still icy, so I jumped in and out quickly and gave myself a head-freeze washing my hair. I was trying hard to go with the flow, but I didn't think I could last for two weeks with hypothermia and the constant threat of carbon monoxide poisoning. My blow dryer wasn't working because the electricity was going on and off, so I just covered my wet hair with a black shawl.

I took a cab to Zaeef's mansion in Kabul's Khushal Khan neighborhood, feeling very nervous about meeting the outspoken former Taliban ambassador. I'd gotten in touch with Zaeef through local journalists who had written about him and who had helped me request an interview. As I got out of the taxi, I counted ten armed guards outside the ambas-

Abdul Salam Zaeef's guards outside his Kabul home. *Author photo.*

sador's gated complex. Some were wearing camouflage and boots, but one wore plastic sandals with socks. Two were sitting in blue plastic chairs with their legs crossed. Another squatted in the driveway holding a gun. They seemed to be expecting me and were at ease. A man waiting by the gates escorted me into a room lined with gray sofas, where I sat down to wait.

Zaeef became notorious when he made himself the public face of the Taliban by holding regular news conferences after September 11. While he publicly condemned the attacks on the World Trade Center and the Pentagon, he maintained that Osama bin Laden was not responsible. When the situation got a bit dodgy in Afghanistan, Zaeef fled from the bombs to neighboring Pakistan, where he sought asylum and continued his media attacks on the U.S.-led war. Soon after, he was arrested in Islamabad by the Pakistani Secret Police, handed over to the U.S. military, and eventually wound up at Gitmo.

I was particularly curious about him because of his former political affiliations. I wanted to pick his brain about his former job as ambassador for the Taliban. Dechert was supposed to have represented Zaeef, but he was released in the summer of 2005 before Peter Ryan and I ever had the chance to meet him. I also thought it was peculiar that he'd been arrested at all, since international law dictates that he should have received diplomatic immunity.

When he walked in and greeted me, my nervousness didn't immediately dissipate, although I was surprised to find him very soft-spoken. He was a tall, big-boned man with a thick, dark beard and eyeglasses. He was wearing a light-colored blazer over his Afghan clothes. He sat down across a glass table from me, and I was relieved that he apparently had no qualms about a woman interviewing him, although all he could see of me were my face and hands. A thin man came in and poured us green tea. I was freezing and quickly took a gulp, burning my lips.

Zaeef curled up in the sofa chair, drawing in his sock feet. He told me he was through with politics and was happy at home with his two wives and six kids, writing another book.

Over the next two hours, we downed a pot of green tea, and I picked his brain. I started off with questions related to his experiences at Gitmo and worked up the courage to ask him about how he'd justified working for a regime that allegedly executed women in a sports stadium.

Here are some excerpts of our chat:

Q: You were at Gitmo for three years and five
    months. Did you always cling to a hope that you
    would go home?

A: No, in the beginning, I had no hope. When I was
    first brought to Guantánamo, it brought back
    memories of the Russian invasion of Afghanistan.
    Thousands of Afghan men disappeared [during
    that war]. I feared a similar fate. It was only after I
    saw other Afghans going home that I slowly al-
    lowed myself to hope that I might too. I knew I
    had not committed a crime, so I had hope that
    someday I would be released.

Q: What was it like when you were finally released?
    How did you get the news?

A: I was in Camp 4 with Haji Nusrat and his son
    Izatullah when I got the news. The soldiers came
    with the Red Cross and told me I would be going
    home. All of the other prisoners congratulated
    me. They asked me to visit their families and con-
    vey their greetings.

Q: Tell me about actually going home. What was the
    plane ride like? I've heard that prisoners are sent
    home in shackles. Were you shackled on the way
    home?

A: Well, I had never seen the Guantánamo Airport
    before because prisoners are always moved around
    in special windowless vehicles. It was night time,
    and when I got there, there was a general standing
    on the tarmac. His name was written on his shirt,
    but I don't remember it. . . . He congratulated me.

He told me I'd been through a lot of hardships but
that I was a good person and that I was headed
home. Then, he told two soldiers to free me. They
cut my plastic handcuffs. There was a soldier on
each side of me, and they led me to the plane.
There was also a delegate from the Afghan government there, and he congratulated me.

Q: What did it feel like to be unshackled for the first
time in years?

A: I thought I was in a dream—that none of it was
real. I was in a special plane; I was unshackled. It
was the first time in years that I could eat and
move my legs freely . . . and decide when I
wanted to eat. It was a strange experience.

Q: What did you feel?

A: I felt many things. I was feeling guilty for everyone left behind. I was excited to be leaving Guantánamo. But at the same time I was very anxious,
very nervous.

Q: Nervous how?

A: I was nervous about where I would be taken. I
was afraid I might be jailed somewhere else.

Q: Are you able to separate the American people
from their government?

A: It is hard to separate the two. Right now, I am hat-
ing most Americans.

Q: Why?

A: Initially, I thought it was the policy makers and
the American government that were to blame—
not the American people. But the American peo-

ple voted for Bush a second time. Although I do believe the American government has taken the American people hostage. They live in fear of their government's lies.

Q: Would you ever visit America?

A: No. I have no interest in that.

Q: How do you justify your work as a representative for a regime that executed women in the sports stadium?

A: That incident was televised all over the Western media, but what Americans do not know is that this lady was sentenced to death for murdering her husband. It had nothing to do with adultery. Don't Americans also have the death penalty? Would it make it better if she were executed in private?

Q: Tell me about some of your interactions with the guards at Gitmo.

A: I was always talking to them. I was explaining my situation to them and I was always inviting them to Islam.

Q: How'd that go over?

A: Sometimes they listened. Sometimes they didn't. I always told the guards that if they had objections to Islam, I was ready to speak to them about it. Some people had no idea what Islam was really about. I thought it was my responsibility to expose them to true Islam. *Alhamdulillah*—praise be to God—two became Muslim.

Q: Tell me about that.

A: Two white soldiers, they accepted Islam after speaking with me for three or four months. They kept it a secret. They would come to me, wake me up, and I would talk to them. I wish I could meet those two again, but I don't know their addresses or how to find them.

Q: What were their religions before?

A: One was an atheist, and the other was Christian. There were other soldiers who didn't convert but were intrigued enough to listen to me and told me they would speak to an Islamic scholar when they returned to America. I was always trying to educate people about the religion; they know so little and have been so prejudiced. When I was called into interrogations, I would do the same thing there. Sometimes they would tell me they weren't interested in listening, but many of them were open minded.

Abdul Salam Zaeef rereading family letters received at Guantánamo. *Author photo.*

Before I left, I photographed Zaeef sifting through a thick stack of his Guantánamo letters, many of them covered in dark censor strokes. He told me that letters were everything to prisoners. Now, they evoked painful memories, but he hung on to them. He echoed what so many of the released have said about Guantánamo: "It's a part of me now."

He also showed me a photograph of his daughters that he
kept in his cell at Gitmo (at
right).

As I hopped into a cab, I decided
to check out of my hotel and go
someplace with a generator and
central heating. I asked the
driver to take me to the Inter-
Continental Hotel. It was only

A photo of Zaeef's daughters, which he
kept in his Gitmo cell. *Courtesy of Abdul
Salam Zaeef.*

ten minutes away, but traffic was very heavy, and it ended up
taking half an hour to get there. The driver made small talk. He
asked me what I was doing and where I was from. I told him a
bit about myself but omitted the part about America. But that
was the part he was wondering about.

"But where is your home?" he asked. "You sound like you
have spent time abroad."

"*Amreeka kay usaygam*—I live in America," I finally said.

He looked at me in the rearview mirror and smiled. "How
fortunate you are."

"This is my first time in Afghanistan. It's really beautiful," I
said.

He started to tell me about his troubles. He had salt-and-
pepper hair and six- or seven-day stubble. He wore an embroidered hat and honked the horn brazenly as he wove through
traffic, all the while telling me about an entire generation of
Afghan youth left without education because of war.

"Without education, sister," he said, glancing back at me, "our future is bleak."

Afghans hated the Taliban and lived in fear during their rule, he said. "God damn them for what they brought upon us," he said angrily. Unlike many others, he could not afford to flee to Iran, Pakistan, or overseas. He told me that I should know about the hardships all Afghans face every day. He told me about his struggles to take care of his young children and his wife. We talked about the Russian invasion, the Taliban, the land mines littering the country, warlords, and U.S. bombs.

He drove onto the InterContinental's long uphill driveway, stopping at several gates and various levels of security check-points where armed guards questioned him and peered into the trunk. They waved us through. When we pulled into the hotel parking lot, I handed him some extra dollars. He put his palm against his chest and nodded. According to the Afghan ministry of finance, the average Afghan makes about eighty cents a day. Up to that point, I had only known about the economic, social, and psychological effects of perpetual warfare from accounts by journalists, historians, and statisticians. I knew that the separation between the rich and poor was great, but beyond the dates and figures, I had no experience of it.

I had also heard a lot about developments in infrastructure, commerce, and education since the Taliban had been ousted, but I was still surprised when I saw the InterContinental. The taxi driver insisted on walking me in with my bags. We passed a large sign with a picture of a machine gun and a large red X drawn over it. "No Weapons," it read. A doorman held open the glass doors to the lobby. I stood behind a barricade of red velvet ropes. The doorman told the cab driver to put my luggage on the table, where it was searched. Then, another man with a black mustache, wearing a blue suit, instructed me to walk through a metal detector into the chandeliered lobby.

I had no idea that Kabul had such a revamped hotel. I quickly discovered the InterContinental's ostentatious list of amenities. All of a sudden, my taxi driver looked out of place in his tattered clothes and dusty shoes. He must have felt it too, because he hurriedly gave me a small card with his number, in case I should need him again. I thanked him profusely and said goodbye.

The hotel is a huge complex; all charges were to be paid in dollars only. I was surprised to see an ATM machine in the lobby—and further surprised when it dispensed U.S. dollars. The restaurant and room service menus listed a variety of American and Afghan cuisine with prices listed in U.S. dollars. An "American hamburger" was $8.

The complex included a spa, a business center—which charged by the minute, in dollars—a team of imported young Thai masseuses, a hair and nail salon, a ballroom, a swimming pool, restaurants, a tea and coffee house with huge dark leather couches, and a wide variety of imported teas and coffees. The hotel was full of businessmen, tourists making weekend trips from Dubai, and, as a hotel employee would tell me later, Afghan and U.S. intelligence spying on guests. Some of the rooms, I learned later, were bugged.

The hotel also had an airline counter and numerous small gift shops. When I asked one shop keeper how he justified his ridiculously inflated prices, in dollars, he told me that a small gift shop space at the hotel was $800 a month—and highly coveted.

The clerk at the front desk quoted me a rate of $160 per night. It seemed obscene for Afghanistan. I looked at him in disbelief and started to haggle. "I can't afford more than $100," I said firmly.

"Okay. We accept cash only. Dollars," he said.

He asked me to pay for a few days in advance.

I was surprised when he handed me a modern key-card to my room. As I walked across the lobby to the elevators, I saw Westerners in jeans standing around speaking French. There were couples sitting on couches being served big slices of yellow cake and tea. The place was crawling with North American Treaty Organization soldiers, European adventure seekers, and other tourists browsing the antique jewelry shops. It was a weird oasis.

At the elevator, I was greeted by a guard.

"Which floor, madam?" he asked in English.

"Eight, please."

Hardly anyone at the hotel wore Afghan clothes. None of the women covered their hair, and all of the employees spoke English. It was often broken English, but they were obviously instructed to speak it.

In my room, I plugged in my laptop and went online. I felt guilty paying so much for a hotel room when most Afghans didn't have running water or electricity in their homes. Here, I had central heating, a huge bathroom with hot water, and high-speed Internet.

I e-mailed my family to let them know that I was fine. Then, I slipped into a pair of flats, wrapped myself in a pashmina, and prepared for my meetings with the families of detainees. Each day, I visited a former Gitmo prisoner or the families of men still imprisoned. The families were instrumental in helping gather evidentiary documents used in the detainees' defense. For example, the U.S. military didn't seem to buy that Abdullah Wazir Zadran was a shopkeeper selling tires in the Khost bazaar with his family. So, I asked his older brother Zahir Shah to collect photographs of the tire store. We also discussed getting affidavits of neighboring shopkeepers to give to the military courts. Zahir Shah brought a stack of about fifty photographs of the tire store with the family name clearly written on the sign above it. I held many of these meetings at the hotel because I was nervous about venturing into southern Afghanistan.

After my work for the day was done, I headed into the city. I loved the hotel's comforts but was eager to get outside its gates. I wanted to see the real Kabul.

At the front desk, I asked one of the mustached men to help me hail a cab so I could explore the city.

"Are you going alone?" he inquired. "We can send someone with you if you prefer."

The hotel's Ariana Airlines desk officer closed the office and said he'd take me around. He had a short beard, and I immediately noticed a huge scar along the left side of his face and wondered what it was from. When our discussion eventually turned political, he explained that he had been beaten by the Taliban years before. He couldn't afford to flee, as many of his friends had.

"There is no way I could have walked the streets with this short beard," he said. "And there is no way we could have walked together. It was a terrible time."

He took me first to Chicken Street, a narrow lane lined with small shops selling everything from antique water jugs to handcrafted Afghan rugs, as well as the imported Persian variety. I picked up two, one for me and one for Peter Ryan. I wandered from store to store, checking out the antique jewelry, embroidered shawls, and jeweled, wooden boxes with hand-painted Persian hunting scenes. I picked up a rabbit fur jacket for $30 and a bunch of large dangly antique silver earrings. While the prices on Chicken Street were much more reasonable than at the gift shops at my hotel, I still wondered how Afghans could afford Kabul. Everywhere I went, I saw European men and women shopping.

After Chicken Street, my guide gave me a tour of Kabul. It seemed like everywhere we looked, there was bogus development. I saw little evidence of urban planning, or a desire to close the open sewage lines, or hospitals or schools. Instead, the city had seen a spike in high-end hotels, Internet cafes, bars, and swimming pools, which I was told were surrounded in the summertime by European women in bikinis. At first, I didn't know what to make of it all. But the more I saw, the more it irked me. Living costs in Kabul are just as high as (or higher) than they are in the United States.

Before the U.S. invasion, it would have cost $50 to $60 monthly to rent a small house near Kabul City. Now the price had been hiked up to $1,500 a month. But in the upscale Wazir Akbar Khan district of Kabul, prices were insane. It used to cost about $300 a month to rent a nice house there. Now, prices had soared from $5,000 up to a whopping $15,000 a month—higher than the cost of living in most areas of Beverly Hills.

All this so-called development wasn't for Afghans or even for Afghanistan. It was for European and American NGOs, for people who chat up their sat phone bills and hook up their Sony Vaios at cybercafes. These were the sorts who stayed at the InterContinental—or Kabul's new decadent Serena Hotel, where guests could drop $350 a night for a room or $1,200 a night for a presidential suite. The average Afghan would have to work for more than four years to be able to afford a single night there.

When I visited the Kabul City Centre, a massive, multimillion dollar megamall with shiny golden escalators and glass elevators, it was more of the same. Rich Europeans, Americans, and Afghans who lived abroad were passing their time shopping for high-end electronics, designer clothing, precious stones, Swiss watches, and antiques. The stores displayed limited-edition U2 iPods and multiple-stranded ruby and emerald necklaces. The only currency accepted was dollars. With the holiday season fast approaching, there were signs for Christmas specials everywhere. It seemed a little odd in a predominantly Muslim country.

Outside the mammoth mall of decadence, it was another story. The typically proud Pashtuns had resorted to begging. It was the only way to benefit from the grand development going on all around them. Afghan boys and girls in tattered clothing gathered in the piercing cold winter winds. They held out their dirty hands, hoping that a wealthy shopper would take pity. Some had lost legs to land mines and dragged their bodies across the icy pavement as shoppers mostly averted their gazes and walked quickly toward warm waiting Land Rovers.

The UN Department of Humanitarian Affairs estimates there are about ten million land mines scattered throughout

Children playing in Kabul. *Author photo.*

Afghanistan, many of them remnants of the 1980s Russian invasion. An estimated eight hundred thousand Afghans have
been maimed by the devices in the ensuing decades. UNICEF
estimates that twenty to twenty-five people are wounded
every day and that 4 percent of the Afghan population has
been disabled by exploding land mines. You could see the legless people on crutches or in wheelchairs everywhere.

Next to Wazir Akbar Khan's megamansions are Kabul's
slums, lined with mud houses and open sewage canals. They
have no electricity, no running water, not even any heat to stave
off the subzero temperatures. The average Afghan lives in ab-
ject poverty. As we drove through this neighborhood, I watched
children pushing each other in a wheelbarrow and playing in
mounds of garbage. They had no playgrounds, day care, or
clean clothes like American children. Little boys and girls ran to

the car, holding up a finger in a request for some change. Some were so young they could barely reach the window.

Afghanistan's children bear the brunt of the nation's poverty. While there have been improvements since the Taliban were ousted, the country still has the second highest infant-mortality rate in the world, preceded only by Sierra Leone.[1] The great majority of Afghan women do not receive any prenatal care and give birth at home without the help of a midwife or a doctor. As a result, Afghanistan has the distinction of having the highest life risk for maternal mortality. One in six Afghan women die in child birth every day. One in four children dies before age five.[2] The life expectancy for men is forty-five; for women, forty-four. Almost 90 percent of Afghan women are illiterate.[3] Most Afghan women are married before the age of eighteen. Many are forced into marriages for various reasons, including to settle feuds or repay debts.

When I saw the scale of deprivation, I was again reminded of my own good luck that I was born and raised as an American. What if my parents hadn't been educated, had never emigrated to the United States? For the first time, I understood that the opportunities in my life were a windfall. The old taxi driver had been right about my good fortune.

While most of the Afghans I spoke with were grateful that the Taliban were gone, some bore an untempered anger toward the U.S. armed forces for the destruction of their land. A few times during my stay, I heard about inexplicable cancers and strange diseases that people seemed to have developed. Some believed that it was all due to the U.S. bombs.

I contacted Mohammad Daud Miraki, a local and international expert who has researched the mysterious illnesses. He works closely with Asaf Durocovic of the Uranium Medical Research Center (UMRC) in Washington, D.C. Durocovic sent a team of field workers to Afghanistan immediately after the coalition bombing of Afghanistan in Operation Enduring Freedom in 2001. UMRC studied the presence of depleted uranium in populations bombed by coalition forces in targeted cities such as Tora Bora, Jalalabad, Spin Gar, and Kabul as compared with untargeted populations. Durocovic consistently found that the residents of heavily bombed areas had a uranium concentration in their urine that was twenty to two hundred times larger than that of the control group.

While no direct scientific data correlates the increase in uranium with the illnesses, Miraki saw no other explanation. "There is nothing 'depleted' about depleted uranium," he told me. "It gives off ionizing radiation that damages DNA and genes. The damage can be seen most readily with cells that are dividing and growing rapidly, like those in a human embryo."

Following Durocovic's published study of radioactive warfare in Afghanistan, Miraki sent his own team of field workers to catalogue the anecdotal incidents. He traveled to the Operation Enduring Freedom bomb sites and collected photographs of severely deformed infants. Many were limbless and died soon after birth; some were born without eyes, with enlarged heads or with massive tumors protruding from their bodies. Miraki and his field workers also recorded interviews with locals in the noncontrol areas.

Assadullah, an Afghan from Paktia province, said that his wife gave birth to a boy with melon-sized tumors growing where his eyes should have been. "When I saw my little boy with those monstrous red tumors, I thought to myself, why is it difficult for Americans to understand that they are hated in our country? If I did this to the child of an American family, that family would have the right to pull my eyes out of my sockets," he said.

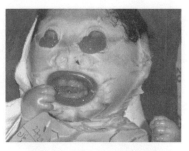

Jooma Khan's deformed grandson, who was alive for several hours after birth but died shortly after this photograph was taken. *Courtesy of Mohammad Daud Miraki.*

Sa'yed Gharid of Tora Bora became angry as he spoke about the horrors he had witnessed. "What else do the Americans want? They killed us; they turned our newborns into horrific deformities; they turned our farmlands into graveyards and destroyed our homes," he said. "On top of all that, their planes fly over and spray us with bullets. We have nothing to lose; we will fight them the way we fought the previous monster," the Soviet Union.

Jooma Khan of Lagman province said his grandson was a victim of unconventional U.S. warfare. "When I saw my deformed grandson, I realized that my hopes for the future have vanished for good, different from the hopelessness of the Russian barbarism," Khan said. "We are part of the invisible genocide brought on us by America, a silent death from which I know we will not escape."

About a week after my arrival, a snowfall covered Kabul's dirty slums in white. I fell in love with wintertime in Afghanistan. At night, I would fall asleep to the light rhythm of snow falling,

Afghanistan's winter lull. *Author photo.*

and every morning before sunrise, I would jump out of bed and pull back the curtains to photograph the sunrise over the city or the big white snowflakes falling from the sky and covering Kabul in a glittery blanket. Afterward, the roads were blocked, shops were closed, and the city slowed to a silent lull.

CHAPTER ELEVEN

DEAD DETAINEES

Suicide by hanging: that was the Pentagon's verdict in the case of Salah al-Aslami, No. 693. But back home in Yemen, his father couldn't believe it. It was murder, he cried.

The official version of the story went like this:

Sometime after midnight, Yemeni prisoner al-Aslami, twenty-seven, and two Saudi prisoners scrawled out suicide notes in Arabic, then hung laundry inside their cages and arranged their beds to look as though they were sleeping, all in an effort to conceal themselves from patrolling cell-block guards. The three then created crude makeshift nooses from bedsheets and clothing and pulled them over their heads. Guards found the prisoners shortly afterward, hanging by their necks in separate Camp 1 cells. All three were pronounced dead after attempts to revive them failed.

Base commander Rear Adm. Harry Harris Jr. immediately issued statements to the media, reiterating that the dead men were dangerous terrorists "committed to killing Americans" who had taken their own lives in a crafty act of war, a planned suicide pact cum public relations stunt against America.

"They have no regard for human life," Harris said. "Neither ours nor their own. I believe this was not an act of desperation but an act of asymmetric warfare against us."

Rubbish, said habeas attorney Clive Stafford Smith of Reprieve in London. "It is asymmetric," he said. "On one side are a bunch of heavily armed soldiers. On the other are prisoners who are unarmed and always shackled. Warfare, it is not."

Al-Aslami's younger brother said he first heard about the suicides on the local news in Yemen but never considered that one of the dead might be his brother. He didn't think much more about the news reports. But the following day, the family was shocked to receive a phone call from an American lawyer who confirmed that Salah was one of the dead prisoners.

The family was hysterical, and Salah's wife, Hayat, may never recover. Their disbelief and shock slowly settled into despair and outrage. Al-Aslami's brother rejected the notion of suicide immediately, believing that something more sinister had taken place.

"We were all stunned by the news," he said from his home in Yemen. "My brother was a simple and gentle sort of guy. Taking his life is very out of character. We have never accepted that this is how he left us."

When I heard about the suicides, they struck me as the ultimate Guantánamo tragedy: three men who had never been charged or given a fair hearing would be going home in caskets.

When I visited the base a few weeks later, it was clear that news of the suicides had made the prisoners anxious and uncomfortable. They wanted to know what had really happened. But no one had any information other than what the Department of Defense had released. There were no independent investigations, and the military refused to release its autopsy reports. So, we could only tell the detainees what we, like everyone else, had heard on the news.

Some of the prisoners listened pensively; others asked thoughtful questions. Taj Mohammad blurted out the conspiracy theory that the others only pondered—or perhaps feared: "I think they were killed."

Since the detention center at Guantánamo Bay opened in early 2002, there have been more than forty-one reported suicide attempts by twenty-three detainees. Many more have gone unreported by the media. Some detainees were accordingly reluctant to accept that three prisoners could have successfully committed suicide on the same night and at around the same time.

Taj Mohammad tried to hang himself several times. Shah Mohammad, a twenty-two-year-old Afghan prisoner, also tried to take his life.[1] He was reportedly put into solitary confinement when all the regular cells were occupied. There, he tried to commit suicide four times. In 2003, he was released to Pakistan, where he told reporters that the U.S. military gave him injections prior to his interrogations to make him talk.[2] The abuse was more than he could manage. Around the time Shah Mohammad was released, another twenty-three detainees tried to commit suicide en masse—unsuccessfully.

In the aftermath of the suicides, the Department of Justice alleged that the detainees may have used paper provided by lawyers to plan their suicide pact. It asked a court for permission to seize and review privileged attorney-client documents. The move outraged the habeas legal squad, which considered it an excuse to invade the detainees' and lawyers' privacy.

"This is nonsense," said habeas attorney Stafford Smith, who represented thirty-seven prisoners. "For an organization intent on people taking responsibility, they sure don't want to do it themselves."

There were only two explanations for how three men might have died on the same night and at roughly the same time: they were killed, or they committed suicide in a joint pact.

I don't know what happened in the early morning hours of Saturday, June 10—whether it was desperation that brought the three young Arabs to suicide or whether, as many in the "non-American" world tend to believe, something more sinister happened. But three prisoners were dead, and I wanted to know about their lives. I was particularly intrigued by Salah al-Aslami because he was just twenty-three when he was brought to Gitmo. I wondered how his parents had reacted to the news of his suicide and wanted to know more about his childhood, why he'd left Yemen, and what had led him down the road that ended in his premature death.

So, I Googled the dead Yemeni, hoping to learn more. When I tried to get transcripts of his military hearings, there was nothing. Al-Aslami had had a combatant status review tribunal, but the military refused to release the transcript despite a court order that resulted from an Associated Press Freedom of Information Act lawsuit.

I was able to locate a record of his military Administrative Review Board transcript, but it was entirely redacted and disclosed nothing, not even the allegations against him. There was, however, a brief mention of al-Aslami in the military transcripts of another Yemeni prisoner, Fahmi Abdullah Ahmed, No. 688. The two had been picked up together in Pakistan.

From the transcripts, it appears that Ahmed was twenty-two years old and, like al-Aslami, in Pakistan on business. The two met soon after Ahmed's arrival and hit it off right away. Al-Aslami invited his new friend to come live with him in a communal house shared by a group of students, many of them also from Yemen. Ahmed told the tribunal that he had never been to Afghanistan and that as far as he knew, al-Aslami hadn't been either.

The two lived together for just two weeks before their house was raided by Pakistani police, who seized the group of young Arabs and handed them over to U.S. armed forces. Eventually, both wound up at Bagram before being brought to Guantánamo.

For Tom Wilner of Shearman and Sterling, who represented several Arab detainees, the Pakistani police raid scenario was déjà vu all over again. Eighty-six percent of the detainees had been seized in Pakistan, according to declassified Defense Department documents.[3] It's believed that a great number, if not all, of these men were sold into captivity.

"None of my clients were captured on any battlefield or are even accused of engaging in any hostilities against the U.S.," Wilner said. "Each was sold into captivity for bounties."

Al-Aslami was one of the first prisoners brought to Guantánamo Bay, and according to news reports, military officials
said he was a regular hunger striker who protested his detention and encouraged others to do the same. Back home in
Yemen, his parents prayed that he would be released soon, as
other Yemeni detainees had been.

The family was reassured of their son's well-being when
they received occasional calls or letters from released detainees who had been imprisoned with him in Guantánamo.
Former Kuwaiti detainee Saad al-Azimi and several released
Saudi detainees told the family that their son was in good
health and felt confident that he would be headed home soon.
Nothing could have prepared the family for the news of his
suicide.

With the help of lawyers at the Center for Constitutional
Rights, I was able to speak with al-Aslami's family in Yemen.
His father, Ali Abdullah Ahmed, who now prefers to be called
Abu Salah (in Arabic "father of Salah"), was adamant that his
son was a devout Muslim who had memorized the Qu'ran
and would never have committed suicide, which is a grave sin
in Islam.

"My son was murdered by Americans," Ali Abdullah told me
through an Arabic interpreter. "This idea of suicide is a lie."

Al-Aslami was born into a large, tight-knit family of eight
brothers and four sisters. When he was a child, the neighbors
often saw him playing soccer in the streets with his brothers
and friends. He loved the sport, and the boys competed in a local neighborhood league.

"Salah was a good brother," his younger brother, Amar, said. "He never got upset with me, even when something was my fault."

As a boy, al-Aslami enrolled in the village elementary school, Abu Bakar bin Sadiq, where he excelled in math and science. Even then, his father said, he was very precocious and business minded. He wanted to earn a living and was always coming up with new business ideas.

"It pleased me that he was so bright at a young age," said his father.

While attending school, the boy got a part-time job at a neighborhood store called Salameen Groceries, where he made pocket money selling nuts, yogurt, and meat. He often came home with jars of fresh honey for the house. A cook at the store became fond of young al-Aslami and regularly made him his favorite foods—spicy fish, rice, and meat.

Al-Aslami also helped his father around the family farm, feeding the animals and playing with the sheep. "I shared so many little moments like that with him," his father said. "Now I wait patiently to see him again in the hereafter."

Al-Aslami continued to work at the grocery story for years, until he eventually saved up enough money to buy it. He wanted to get married and provide for a family. When he turned fifteen, the family arranged a marriage to his first cousin, Hayat Warshad Ali. The two grew to love each other, and the elder al-Aslami described his son as a devoted husband who liked to make his wife laugh. "His biggest joy was pampering her and his mother," he said with a chuckle. It was the only moment of happiness I sensed during that long-distance call.

Al-Aslami wanted to expand his shop and import spices and perhaps textiles, so he planned a trip to Pakistan, which was just a short flight away.

"My son went to Pakistan to expand his business," his father told me. "Nothing more."

The family didn't think anything of the young man's trip. Many Arabs travel to neighboring countries for commerce and to do charitable work. But it would be the last time that they would see him.

The family became worried as weeks and months went by without a phone call. Then, one day, the Red Cross delivered a letter. "I am in Guantánamo Bay, Cuba," al-Aslami wrote. "This is a place where there are no rights, and there is no justice. I'm afraid there is nothing I can do, so I leave my fate and my freedom in the hands of the Almighty. Please write to me and send me letters."

The family was relieved to know where he was and hoped that the U.S. military would investigate and soon release him. After all, "America was known around the world for its justice system," Amar said.

The family replied to Salah's letter countless times—first writing long letters and then simple short ones, simply pleading for another word.

"I don't remember how many times we wrote, but we never heard from him again," the elder al-Aslami told me quietly. "We never got another letter. We only received his body."

Six days after the alleged suicides, the U.S. military shipped the bodies back to their home countries for burial. Al-Aslami's corpse was accompanied by a death certificate listing hanging as the cause of death. But al-Aslami's father said that he would not bury his son until an independent autopsy was conducted by a neutral international medical team. The family got in touch with the Geneva-based nongovernmental organization Alkarama for Human Rights, which coordinated with Lausanne University's Institute of Legal Medicine to conduct a second autopsy.

The procedure was conducted at a military hospital in Sanaa, the Yemeni capital, on June 21, 2006, eleven days after the young man's death, by a Swiss medical team led by forensic pathologist Dr. Patrice Mangin.[4]

In his autopsy report, Mangin stated that al-Aslami's body was remarkably well preserved. It had been transported from the United States to Yemen in a state-of-the-art aluminum container in which the body was kept frozen.

To its surprise, the Swiss team reported, organs essential to its investigation had been removed from the body. "Some of the organs in the pharynx, larynx, and the throat were missing," Mangin stated in an interview in Geneva. "These are often the most important parts to examine when there has been a hanging."

The pathology team also detected traces of pressure around the neck, bruising on the back of the right hand, a punctured vein as well as other injuries, lesions in the mouth, and a lower front tooth that had probably been broken when the victim was alive. There were also indications that al-Aslami had been given intravenous injections, but the Swiss medical team was unable to determine what these injections might have been, and toxicology reports did not indicate the presence of any substances in the body.

While suicide was a possibility, Mangin said that because of the missing organs, other hypotheses could not be ruled out. He further stated that while there was evidence of asphyxiation that could have been due to suicide, it could also have been attributable to other causes.

Mangin said his team didn't have enough information to draw any definitive conclusions. For the pathologists and for the victim's family, many questions remained. "How were the bodies discovered? What was their position? What was the method of hanging? What was their state before death? What was the medical response when they were found? And above all, what was the state of the missing organs?" Mangin asked in European press reports.[5]

The pathology team subsequently made several formal requests to the U.S. military for a copy of the original autopsy, histological and anatomical samples of the missing organs, and information surrounding the nature of al-Aslami's death. But as of this writing, they had received no reply. The pathologists also contacted Dr. Craig Mallak, the U.S. armed forces medical examiner, on numerous occasions and sent letters to U.S. authorities through the U.S. Embassy in Bern, Switzerland.

Mallak said he was not permitted to cooperate with any organization without an explicit authorization from U.S. authorities, and such authorization has not been granted.

The U.S. military's refusal to cooperate baffled the Swiss team. "It is surprising. On the one hand, they have taken so much care to send us the body in an extraordinarily well-preserved state, which would have involved some serious work. On the other hand, some key information is missing," Mangin said.

The pathologists were further puzzled by al-Aslami's fin-ger- and toenails, which were cut short. Under medical law, fingernails may be cut to test for DNA traces of an attacker, but Mangin said cutting the toenails was "truly bizarre." He speculated that the organs may have been removed to pre-serve them as evidence.

"It is really regrettable that we cannot have access to the American medical reports," he said.

But Mangin's examination led to some concerns. "Accord-ing to the testimony of former prisoners in Guantánamo, they would never be left alone for more than five minutes without a warden checking on their cell," he said. "In this case, the timing does not add up. It takes at least three minutes to die from hanging. So, someone would only have had two minutes to set it up. And three deaths from hanging the same day?"

Said al-Ghamidi, chief forensic pathologist at the Riyadh Center for Forensic Medicine in Saudi Arabia, conducted autopsies on the bodies of the two Saudi detainees, Yasser Talal al-Zahrani, twenty-two, and Mani Shaman al-Utaybi, thirty. His reports indi-cate that in addition to missing throat organs, the brain, heart, liver, and kidneys were also removed from both men.

The Saudi families similarly dismissed U.S. claims that their sons had committed suicide. Yasser's father told local Saudi journalists that his son's letters from prison said that he was looking forward to a big family reunion and indicated that his faith was steadfast. Released detainees told him that his son had encouraged them to deal with their situation with patience.

Back in Yemen, Amar was appalled when he was finally allowed to see his brother's face. He didn't want to view the rest of the body because he didn't want to see the autopsy scars.

"My brother had bruises on his face. It was obvious that he had been beaten badly," he said. "We believe that he was tortured to death. It was very hard to see him like that."

After the viewing, mourners packed the local village cemetery as al-Aslami's family, community, and friends offered him the Salat-al-Janaza, the funeral prayer before burial.

"My son is finally free now," his father said.

Al-Aslami's young widow, Hayat, took the news worst of all. She had been hopeful that her husband would come home one day, but after receiving the news of his death, she fell ill and became bedridden.

Surprisingly, though, the family wasn't implacably angry with America or Americans.

"By God, there is a big difference between the American government and the American people," Amar said. "The American people are great and friendly people. The proof of this is the lawyers who have taken up our cause."

But his father wasn't timid about expressing hostility toward the Bush administration, referring to its members as "murderous hypocrites" and calling on the international community to help close Guantánamo Bay.

"By God, I have said this before, and I say it again, all of the officials in that 'black house' should fall, and all secret prisons should be filled up," he said.

The family doesn't want an apology. "We would just like them to confess and to acknowledge how they have hurt us," Amar said, without sounding as if he believed he would ever hear any such thing.

Amar told me that he believed his brother was in heaven and that he and the family would be able to see him there one day. Until then, Salah visits them in their dreams once in a while. In one dream, Amar saw his brother alongside the Prophet Mohammad in heaven, the ultimate consolation.

"He has never spoken to me," Amar told me, "but he is always very happy and peaceful."

CHAPTER TWELVE

HABEAS HURDLES

Lawyers usually get a total of only five or six hours to spend with their clients in meetings on each trip, hence the extreme frustration whenever the meetings were delayed, as they frequently were. On one occasion, the guards led several attorneys and me into Camp Echo but then made us stand around in the hot sun for a good two hours before allowing us to see our client. I was wearing a heavy shawl and felt as though I might pass out in the 90-degree heat, so I asked one of the guards whether I could seek a little relief in their air-conditioned, armored booth. "Sure," he responded. "Go ahead."

The guard's booth was a tiny, tan-colored steel room, about three feet square. I was told that it had once been used in Iraq, which explained the two bullet marks in the bulletproof glass. When I went in, I noticed a piece of paper taped to the inside of the door. It was the U.S. Army Soldier's Creed, which reads in part,

> I am an American Soldier.
> I am a Warrior and a member of a team. . . .
> I stand ready to deploy, engage and destroy the
> enemies of the United States of America in close
> combat.

Obviously I support the idea of defending the United States of America, but this message struck me as terribly out of place at Gitmo. Hanging it in the detention camp suggested that the prisoners were "the enemy" and presumed their guilt, despite the absence of charges or due process. It encouraged the notion that soldiers should hate the men they were guarding.

I slid the door open a crack and said to the guard somewhat sarcastically, "I love this thing on the door. Can I get a copy?"

"Why? You wanna be a part of the team?" he asked equally sarcastically.

"Absolutely. And I want to be a warrior and kill the enemy in close combat," I told him. "Can I have this?"

"No, but I'm sure you can download it online."

I made a mental note to myself to Google the Army creed.

After two hours of waiting, the guard told us that we could meet with the prisoner. By then, I had the creed committed to memory. I gathered my belongings and a tub of liquefied ice cream and followed him. As he marched us to the meeting room, I couldn't help myself. I started to chant the creed.

"I am a warrior. I stand ready to deploy, engage, and destroy the enemies!"

The guard looked at me. "You find that funny?" he asked.

"Absolutely not: deploy, engage, and destroy the enemy in close combat!" I said, flashing him a big smile, and walked into the meeting room.

To deflate the rigid orderliness of Gitmo, the attorneys and the interpreters often made small, subtle attempts to break the regimented monotony.

Every time we gathered outside Camp Echo, for instance, it was part of the military escort's song and dance to announce "Habeas on site" into the intercom in stentorian tones. But one afternoon, attorney Charley Carpenter had an epiphany when he heard those magic words.

"Is that a signal for you guys to stop torturing the detainees?" he asked.

All the lawyers started laughing, and it broke the order of things.

But the soldiers on duty weren't amused by this attorney who had come from afar to "help the enemy." Charley's wisecrack soon landed him in hot water. The incident went up the military chain of command, and orders were issued that he be reprimanded. Charley was pulled aside by the captain in charge, who informed him that further indiscretions would result in his being thrown off the base. Charley quickly apologized. But he didn't take the scolding personally. Those harsh words, like everything in the military, came from above.

When lawyers were first given access to the military base in 2004, the government allowed them to meet prisoners from 8 AM to 5 PM, seven days a week, for a total of sixty-three hours weekly. But then things changed. The military cut out weekend visits, forcing lawyers to leave the island on Thursday since there weren't any Saturday flights out. Daily meeting times were also slashed in half so that lawyers were lucky to get two and a half hours in the morning and three and a half hours in the afternoon. Most people didn't even get that.

There was always a long search both on the way in and on the way out with ever-changing rules about what you could bring in. Things hadn't been so rigorous in the beginning. No one cared what we wore; guards didn't look through papers and glanced only briefly into bags. Then, they started telling us to spread our legs, wanding us down for metal, yelling if anyone got too close to the table while they rifled through our stuff and sometimes confiscated family photos.

In 2006, I had no problem carrying in ceramic plates, silverware, and dishes filled with Afghan rice and lamb. By 2007, the dishes and utensils were banned. I resorted to paper and plastic, which was okay for a few weeks. Then, the rules changed again: no plastic forks or knives. They could be fashioned into weapons. (There's no evidence from Guantánamo that they ever have been.) I started bringing just plastic spoons. Predictably, the spoons were eventually banned too— for reasons of security, of course.

"We'll supply the utensils," the guard told me.

He threw out the plastic spoons and came back with sporks, which I found odd because the only difference between a spoon and a spork is that a spork, while shaped like a spoon, has spikes on the end. Didn't that make it more dangerous than a spoon?

Soon enough, I was asked to start taking out my hair clips.

"What's wrong with them?" I protested. "They keep my hair out of my face."

"They can be fashioned into makeshift keys to open handcuffs," the guard responded.

I found that comical. Even if a prisoner were able to get out of his cuffs, where would he run to? The locked cell door?

I learned never to carry eye drops, medication, or extra pens. Once I had just visited my dentist and had X-ray slides of my teeth in a zippered purse pocket. That caused a big to-do with the guards, who confiscated my X-rays. You'd think my dentist had encoded messages for the enemy in them.

During one particularly long and unexplained delay, followed by an even longer search, one of the attorneys and I started joking about whether the McDonald's french fries he had brought could be considered a weapon too. As the guards meticulously rifled through lunch bags and legal papers for contraband, we speculated about how deadly some of the crispier french fries or plastic straws could be. As the search went on for a good forty minutes, the young attorney, a law professor at an East Coast university, struck up an impromptu rap accompanied by a human beat box and broad arm movements:

"Ice cream's gettin' soupy—my fries are gettin' droopy. It's the *H* to the *A* to *B-E-A* and *S*. Yo habeas! Yo habeas!"

We spent almost an hour coming up with rap lyrics and crying from laughing so hard. 50 Cent and Snoop D, O, double G would have been proud.

A few weeks later, plastic straws were banned too.

Most lawyers who visit the base are working pro bono, spending large amounts of money and time away from work and family to visit prisoners. Some fly in from as far away as Europe. So, any additional military obstacles are highly frustrating.

Attorneys who made the mistake of bringing lots of documents into the room usually ended up kicking themselves as the guard went through hundreds of pages one by one, searching for contraband. Sometimes the guards even confiscated maps of Afghanistan—as though the Afghans didn't know the geography of their own country. Rebecca Dick of Dechert's Washington, D.C., office was livid when, for security purposes, they took away a wallet-sized photograph of her blond babies building sand castles on the beach.

Different lawyers dealt with this frustration differently. Some flew off the handle, threatening to file motions—which was sometimes very effective. Others just took a deep breath and tried to be as cooperative as possible.

Besides my brief banishment from the base, I had a few other hiccups while visiting there. I wore open-toed shoes for eight months. Then, on one visit, the notoriously mean skinny guard with rodent teeth told me that I wouldn't be allowed into the camp without proper shoes. I went a little nuts, embarrassed to be holding up the entire group.

The lawyers put their heads together. They asked whether I could wrap garbage bags around my feet to get around the no-open-toes rule. Rodent face said no. I ran back to the bus and begged the military escort to give me his shoes for the morning. He refused. One of the older captains, a very nice guy, was also on the bus, and to my great relief, he took pity on me. He walked me back into Camp Echo, where Bucky Beaver guard saluted him.

"Honor bound, sir!" she said, standing at attention.

The captain saluted back and asked her to let me in until I got other shoes.

I was sad when that captain left Guantánamo. I stayed in e-mail touch with him after he left the military and became a civilian lawyer.

Reading material for the prisoners is the subject of an ongoing tug-of-war between the Department of Defense (DOD) and the attorneys. The DOD used to review books that lawyers wanted given to their clients. Many were rejected and sent back. Among some of the censored books were *Hidden Agendas* by John Pilger, *Blair's Wars* by John Kampfner, and *I'm Not the Only One,* by George Galloway. These selections were probably considered too political for the prisoners. But it's less clear why "Puss in Boots," "Cinderella," "Jack and the Beanstalk" and "Beauty and the Beast" were also nixed.[1]

In September 2005, habeas lawyer G. T. Hunt sent his sixty-one-year-old Pakistani American client Saifullah Peracha a copy of the Bible after the detainee made multiple written requests for it. While Peracha was a practicing Muslim, Islam overlaps with many biblical beliefs, and he wanted to further his religious understanding. Hunt mailed the Bible to the Unitarian chaplain at the base and requested that he deliver it to Peracha by hand. But the Bible was intercepted by the military. The next time Hunt was at Gitmo, he got an earful. "We are trying to run a prison here!" one of the officers on duty told him.

"I got reamed," Hunt told me, not understanding why the military would refuse to deliver a Bible. "I thought it represented colossal gall, even from a government claiming the right to lock up anybody anywhere forever."

The military attempted to ban several lawyers from the base, but habeas counsel were a zealous bunch of more than five hundred attorneys who didn't get steamrolled easily. They had inexhaustible access to courts and legal resources. Collectively, they were a legal powerhouse and a highly influential force.

On one occasion, DOD told Tom Wilner of Shearman and Sterling that he was going to be banned from the base because of an interview with a detainee that his office had allowed the BBC to broadcast. DOD said that Tom had violated the base protective order. Tom wasn't pleased.

"There was no violation, and I told them to go to hell," he told me by e-mail, maintaining that everything his firm gave the BBC for their broadcast had already been cleared by the DOD and stamped unclassified. He said the BBC interview "pissed [DOD] off mightily." Notoriously outspoken to the press, Tom said the interview was an excuse to attempt to shut him up and cut off face time with his prisoner clients. The matter was eventually settled at the prisoner's insistence, and the lawyers agreed to inform the military beforehand the next time they decided to publicize an interview.

The DOD tried the banning tactic with a large New York firm after it informed a prisoner that the military had no legal right to force-feed him while he was on a hunger strike. The firm's legal advice was correct: more than thirty years ago, the World Medical Association declared it unethical to force-feed a mentally competent hunger striker. After the attempted ban, the firm's lawyers brought the issue before a federal magistrate, and the threat to ban the firm from the base was withdrawn.

Other obstacles arose when the prisoners got visits from interrogators disguised as doctors, lawyers, or delegates from their home countries telling them that they were going to be released. Prisoners never knew who was telling them the truth. They had also been told a wide variety of things that the military believed would incite mistrust in their attorneys. The military told Clive Stafford Smith's South London client Shaker Aamer that Clive was Jewish, and they told his Jordanian client Osama Abu Kabir that he was gay.

"I think it's extraordinary, puerile, duplicitous, and wicked, all in the same breath," Clive said.

Clive also experienced obstacles of another kind. On a trip to the base in 2005, shortly after several detainees began a hunger strike, he was pulled aside into a meeting room by Captain [name redacted], who told Clive that, based on information from the detainees, he believed that Clive was orchestrating the hunger strike. He pointed to a steel mesh cell, threatening to put Clive in it.

"I was really incensed by that," Clive told British reporters. "I wrote them a letter saying, 'I don't want to hear anything more about this, or I'll be suing you people.'"

Then came the next accusation: In addition to the hunger strikes, Stafford Smith had orchestrated the camp suicides. According to press reports, the U.S. military claimed that a prisoner had said Clive masterminded all of it. It was scary stuff, being framed by the military. It could ruin your life.

Clive responded by going to the media with the threats. He spent a great deal of time dissuading suicidal clients from attempting to take their lives, he said. He had no intention of encouraging anyone to leave Guantánamo in a casket.

"I think they're targeting me over these suicides in Guantánamo because the military doesn't want to accept that the prisoners got depressed because they've been treated so badly," Clive told British reporters. "So, they want to point the finger of blame wherever they can."

In April 2007, the Department of Justice asked a federal court to put more limitations on the lawyers representing Guantánamo prisoners. The government wanted to limit the number of times a lawyer could see a client to four, it wanted permission to read attorney-client-privileged mail, and it wanted more control over what lawyers could discuss with their clients.

The government made this move, claiming that lawyers were directly responsible for inciting hunger strikes and unrest through their communications with prisoners during visits and in legal mail. But this attempt to throw attorney-client privilege out the window outraged lawyers and civil liberties groups nationwide. The American Bar Association called on its members to protest the continued erosion of U.S. law and ethical standards.

Perhaps the biggest hurdle has been learning the military's sneaky speak. Here are a few interpretations: Enhanced interrogation technique: torture; manipulative self-injurious behavior: suicide attempt; voluntary fast: hunger strike; contraband: flowers, hair clips, straws, plastic spoons, plastic forks, staples; rendition: kidnapping; assisted feeding: force-feeding hunger strikers by shoving a plastic tube up nose; asymmetric warfare: suicide; self-harm: attempted suicide; hanging gesture: suicide attempt; law fare: legal motion; comfort items: soap, toilet paper; recreation time: placed in a cage by yourself with a ball; high-value detainee: individual secretly imprisoned and tortured by the CIA.

The following are from the 2004 Camp Delta Standard Operating Procedures (Unclassified/FOUA): Document exploitation: detainee mail screening procedures; Behavior Management Plan: to enhance and exploit the disorientation and disorganization felt by a newly arrived detainee in the interrogation process; Roving Sally: a unit responsible for opening and closing the cell-block gates with haste whenever an IRF team is "requested." There are also special procedures for "Military Working Dogs" (MWD) gone wild: First person to notice a loose dog will call out: LOOSE DOG! Everyone in the area will stop movement and remain still. In the absence of the assigned handler, the person nearest the dog (in some cases this might be the detainee) will attempt to restrain it. There is no protocol for a failed attempt to restrain the MWD except calling in the Roving Sally to facilitate a quick escape.

And finally, Guantanamo Bay, Cuba: United States.

CHAPTER THIRTEEN

SAMI AL-HAJ

Sudanese journalist Sami al-Haj was covering the war in Afghanistan when he was picked up by U.S. armed forces. He'd been hesitant to head into a war zone, but like so many rookies in search of a scoop, he'd decided that the potential career boost outweighed the risks. But what he thought was the road to celebrity journalism landed him instead in a seven-by-nine-foot cage at Guantánamo Bay.

After that, the thirty-eight-year-old prisoner No. 345 could only share stories in letters or in meetings with his lawyers, Clive Stafford Smith and Zachary Katznelson of Reprieve in London, who visited every six weeks. But al-Haj documented as much as he could about his detention and what he saw at Guantánamo. He said he was willing to be the last man out of the camp if it meant that he could tell the world the truth about what was happening inside its prison walls.

Sami al-Haj. *Courtesy of the family of Sami al-Haj.*

Writing also helped him cope. In a letter to his attorneys, he imagined "small, iron" cells like the one that imprisoned him at Guantánamo lining the foot of the Statue of Liberty: "Inside there are creatures wearing orange clothing. It hardly seems possible that they are human (but) they breathe, just as we breathe, they have feelings just as we have feelings, sentiments and emotions," he wrote.

> Will the world stand for a moment of silence one day beside that colossal wreck saying, "There was once a stone statue here—a statue called Liberty"? . . . The enormous statue cries out to the world, "Liberty and Justice for All!" Yet despite the floodlights all around Lady Liberty, her voice becomes weaker, and the world begins to see that she is either deceiving or deceived. Else how could she allow those cells to be built in her very foundation? Sadly, the flame in her hand is sputtering in the storm. Will, first, the light go out on the world, and then the statue crumble?

In April 2000, al-Haj responded to an employment ad run by the Middle East broadcasting network Al-Jazeera. He had no formal training in journalism, but he was ambitious, fluent in

English, knew about computers, and had a natural command of language.

He started as a freelancer, then jumped at the chance to prove himself on the frontlines as a cameraman in Afghanistan. More seasoned journalists shied away from the assignment, but al-Haj saw it as his moment to shine.

From Pakistan, he headed west to Afghanistan with the rest of the Al-Jazeera news team to cover the conflict for more than two weeks, sometimes working fifteen hours a day, before returning to Pakistan. He made several trips like this, sometimes crossing the border at Chaman and other times at Spinboldak. In December 2001, the station sent him to cover the inauguration of interim Afghan president Hamid Karzai. But the crew was stopped en route by Pakistani police, and al-Haj was detained. His passports, travel visas, and press cards were taken. It was the last time his crew saw him.

Three weeks later, on January 7, 2002, the Pakistanis handed him over into U.S. custody. Al-Haj described the event in his writings:

> They put black hoods over our heads, tied our hands and feet and loaded us into a vehicle. They drove away, and we lay there, still, with no idea where we were going, or what our destiny might be when we arrived. After some time, the vehicle stopped and the engine shut down. There was a frightening silence that echoed around us for the longest ten minutes of my life.
>
> The terrifying silence turned into even more disorienting activity. The doors opened, and hands began dragging us, throwing us out of the vehicle. Every part of my body was forcibly searched. Each of

us received a quick series of punches and kicks—a
warning that now we were in different hands. The
sale was complete—one era of our suffering was over,
a new one about to begin.

His American captors transported him by plane to Bagram
Air Force Base. When the plane landed, he was thrown onto
the tarmac by a U.S. soldier. The impact tore the tendons in
his knee, which never healed.

The next sixteen days at Bagram, he said in terms we heard
from so many of the prisoners, were "the worst days of my
life." He said he was severely tortured, attacked by dogs, held in
an icy cage, and fed frozen food. He was later moved to a dark
prison infested with rats in Kandahar, in southern Afghanistan,
where his physical and psychological torture and abuse continued: he was subjected to multiple full-cavity searches, forced
into stress positions, made to kneel for long periods on concrete
floors, and mercilessly beaten on a regular basis.

Amnesty International further reported that the hairs on al-
Haj's beard were plucked, that he was not allowed to wash for
months on end, and that he was infested with lice and threatened with rape.

June 13, 2002. Along with dozens of other prisoners, al-Haj
was hooded, shackled, gagged, and hauled onto a dark, windowless military plane.

Guantánamo Bay. On arrival, he was intimidated by ferocious dogs, the beginning of the abuse he would suffer. He

was denied medical treatment for throat cancer and rheuma-
tism. He said he witnessed numerous desecrations of the
Qu'ran. Some guards didn't even bother to refer to him as No.
345; they just called him "nigger" because he's black. Al-Haj
thought that some of the black prisoners were denied recreation, and depending on which soldier was on duty, their
meals were often delayed for long periods.

In 2007, he was moved to Camp 6, the newly built maximum-
security section of the prison where prisoners were confined
to eight-by-ten-foot cells for at least twenty-two hours a day
and allowed out only infrequently to shower or to exercise in
enclosed areas surrounded by high concrete walls. There were
no windows to the outside, and the prisoners complained that
the cold was unbearable.

At 9:30 AM on January 7, 2007, the fifth anniversary of his imprisonment, al-Haj began a hunger strike. He wrote to the
base admiral and to his interrogators, saying that his protest
would continue until the following five conditions were met:
(1) the U.S. military agreed to respect the prisoners' religious
rights, (2) the Geneva Conventions were properly applied, (3)
those held in total isolation were allowed to rejoin humanity,
(4) there was a full and fair investigation into the fate of the
three prisoners who died in custody on June 10, 2006, and (5)
he was either set free or allowed a fair trial in a civilian court
in the United States.

He received no response to his requests.

At least thirteen prisoners went on strike along with him to
protest the harsh Gitmo conditions. Al-Haj's lawyers worried
as he lost more and more weight and his orange uniform

hung more and more loosely on his shrinking frame. He experienced dizzy spells and started to have trouble standing up. His pulse dropped to seventy-six, and his hearing started to deteriorate, as did his eyesight. As punishment for going on strike, the military took away his glasses. If he tried to read the Qur'an, his eyes watered badly, and he got splitting headaches. He started finding it hard to concentrate and to sleep.

The guards also confiscated his knee band, and his knee caused him constant pain. He was force-fed twice daily in sixteen-point restraints. He always prayed that the process would go smoothly, but the tube was often jammed into his lungs instead of his stomach. Water that was poured down the tube to see whether it was properly positioned would often spurt up his airways and into his nose.

The force-feeding was designed to make things as difficult as possible for the strikers in an effort to induce them to stop. In the early years, many did. But the prisoners toughened over the years, and the force-feeding ceased to be an effective deterrent.

The thirteen hunger strikers in 2007 were tough, so the military changed the force-feeding times to 8 AM and 11 PM to disrupt the prisoners' sleeping schedule and exhaust them. Eventually, four of the strikers would give up. But even at the end of the year, nine, in addition to al-Haj, were persisting in their protest.

Even during the hunger strike, al-Haj continued to write. He also kept a diary of his strike, which his lawyers recorded for him. Declassified by the Defense Department, it reflected the experiences of numerous other detainees who had protested in similar fashion. Here's an excerpt:

If the prisoner misses three meals, he is immediately punished without any recourse. This begins with the removal of his mattress and its replacement with a thin isomat, as well as the confiscation of his letters and his pen.

When the prisoner has missed five meals, he loses the bottles of water that he is normally allowed between meals, and he must drink the yellow tap water—despite the agreement the military made in July 2005 [that the prisoners would get three bottles of clean water each day]. He also loses his soap and toothpaste.

When the prisoner has missed six meals, he loses his prayer beads, his prayer rug, his sheet and blanket (except between the hours of 10 PM to 5 AM), his library books and his cup. In my case I also lost my glasses and the knee brace that had been prescribed by the doctors [for the knee injury I sustained when I was thrown on the Bagram tarmac]. I was suffering with my knee a lot when I had to bend to use the toilet, but thanks to the strike I now use the toilet much less, so the pain is reduced.

They have taken my pen. I have been allowed a pen only for 30 minutes each time, on January 11th and January 18th, to write to my lawyer. I received a letter from Amnesty in Belgium—a place called Louvain-la-Neuve. It had been sent on November 21, 2006, but I cannot reply. I am sorry.

At this point, the prisoner is left with just his Qur'an, the isomat, and the clothes he is wearing. He is allowed only five minutes when he takes a shower, and he is denied all recreation time. . . .

They are force-feeding me now.

I was 204 pounds when I began. . . . After 11 days, I was already down to 176 lbs. Every day they drew my blood. After 18 days, they took me to the hospital. They asked me if I wanted to eat, and I told them no. They said I needed an IV. I said I did not want it. They made me drink two bottles of water in front of them and then took me back to my cell.

On the Saturday [January 27], which was the 21st day of my strike, they took me back to the hospital. I was 168 lbs. They told me there was no sugar in my blood, and that I would die.

"I know I will die," I replied.

They said I needed an IV. I said I would not have one. They said that water was not enough, and they would force me, so I complied. They said they would put an IV in and give me one bag [of nutrients]. The IV was in my elbow. They put one bag in. When it was done, they brought another bag. I said they had promised only one. But they gave me a second. Then, they brought a third, which they said was vitamins. I said they had lied to me, and I would rip the IV out with my teeth.

"We will put you in 'The Chair,'" the officer said. [This refers to the chair used to strap the prisoners down for forced feeding. The prisoners call it the "Torture Chair." Advertisements for the chair available on the Internet say it as "like a padded cell on wheels."] It was the time for prayer, so I asked the of-

ficer for five minutes. I asked them to remove the IV
while I prayed. They refused. I missed two prayer
times there. They cared more about their IV than for
my prayer.

When I had missed 70 meals, the doctor said that
my condition was very bad. It was more than 500
hours since I had last eaten food. He said they would
force-feed me or I could die within hours. I said I did
not wish to eat. I told him that I knew my rights under the Tokyo Declaration—they could not force-
feed me consistent with their ethics, because they
knew I was competent, and they knew I made the decision voluntarily.

"I wish to go back to my cell please," I told them.
There was a nurse, who let me pray.

On Monday [January 29] they told me that they
would not let me die. They brought in a 12 mm tube.
It was yellow. They pushed it into my left nostril, all
the way down until it reached my stomach. They
force-fed me by machine, 250 ml of Ensure. I was
there for 14 hours with the tube in my nose. It was
1:30 AM. I wanted to sleep and asked them to take it
out, but they refused. I said I would begin to scream
unless they took it out. They finally did.

On Tuesday [January 30] at 8 AM, they forced the
tube in again. This time it was 900 ml of Ensure. The
whole time they had an IV in me. The first day they
had forced it in at 20 ml per hour, but the second day
it was 100 ml an hour. It took almost ten hours in total. It did not finish until about 6 PM.

I slept.

On Wednesday [January 30] a doctor came in and asked how I was.

"Please take me out of here," I said. "I want to go back to my cell." He ordered them to give me 600 ml of Ensure and a bottle of water through the tube, along with something else. I was very tired. Nothing comes out any more when I go to the toilet.

By the time anyone is allowed to read my words, I will have had my birthday on February 15. I will celebrate it in the Torture Chair this year, I think.

It is sad to be on this strike. I have no desire to die. I am suffering, hungry. The nights are very long, and I cannot sleep. But I will continue the struggle until we get our rights. The strike is the only way that I can protest. The military administration treats us all so very badly.

I saw my lawyer Clive in a dream. He was in Sudan, and I had invited him. He came to my home for dinner. We spoke. I said, do you remember those days in Guantánamo? It seemed so far away, such a long time ago.

Many dreams here become reality. One day I dream of playing with my son Mohammed. Meanwhile, to my wife and son I say, "Don't worry, what will happen will happen." One day the sun will shine again, and we will be free. Facts are facts, and at last we will prevail.

The following entry was recorded by Clive Stafford Smith during his March 1, 2007, visit with al-Haj:

Food is not enough for life. If there is no air, could you live on food alone? Freedom is just as important as food or air. Give me freedom, and I'll eat. Every day they ask me, when will I eat. Every day, I say, "Tomorrow." Every day. It's what Scarlett O'Hara says at the end of *Gone with the Wind*: "Tomorrow is another day." I am being force-fed at 10 AM and 3 PM each day. . . . They take notes all the time, so I know they have a long record of what they are doing to me.

They slam the prisoners into the chair. They tighten the straps so they cut into us. They have new padded shackles for moving the prisoners now, which are much better, but for the hunger strikers they use the old ones that cut in.

They begin with the feet first, then the waist. Then, they do one wrist at a time. There is one band around each shin. One on each wrist. One on each elbow. One strap that comes down over each shoulder. Three on the top of the head, so that the head can't move. The ankles are shackled to an eye on the chair. They pull hard on the wrists in particular.

They pull a mask over your mouth, apparently to stop people from spitting.

In the morning they use my left nostril, in the afternoon, my right. The pain of putting the tube up my nose depends on the shift. As it goes in, at first you are gagging on it. As it goes down, they blow air into it to hear where it is. They put a stethoscope near my heart to listen—I am not sure why. I prayed to Allah when they first did that!

I worry that these people are not nurses at all. Abdurrahman said that the IV was put in him by a guard, not a nurse. Some days they put the tube in okay, so it does not hurt too much. But some days I suffer until the tears stream down my cheeks. They have had two trainees who have practiced on me. One was a white woman, fat, short, something over thirty years old.

The other was a captain nurse, a white man, over forty years old, blond, with a moustache, average build, about five foot nine, with green eyes. You saw the eyes when he was putting the tube in. He came three days in a row, and after the first experience, I prayed to Allah that it would not be him each time. He said, "Are you ready?" I said, "So, what if I am not? You will force me anyway." Three times they have inserted the tube the wrong way, so it has gone into my lungs. They put water into it, and it made me choke. Water started coming out of my nose. One time the nurse wiped my nose. Another time, they did not seem to care.

They use the same pipe (I can see it is the same number) for about two weeks at a time. It makes me nauseous to see the same one going in each time. Sometimes the guards come by and knock the pipe when it is in my nose. It is very painful.

Most say nothing at all to me. Never once has one of them said "I'm sorry" when they have hurt me, or said, "I hope this doesn't hurt." Even when they put it in my lung.

They force me to accept two cans of Ensure liquid nutrient, each of 236 ml, and 250 ml of water each time, for a total of 722 ml that they force through my nose. There is no taste of anything. It has been a long time since I knew the flavor of food.

They hold you for an hour in the chair after being fed, to make sure you don't throw up. If I do throw up on myself, which happens frequently, I am given no clean clothes, and I cannot even clean myself, since they keep the water turned off when we get back to our cells.

My stomach is causing me all kinds of problems. Now I am experiencing constipation and diarrhea alternately—for roughly three days each at a time. I feel dizzy and in danger of collapse when I stand up. . . .

As of today, I have been held as a prisoner without trial for One Thousand Nine Hundred and Two days. Sometimes I wonder what a human being would have to be given to go through this voluntarily. When I was sent on assignment to Afghanistan, Al-Jazeera was paying $600 a day for dangerous work abroad. At that rate, it would be $1,141,200 for the time I have been away from my wife and son. Would I accept the suffering I have been through if I had been promised more than a million dollars? Never. Not at all.

According to al-Haj, hunger strikers suffered the worst abuse in "India Block." There, the air-conditioning was cranked up high, and prisoners were pepper-sprayed without warning, then doused with cold water so that they could never relax. They were forced to shower naked in full view of the guards, denied shorts or even towels.

Systematic forced nudity was used to demean and dehumanize the prisoners, said lawyer Zachary Katznelson. That sort of prolonged degradation couldn't be justified under the guise of a security threat. It brought to my mind images of Iraq's Abu Ghraib prison. The only reason U.S. soldiers were charged in connection with the abuse that went on there was because someone made the mistake of taking photographs.

But forced nudity wasn't the only means of demoralizing prisoners like al-Haj. According to Katznelson, a number of prisoners reported that they were humiliated by soldiers repeatedly inserting their fingers into their anuses. One even claimed that a stick had been shoved into his rectum.

Al-Haj was held for more than five years on the basis of secret evidence, never charged with any crime. Until the Associated Press sued the Pentagon in 2005, the military wouldn't even acknowledge that it was holding him. His family had no idea what had happened to him and was unaware that he had been taken to Guantánamo until six months after his arrest, when his wife, Asma, received a letter through the Red Cross.

Contact after that was strained. Al-Haj's letters took several months to reach the family. It was even worse on his end. He went an entire year once without hearing from his wife. Another time he was given a letter from his brother—dated two years earlier. On average, Katznelson said, it took seven to nine months for his client to receive a letter—and then it was often heavily censored.

In his military hearings, al-Haj was accused, among other things, of running a terrorist Web site, of entering Afghanistan illegally, of interviewing Osama bin Laden, and of supplying arms and funds to Chechen fighters. Attorney Clive Stafford Smith, who was not allowed to attend these military proceedings, called all the allegations "nonsense" and the hearings process itself "un-American."

"Al-Haj is no more a terrorist than my grandmother," Stafford Smith said. "There is absolutely zero evidence that he has any history of terrorism at all."

During his more than six years at Guantánamo, the allegations against al-Haj changed repeatedly. The military found that he never interviewed Osama bin Laden, so that allegation disappeared. There was no jihadist or terrorist Web site, so that allegation too vanished, as did the charge of funneling arms to the Chechens.

Again and again, the allegations proved false. "There is no evidence that he is guilty of anything," insisted Stafford Smith. "And the U.S. has clearly shown that by the fact that they never even interrogated him about his alleged guilt—until he begged them to."

Strangely, the military showed scant interest in al-Haj's alleged terrorist connections. Instead, most of his more than two hundred interrogations focused on pumping him for information about his former employer, which confused al-Haj. Eventually, he pleaded with interrogators to ask him about the alleged crimes he was being detained for, but their focus remained on Al-Jazeera. He was asked about the news staff, who paid its salaries, who paid for travel, where the money came from, and whether the network was really a front for al-Qaeda.

The military made clear what it wanted, said Stafford Smith: for al-Haj to turn spy and inform on Al-Jazeera.

Al-Haj refused.

It's no secret that Washington doesn't like Al-Jazeera. The network angered U.S. officials with its unsanitized approach to covering combat. In its typical no-holds-barred reporting style, Al-Jazeera filmed and televised Iraqi war victims, dead U.S. soldiers, and scores of civilian casualties. Former defense secretary Donald Rumsfeld publicly called its coverage of the war "vicious, inaccurate, and inexcusable." The news team defended its broadcasts by stating that "the pictures do not lie."

The network, which has millions of Middle Eastern viewers, is also known for broadcasting videotapes sent in by al-Qaeda and Osama bin Laden. As a result, Americans have come to suspect that Al-Jazeera is in the business of aiding terrorists, even though the same videos are usually replayed by U.S. networks.

When Al-Jazeera's Kabul office was wiped out by U.S. bombs in 2002, and when U.S. air strikes took out the Baghdad office a year later, killing Al-Jazeera reporter Tareq Ayyoub, the news staff began to suspect that they were a target of U.S. armed forces.

Al-Jazeera producer Ahmad Ibrahim told me how terrifying this was for his staff. Al-Jazeera journalists, he said, are no different from other reporters and have never been tied to any political groups.

"We have operated in the most professional manner throughout our ten-year history," Ibrahim said from his office in Doha, Qatar. "There is not a single instance where Al-Jazeera has operated in a way that favored any group, political party or country over another."

He said that Al-Jazeera never agreed with the concept of "embedded" journalism, that is, allowing a news reporter to travel with a military unit involved in armed conflict. Embedding during the 2003 invasion of Iraq was Washington's response to the broad and sometimes unfavorable coverage of the 1991 Gulf War and the 2001 invasion of Afghanistan. But Al-Jazeera staffers wouldn't go along with the way Washington wanted them to conduct their journalism.

"[Washington] wanted us to operate as embedded journalists—seeing the world from their Humvees or aircraft carriers—and treating that as the only opinion," Ibrahim said. But "our motto is 'the opinion, and the other opinion.'" Reporters should gather news independently, he said; embedding with the military would provide an incomplete and lopsided view of the war.

As al-Haj's lawyers saw it, his continued detention was a political game that had little to do with him. "He is a clearly a pawn in a game much bigger than he is—human collateral in the United States government's grudge against the television station," said Katznelson.

A transcript of al-Haj's Annual Review Board hearing on August 12, 2005, quoted the prisoner pleading for mercy and stating that he would like to return to his family. He had been arrested in error, he told the board.

"I can say without hesitation that I am not a threat to the United States or to anyone else," he said. "I strongly condemn any act that is taken against innocent people, and I strongly condemn the tragic attack on the World Trade Center in New York. Islam properly understood would never allow the killing of innocent people in this way."

Al-Haj's imprisonment frightened his coworkers and threatened their profession globally, they said. They think twice now before covering a subject that might anger the United States. Many fear that they too could be targeted.

"All journalists feel less safe now than before," said Ibrahim. "Personally, I think twice before I head to cover certain events in certain places, but I go anyway."

Still, al-Haj's colleagues stood behind him. His face became familiar in the Middle East as Al-Jazeera carried frequent news updates on his case. A documentary detailing his arrest, torture, and detention called *Prisoner 345* caused public outrage and led to calls for his release.

His imprisonment also got the attention of Reporters sans frontières (Reporters without Borders), an international group headquartered in Paris that defends press freedom and the rights of journalists all over the world. The watchdog group has advocated tirelessly for al-Haj's release.

Sudanese government officials also followed his hunger strike and imprisonment. In April 2007, Sudanese minister of justice Mohammad Ali al-Marazi publicly condemned al-Haj's imprisonment without charge or trial. The United Nations, Amnesty International, Human Rights Watch, and a parade of world leaders also condemned it.

When you arrive at Guantánamo Bay, you're greeted by a large plaque inscribed "Honor Bound to Defend Freedom." Every time I saw it, I wondered whether the men in charge of that colossal operation had any true concept of honor, or that freedom might be a universal, not narrowly American, right.

CHAPTER FOURTEEN

THE DRAMA

Every trip to Gitmo was full of drama, with boozy beachside barbecues and endless storytelling. In and outside the detention camps, the military base is a surreal place, peopled with curious characters. I often found myself wondering who the people around me were and why they were at Guantánamo Bay.

Like the legless man.

Each morning, when I took the ferry to the windward side, I would see a young Cuban man with prosthetic legs. He always wore shorts, so I'd catch myself sneaking peeks at his plastic legs and wondering what had happened to him. One day, he told Peter Ryan and an Arabic interpreter his incredible story.

His name was Amadoo. One day, he'd decided to flee Fidel Castro's Cuba. But instead of trying to sail to Miami in a makeshift raft, as most refugees do, he thought he would go over land and try to reach Guantánamo Bay, where he would ask the Americans for asylum. Unfortunately, Cuban soldiers spotted him from a guard tower as he neared the base and shot him in the leg. The gunfire drew the attention of U.S. border guards, who ordered the Cubans to pull back and allow him passage. The Cubans refused, and a standoff ensued.

A U.S. and a Cuban helicopter both flew out and hovered over him for a time. Finally, perhaps not wanting to create an international incident, both choppers retreated, and Amadoo dragged himself as quickly as he could toward the American side.

There were once seventy-five thousand land mines placed by U.S. troops across "no man's land" between the U.S. and Cuban border, creating the second-largest minefield in the world and the largest in the Western Hemisphere (the first largest is in Afghanistan). But President Bill Clinton ordered them removed in 1996, and they have since been replaced with motion and sound sensors to detect intruders. Unluckily for Amadoo, however, the Cuban government hadn't cleared the minefield on its side of the border. As he hobbled along, trying to make his way to the U.S. side, a Cuban land mine took out his other leg.

For hours he lay unconscious, slowly bleeding to death, as neither U.S. nor Cuban soldiers made any move to help him. Finally, that night a Cuban soldier, assuming that Amadoo was dead, picked him up and threw him into a nearby cemetery. He was discovered the next morning, barely breathing, by other Cubans, who took him to a hospital, where he was fitted with his artificial legs. As soon as he had recovered, he fled again. This time he made it across the border. He'd been living at Gitmo ever since. He was eventually granted political

asylum in the United States, but his wife and children remained in Cuba.

There was a sizable Cuban community on the leeward side of
the base, and more Cubans dropped in all the time. One day,
two surrendered to one of the Arabic interpreters, who was
chain-smoking outside the Combined Bachelors Quarters
when they came ashore. The elderly translator was the first
person they saw, so they threw their bags down and put their
hands up in the air.

A number of Cubans who'd been intercepted by the Coast
Guard while trying to make it to Florida were also living on
the base. Cubans who reach U.S. soil are allowed to stay, but if
they're intercepted at sea, they're sent back to Cuba on the basis of so-called wet-foot, dry-foot statutes. Instead of sending
some refugees back to Cuba, though, the Coast Guard
brought them to Guantánamo.

On my first trip to the base, I saw an adorable little brown-
haired boy carrying a red Spiderman backpack on the morning ferry. His older brother was playing video games on his
Sony PSP. His father wore a red polo shirt with a yellow Mc-
Donald's insignia. Over the months, I got to know little Jordan
Lopez. His father, Jorge, said the family had fled Cuba on a
homemade motorized raft that had run out of fuel just a few
miles from Miami. They'd been picked up by the Coast Guard
and brought to Guantánamo Bay, where Jorge worked at Mc-
Donald's. He looked over his shoulder constantly as he spoke
to me. Immigration officers were always monitoring them, he

explained. After spending about a year at Guantánamo, the family was finally granted political asylum in the Czech Republic.

Alex, another Cuban, was not so fortunate. He pulled out military papers to show me that he had been reprimanded for "familiarizing with a Jamaican." After three separate violations, Alex said, he was thrown into solitary confinement for several days with only one hour of recreation each day, during which a guard would give him a ball to kick around. The Cubans, Alex complained, were treated like the detainees, their letters home censored and their phone calls monitored. "I am not a criminal," he said. "But they treat me like a spy."

I was always glad to see the familiar faces of our military escorts, who became like old friends over the months. They always greeted me with happy smiles or hugs.

"Long time!" they'd joke sarcastically. I'd come in expecting the captains and escorts to be hostile, robotic jerks. I was so wrong, just as I had been in my prejudgments of the detainees. I grew to genuinely like many of the military guys. I learned about their families, their plans to go to college, their relationships, their divorces, and their affairs. They told me about the girlfriends and fiancées they missed back home. I keep in touch with some who have left the military and have invited others to my home in San Diego. One soldier told me that she hated it when people insulted "the military." "It's always the soldiers at the bottom who feel the brunt of the criticism," she said, not the men who make the rules.

Once in a while, I'd run into young soldiers who referred to the detainees as terrorists or "the enemy," but most of the time, they had no idea who the nameless, numbered prisoners they were charged with guarding were. Sometimes, when we were delayed in meeting with a detainee, we'd play guessing games with the guards, who were required to remove the Velcro name tags from their uniforms when dealing with attorneys and prisoners.

"So, what's your name?" someone would ask.

"I can't disclose that," the guard would respond.

"Where are you from in the States?"

"I can't disclose that either."

We'd try to guess.

"Are you from Florida?"

"No."

In about twenty minutes, we would have it narrowed down to the Northwest. But then we'd get bored with that game.

"So, what do you all day?" we'd start over.

"I can't disclose that."

"Do you have any pets?"

"Yes."

"What kind?"

"A dog, ma'am."

Sometimes, I'd offer the guards some of the ice cream or Twinkies I'd brought for the detainees. Sometimes, if they were hungry, they'd accept; otherwise, they'd tell me it was against the rules to eat my Klondike bars.

"I am not allowed to accept gifts."

One time, as we waited around again, I asked a guard whether the prisoners treated him well or whether he'd ever received a detainee cocktail, a concoction of feces and urine—shaken and hurled.

"No," he said, shaking his head. "I treat them like human beings, and they respond to me the same way."

"Are there some guards who treat them badly?" I asked, a little shocked that he was engaging me.

"Some of the young ones have tempers and have not acted professionally, but they're often moved quickly," he responded. "I'm just doing my job. I don't think it's my place to judge them."

"That's open-minded of you," I said, meaning it.

"The sooner this place is closed, the better it will be for all of us," he replied.

On the windward side, the base bristled with guard towers, barbed wire, military vehicles, dungeonlike prisons, and U.S. flags waving high. Photography on that side of the island was strictly prohibited, though everyone thought that was an exceedingly stupid rule. After all, you can study the base in minute detail just by going to Google Earth.

On the drive into the detention center, we always stopped at a checkpoint. On one occasion, the Arab interpreters who had been on the base for weeks were itching to mix up the mundane procedures. As armed soldiers approached our vehicle to check our badges, one of the interpreters, a guy in dark shades, shouted out, "Honor bound!" the phrase senior military officials use to greet junior soldiers. Without missing a beat, the guard saluted and replied, "To defend freedom, sir!" As we drove on toward the camps, our military escort tried hard to control his laughter. He told us that we'd probably been mistaken for intelligence.

Most of the detainees—understandably, given the length of time they'd been held—initially assumed their attorneys were interrogators or government agents of some kind. But habeas counsel were probably the only positive face of the United States that many of these men would ever encounter. I think the lawyers had an obligation that went beyond providing legal remedies. They had a duty to treat these men with respect, hospitality, and empathy. In a place like Gitmo, small acts of kindness could be immensely therapeutic.

One lawyer became hostile when his client didn't trust him enough to sign his forms. His colleague and I were both appalled when he abruptly stood up, picked up the wall phone, and called the guards to end the meeting.

When I asked why he'd done that, he said it was a tactic to gain control of the meeting. By walking out, he said, he may have given the detainee the sense that his lawyers weren't coming back.

I think he forgot that these men had been interrogated hundreds of times, had been tortured and continuously humiliated for years on end. They'd been taken, many from their beds at night, halfway around the world and held in secret without any determination that they'd done anything wrong. Many had attempted suicide, suffered religious humiliation, and participated in hunger strikes. Many suffered from depression and trusted no one—certainly not a lawyer who traipsed in demanding a signature on a form after just a few hours, then punished the prisoner by making him feel as though his only lifeline to the world was leaving him.

This lawyer also refused to bring his client food and said he wasn't there to "entertain" him. I tried to explain that food was important in the meetings, not so much to build trust but because hospitality is a central pillar of Eastern culture. The idea was not so much to "feed" the detainee or "entertain" him; it was a matter of hospitality. Attorneys who've visited Afghanistan or the Middle East have always been struck by the extreme hospitality they encountered as they were offered copious amounts of food and tea. Even the poorest Afghans will give a guest the best of what they have. To receive someone empty-handed is an offense that can brand you as *bayghairath*, or honorless.

Over dozens of meetings, I learned that it was vital that lawyers never coerce their clients into doing anything against their will. The message detainees got from their interrogators was often that they'd better answer questions and do it quickly. But it never worked in anyone's favor to pressure a prisoner. That included trying to get names of family members or evidentiary documents in addition to signatures on representation forms. Pressure and coercion only gave the prisoner the impression that he was being subjected to yet another form of interrogation.

The best relationships were formed when a prisoner genuinely looked forward to his meetings with his lawyers as a break from the monotony of jail, punishment, solitary confinement, abuse, and interrogation.

The ultimate attorney-client bond I saw was between Chaman Gul, a charismatic six-foot-three Afghan prisoner, and his American lawyer and investigator. I watched with amazement once as he stood up to hug them before they left. Chaman's legal team worked very hard for him, traveling all the way to Afghanistan and London to collect as much evidence as they could on his behalf. That hug was genuine. The lawyers and the detainee held on with their arms wrapped around each other. The attorneys exchanged letters and poetry with Chaman and genuinely grew to care about him.

I also found that the most comfortable prisoners were those given the greatest levels of control. Detainees had no control over any facet of their lives, including when they woke up, when they saw the sun, when they showered, when they stretched their legs, when they ate, or when they slept. Saying no, even to attorneys, was empowering. Before I went to Gitmo, I studied therapeutic jurisprudence, which emphasizes the importance of collaborating with the legal and psychological needs of prisoners. I thought that the attorneys who applied this model developed better relationships with their clients.

One serious faux pas that occurred on at least two occasions was lawyers' employing interpreters who had worked for the U.S. military in Bagram or at Guantánamo Bay. In one instance, the Arab detainee immediately recognized the interpreter who had been present during his military interrogations. The detainee and interpreter started having a heated dispute in rapid Arabic, which the lawyer obviously didn't follow. Eventually, the irate detainee kicked everyone out, and the meeting was over before it began.

Interrogations were a source of pain, anxiety, and shame for prisoners. It obviously wasn't a good idea for habeas counsel to bring in individuals who'd been present when their client was interrogated or tortured. This was a major setback to ever gaining the prisoner's trust. And it hurt not just the one law firm but had the potential to hurt the entire habeas team.

CHAPTER FIFTEEN

JUMAH AL-DOSSARY

Jumah al-Dossary needed to take a quick bathroom break during a meeting with his lawyer. The guards came and unshackled the Bahraini detainee from the floor and led him to a nearby cell with a toilet. His lawyer, Joshua Colangelo-Bryan, also stepped out of the Camp Echo meeting room and, watching the pouring rain, waited outside for al-Dossary to call out to the guards that he was finished.

Several minutes later, there was still no sound from the prisoner. Colangelo-Bryan began to feel anxious, wondering what was taking so long.

He walked over to the cell, pulled the door open, and poked his head in. Before he could call out his client's name, he saw a puddle of blood on the floor. He threw the door open and rushed in to find al-Dossary hanging from the steel mesh wall of the cage, his face engorged, a noose around his neck. His tongue lolled from his mouth, and his eyes had rolled back into his head. Before hanging himself, al-Dossary had slashed his arm.

Colangelo-Bryan rushed over to the cage.

"Jumah!" he shouted but got no response.

"Jumah!" he shouted again. Panicking, he yelled for help. Guards rushed in and unlocked the cage. They cut the noose, laid al-Dossary on the floor, and ordered the attorney out of the room.

Later that night, Colangelo-Bryan was relieved to learn that his client was in stable condition. He had been revived and given treatment for his injuries, including fourteen stitches in his arm.

It was the thirty-two-year-old's eighth suicide attempt since he'd been brought to Gitmo in February 2002. But al-Dossary told his lawyer that it wouldn't be his last: as soon as he got the chance, he'd try to end his "worthless life" again. Colangelo-Bryan immediately filed a motion, claiming physical and religious abuse, as well as sexual humiliation and vicious interrogations. He asked that the military be ordered to improve al-Dossary's conditions: that he be given books other than the Qu'ran and more recreation time, that he be allowed to see a home video of his family, and that the lights be turned off at night so he could sleep. Otherwise, he faced "irreparable injury," his lawyer told the Washington, D.C., federal district court.

The court never ruled on this motion.

After witnessing his client's grisly suicide attempt, Colangelo-Bryan returned to work in the New York offices of Dorsey and Whitney. Once it was cleared by Department of Defense, he received a chilling reminder of what he'd seen in Guantánamo Bay: the sealed suicide note al-Dossary had given him before his bathroom break. It read,

October 2005

In fact, I don't know how to begin, or where to begin. . . . I feel very sorry for forcing you to see . . . a human being who suffered too much . . . dying before your eyes. There was no alternative to make our voice heard by the world from the depths of the detention centers. . . .

I hope you will always remember that you met and sat with a "human being" called "Jumah" who suffered too much and was abused in his belief, his self, in his dignity and also in his humanity. He was imprisoned, tortured and deprived of his homeland, his family and his young daughter. . . . Remember that there are hundreds of detainees at Guantánamo Bay, Cuba—they are in the same situation of suffering and misfortune. They were captured, tortured and detained with no offense or reason. Their lives might end like mine. . . .

When you remember me in my last gasps of life before dying, while my soul is leaving my body to rise to its creator, remember that the world let us down and let our case down. . . . Remember that our governments let us down. . . . Remember the unreasonable delay of the courts in looking into our case and to side with the victims of injustice. If there were judges who had been fair, I wouldn't have been wrapped in death shrouds now and my

family—my father, my mother, my brothers, sisters and my little
daughter—would not have to lose [me] . . . but what else can I do?

Take some of my blood . . . take pieces of my death shrouds . . .
take some of my remains . . . take pictures of my dead body when
I am placed in my grave. Send it to the world, to the judges . . .
the people with a live conscience . . . to the people with principles
and values. . . .

At this moment, I see death looming in front of me while I write
this letter. . . . Death has a bad odor that cannot be smelled
except by those who are going through its agony.

Farewell. . . . I thank you for everything you have done for me,
but I have a final request. . . . Show the world the letters I gave
you, let the world read them. Let the world know the agonies of
the detainees in Cuba. . . .

Prisoner of Deprivation
Jumah Abdel Latif al-Dossary
Guantánamo Bay, Cuba[1]

The Department of Defense later confirmed that al-Dossary
made another attempt to kill himself. "The purpose of Guantánamo is to destroy people, and I have been destroyed," he
told his attorney.

All al-Dossary's statements and most of the facts in this
chapter are based on his unclassified writings and his lawyer's
unclassified notes. Despite the humiliation he underwent, al-
Dossary decided to speak out about his torture in order to

shed light on what was happening in the prison. His lawyer had written to him about the importance of disclosing his name to the media and of convincing other prisoners to do the same.

"I heard that some American officials deny that human rights violations are occurring in Cuba and deny that there are sexual assaults on detainees and that some journalists are also skewing the facts," he wrote.

Al-Dossary's detailed account of his captivity is one of the strongest claims of prisoner abuse at the hands of the U.S. military.

"How will I write about these horrors, and must I swallow the bitter lump that forms in my throat when I remember them?" al-Dossary wrote. "The revolting torture and those vile attacks . . . whenever I look back on them, I wonder how my soft heart could bear them, how my body could bear the pain of the torture and how my mind could bear all that stress."

Many prisoners shied away from speaking about the indignities they'd suffered, preferring not to relive the shame. Military officials, however, maintain that Gitmo detainees are masters of deceit, carefully following al-Qaeda training manual instructions on how to dupe Westerners.

"These detainees are trained to lie, they're trained to say they were tortured, and the minute we release them or the minute they get a lawyer, very frequently they'll go out and they will announce that they've been tortured," then defense secretary Donald Rumsfeld said in an interview with Fox News in June 2005.

Statements like that angered al-Dossary's lawyer, who watched his client crumble under years of methodical torture.

"So, are the FBI agents and military personnel who have described inhumane treatment of detainees also taking a page out of the al-Qaeda playbook," asked Colangelo-Bryan, "or are they just describing what they've seen?"

Some detainees clearly lied. One Afghan told us on a first meeting that he was illiterate. But when we saw him a few months later, he was reading and writing flawlessly. It was only after perhaps noticing the odd look on my face that he suddenly remembered his lack of education and began to stammer and sound words out like a kindergartner.

Nonetheless, the evidence of torture was extensive. Countless detainees, aid workers, and even U.S. soldiers repeatedly described the use of the same type of torture, sexual humiliation, and religious degradation. Al-Dossary insisted that his story was not contrived in "a flight of fancy or a moment of madness" but was based on "established facts and events," witnessed by other prisoners, the Red Cross, interpreters, and U.S. soldiers, who he said had filmed it all. So, he sat in solitary confinement and wrote a memoir of what he presumed would be his final years.

In his written account, al-Dossary described how his journey to Guantánamo began with a long walk to the Pakistani border in December 2001 to flee the bombs dropping on Afghanistan. He told the Pakistani soldiers at the border that he needed to go to the Bahraini Embassy. They seemed helpful and even welcoming, but instead of the embassy, they took him to a filthy Pakistani jail packed with Arabs and other foreigners, who had suddenly become valuable war commodities. There were no bathrooms and no mattresses, only men crammed shoulder to shoulder, reeking of unwashed bodies and fear.

To protect the prisoners from the winter cold, the Pakistanis doled out vermin-infested blankets. The only food the men received was a hunk of hard bread, which quickly led to malnutrition. The Pakistanis treated him badly, al-Dossary wrote, but the real suffering started when he was blindfolded and delivered to the Americans.

In a long letter to his lawyer, he described how the Pakistanis took him to an airport and handed him over to U.S. soldiers. When the Pakistanis left, a female interpreter came close and told him in Arabic that the soldiers were going to get him ready for the flight to the U.S. military base in Kandahar. He was to keep quiet and obey the commands he was given. Moments later, someone seized him roughly and threw him down on the pavement. The Americans searched his body carefully and violently, then dragged him onto a windowless military cargo plane and bound him with chains to the cabin floor. They ripped off his blindfold, and before they covered his head with a sack, he glimpsed about thirty other prisoners on board.

When all the men were tied down, the cabin door was sealed, and the soldiers began hurling insults and swearing at the prisoners. They cursed "our families and our honor," he wrote to his attorney.

Through the sack, al-Dossary caught quick glimpses of bright light as some of the soldiers apparently took souvenir photographs.

When they tired of shouting obscenities, al-Dossary wrote, the soldiers wove through the rows of chained, hooded men, kicking and punching as they went. One stopped in front of al-Dossary to deliver a few firm kicks to his stomach. The Bahraini howled in pain. He'd had a stomach operation in the past and hoped that his captors would show mercy, but his cries were answered with more blows. He broke out in a sweat and felt nauseated as his mouth filled with a bitter dark liquid, and he began to throw up blood.

"The tragic event on the plane was only the beginning of the horrors awaiting me," he wrote.

At the U.S. base in Kandahar, the men were pulled off the plane and forced to lie face down on the icy winter tarmac as soldiers trampled on them, hit them with their rifle butts, yelled obscenities, and beat them. Then, the soldiers ordered the prisoners to get up and tied them together with wire, leaving about six feet between each man. "Run!" they shouted.

But many of the men were injured and exhausted, and when they tried to run, some simply couldn't keep up and fell to their knees. The soldiers kicked and punched them and ordered them to get back up. Al-Dossary still wore the shackles the Pakistanis had put on his ankles, which caused him to stumble repeatedly. Every time he fell to the ground, he felt a soldier's boot against his body. One time, he passed out, then regained consciousness to find his head under a soldier's boot. He was beaten unconscious again. The second time, he came around to a hot, wet sensation on his head and back. Confused, he turned his throbbing head to see the same soldier towering over him, urinating on him.

"He was roaring with laughter," al-Dossary wrote.

Then, the soldier grabbed a fistful of al-Dossary's hair and kicked his face until his lip split. According to al-Dossary, the soldiers always focused on sensitive spots, such as the eyes, nose, and genitals. During the beatings, he said, the soldiers insulted members of his family and called him a terrorist over and over again.

Al-Dossary spent two weeks at Kandahar, where he claimed that soldiers threatened to kill him and made him walk barefoot over barbed wire or shards of glass. They broke his nose. He was forced to raise his arms backward so high that he was afraid they would pop out of their shoulder sockets. After one especially intense beating, he wrote, he and the others were forced to strip, although much of their clothing had already been torn from their bodies.

"My blood was everywhere, my face was swollen. . . . I had cuts all over my body," he recalled in his letter.

The soldiers began to photograph and film the naked, battered prisoners. Al-Dossary would get to see these photographs much later during an interrogation at Gitmo.

Religious degradation was as much a part of the program as physical abuse. Al-Dossary insisted that soldiers frequently cursed Allah and the Prophet Mohammad. When Red Cross representatives brought the prisoners Qu'rans, the holy books were thrown on the floor during interrogations and sometimes into the plastic buckets that prisoners relieved themselves into. Some soldiers used the Qu'ran as a football, tossing it around in front of the Muslim prisoners. Others tore out pages to clean off their boots.

Meanwhile, the physical abuse became more inventive. One day, al-Dossary had hot liquid poured on his head; another time, he was given electric shocks with a small device that looked like a mobile phone. Individual hairs were pulled out of his beard, and he was made to stand in stress positions for hours at a time and not allowed to sleep. Once, he said, a U.S. soldier put out his cigarette on his bare foot.

"Why are you treating me like this?" al-Dossary cried out. The soldier responded a few moments later by stubbing another cigarette out on his wrist. When he complained to a military physician, some soldiers decided to teach him a lesson. They blindfolded him and took him to another part of the camp. What he witnessed, he wrote, still haunted him.

"I heard an Afghan prisoner scream. He was crying and saying, 'Oh, Allah! Oh, God!'" al-Dossary wrote. That was all he could understand of the man's screams. He was led toward the screaming, which grew louder and louder, and then his blindfold was pulled off.

"I saw an Afghan brother in his fifties. He had a lot of white hair in his beard, and he was tied to the ground. Soldiers were holding on to his shackles, and he was naked lying on his stomach. One of the soldiers was sexually assaulting him. One of the soldiers was videotaping," he wrote.

Al-Dossary was told that he would face the same fate as that "Afghan terrorist" if he dared to speak out again.

The first time I heard about sexual assault or rape, I had a hard time believing that U.S. soldiers could be capable of such brutality. Historically, sexual degradation has been considered an effective way to demoralize prisoners and an entire community. We caught a small glimpse of sexual degradation at Abu Ghraib, the Iraqi prison, where young men and women in uniform posed and smiled for pictures next to naked and humiliated men on leashes, or stacked naked in a pile, or forced to masturbate for a camera while a female U.S. guard gave a thumbs-up and pointed at the prisoner's crotch.

Abu Ghraib caused such a stir when a few of the photos were leaked to the media that the military was forced to investigate. Army Maj. Gen. Antonio M. Taguba was assigned to find out what had happened and spent most of February 2004 in Iraq with his team investigating. In an interview with veteran correspondent Seymour Hersh of the *New Yorker*, Taguba said that he was appalled at what he uncovered. He revealed that the Pentagon forced him to retire in January 2007 as a result of his forceful inquiry into the scandal. Taguba also told the *New Yorker* that the Army's Criminal Investigation Division had kept more pictures, about one hundred, and a video from the public. Americans haven't seen a fraction of what happened at the Iraqi prison, and although only low-level soldiers were prosecuted in that case, Taguba said he believed that the orders for the actions could only have come from above.

Taguba told the *New Yorker* that he saw "a video of a male American soldier in uniform sodomizing a female detainee." The general also said that an Iraqi father and son were sexually humiliated together and that there were images of a female

Iraqi prisoner forced to bare her breasts before U.S. soldiers. The general told the magazine that there were images of male prisoners stripped naked with female guards pointing at their penises, of Iraqi women forced to expose their genitals to the guards, of prisoners forced to perform "indecent acts" upon one another, and of guards physically assaulting prisoners by beating them and dragging them around on chains. There were also reports by an army physician who indicated that an anal fissure on a prisoner was consistent with the sodomy the prisoners alleged.

Many similar reports never reached the U.S. media. Lal Gul, director of the Afghan Human Rights Organization in Kabul, said that U.S. soldiers pervasively raped men and women, regardless of age. Chicago-based sociologist Daud Miraki told me that his field workers attested to multiple cases of rape by U.S. soldiers in Afghanistan too. Miraki has recorded a case of a young woman in Sarobi whose husband was away from home when U.S. soldiers came to search the house and took her to the military base "for questioning." Neighbors informed her husband, and when he went to the base to pick her up, she reportedly told him that she had been gang-raped. Her husband told Miraki that he could no longer accept her as a wife. She went to stay with her parents and committed suicide days later. Some speculate that many rapes in Afghanistan have gone unreported because of the extreme cultural taboo associated with it.

Perhaps it's difficult for soldiers to refuse to obey orders, especially when they're told all prisoners are the enemy. Professor Stanley Milgram, author of the famous experiment that measured participants' willingness to obey an authority figure who instructed them to perform acts that went against their personal consciences, concluded, "Ordinary people, simply doing their jobs . . . can become agents in a terrible destructive process. Moreover, even when the destructive effects of their work become patently clear, and they are asked to carry out actions incompatible with fundamental standards of morality, relatively few people have the resources needed to resist authority."

It's easier to abuse when there's a presumption of guilt, an assumption that the prisoners are terrorists. Was this what provoked the torture and sexual humiliation that led Jumah al-Dossary down the path to self-destruction?

"I spend many hours trying to convince Jumah that he shouldn't kill himself," his lawyer Colangelo-Bryan told me. "I tell him that he'll go home one day and be with his family again. He asks when that will happen, and, of course, I have no answer. He reminds me that he has lived for years alone in cells . . . and has been told by the military that he will live like that forever. All he can see is darkness. For me, his words bring on a feeling of crippling powerlessness."

The next states of al-Dossary's captivity began when a soldier cut off all his clothes with a pair of scissors, and his head and face were shaved clean. Naked, he was led into a large tent holding a group of men just like him, all bald, naked, and hairless. Soldiers instructed them to don orange prison jumpsuits, and they were fitted with sound-blocking ear muffs and blackened goggles. It was a bewildering experience to be deprived of basic sensory input. The men were then left in the room for hours, from noon until nightfall, to wear them down physically and mentally for the long flight west.

"We sat without food or drink, [and we were] unable to re-lieve ourselves or pray," al-Dossary reported. But the men did pray, trying their best to make the motions. Very late that night, they were led onto a plane and tied by the legs to the cabin floor or to the seats. Al-Dossary's forehead and nose were injured by the tight goggles, and his hands and legs swelled from the pressure of the shackles.

"Then, the plane took off and flew for many hours. I do not know how many," he wrote. "[It] landed in a country where the weather was hot."

They were moved to another plane and flown further west.

When they landed in Guantánamo Bay, the men were un-loaded onto a military bus.

"You are at an American base. You must not speak or move. You must keep your heads down," a translator shouted in Ara-bic, warning that prisoners who moved would be beaten.

"When it was my turn to get off the bus, I could not move because I was extremely stressed and exhausted," al-Dossary wrote. "They told to me get up right now and shouted at me. When I wanted to tell them that I could not move, they started hitting me and told me again that I was not allowed to talk." Two soldiers picked him up and threw him out of the bus.

The men were taken to Camp X-ray and left there until the following night, when they were led one by one into a large tent to be photographed and fingerprinted. Next, they were taken to a "cement building" to take a shower.

"They stripped me of my clothes and gave me soap but did not take the goggles off my eyes," al-Dossary wrote. Though the water was very cold, he was relieved to be bathing. But just as he was lathering his hair, he was ordered out of the shower.

"They were well aware that I had not bathed in over a month and a half," he wrote.

The years of abuse in Guantánamo broke him, al-Dossary wrote.

He had been interrogated at gunpoint several hundred times. Soldiers had threatened to rape him and to harm his family in the Middle East. He was told that his young daughter Nura would be kidnapped and that if he was sent home, he would be murdered by U.S. spies in the Middle East. He was also threatened with being sent to a jail in the United States.

"There are American prisoners waiting for people like [you]," interrogators told him.

According to his accounts, he was terrorized by growling police dogs, awakened in the night for questioning, and forced to spend long, cold nights on cement floors. One day, to punish him, he said, the guards poured a "very strong detergent" all around him in the interrogation room.

"I almost suffocated," he wrote.

He described loud music, bright light being shone directly in his face, and being forced to stay in a "very, very cold room" for endless hours. Sometimes, he was denied food and water and not allowed to use the bathroom or to wash before prayers. He said that all the interrogation rooms had a metal ring embedded in the floor. The guards tied his hands and feet to this ring, forcing him to lie in a fetal position.

The worst indignity he suffered occurred very late one Saturday night. He was marched into an interrogation room, shackled to the ring in the floor, and left alone for an extended period. All at once, the door was thrown open, and four soldiers with masks over their faces came in with a female interrogator. One of the soldiers operated a video camera.

"Now we want you to confess that you are with al-Qaeda or that you have some connection to the attacks in America," the female interrogator told him. "Otherwise, tonight we will show you something that you will never forget for the rest of your life."

They were right about his never forgetting. Realizing that something bad was going to happen to him, he pleaded that he'd had nothing to do with September 11.

"I started screaming and shouting so that perhaps one of the brothers would hear my screams . . . [but] the rooms were soundproof," he wrote.

The female interrogator laughed and told him that no one would hear his calls. "It's Saturday, it's the weekend, it's late at night, and there are no officials around," she said.

After a final threat, she issued a command to the soldiers.

They "came and took me off the chair," al-Dossary wrote. "My feet were tied to that ring as I mentioned before. They then laid me out on my back and put the extra shackles on top of my hand shackles and pulled me by them forcefully and brutally in the opposite direction, towards my feet, while I was lying on my back."

They cut his clothes off and threw the shreds into a corner. He couldn't have expected what happened next. The woman began to take her clothes off as the soldiers with the camera continued to film.

"When she was in her underwear, she stood on top of me," al-Dossary wrote. "She took off her underpants, she was wearing a sanitary towel, and drops of her menstrual blood fell on me and then she assaulted me. I tried to fight her off but the soldiers held me down with the chains forcefully and ruthlessly so that they almost cut my hands. I spat at her on her face; she put her hand on her dirty menstrual blood that had fallen on my body and wiped it on my chest. She stained her hands with her menstrual blood and wiped my face and beard with it. Then, she got up, cleaned herself, put her clothes back on, and left the room."

The soldiers proceeded to shackle his hands and feet together to the floor. They picked up his clothes and left him—tied up, naked, and smeared with menstrual blood.

Several hours later, some soldiers came back into the room; he didn't know whether they were the same ones as before, but they acted as if nothing had happened. They unshackled him and led him to a bathroom, where he was permitted to wash and was handed new clothes. He was taken back to the camp just before dawn prayer.

"I was in a hysterical state," al-Dossary wrote. "I almost went mad because of what had happened, how it had happened, and why it had happened."

"If these facts did not need to be documented for the whole world to know what happens in American detention camps, then I would not write this. I was shaken to the core; my body and my mind were shaken."

Parts of al-Dossary's testimony about this incident were corroborated by one of the Guantánamo Arabic linguists, Sgt. Erik Saar, who included an account of it in his book *Behind the Wire*. While it's unclear whether Saar was referring to al-Dossary, his account supports the notion that sexual humiliation of this kind occurred.

Al-Dossary said he wasn't the only one who experienced this abuse, but the others wouldn't allow him to mention their names. "I used to be exactly like them before," he wrote.

Al-Dossary said that, strangely, the interrogators who took part in sexual assaults were often never seen again afterward, "almost as if they were specialists in these types of crimes and assaults."

Al-Dossary spent prolonged periods in solitary confinement, suffering the kind of social and sensory deprivation that, according to the *American Journal of Psychiatry*, often leads to mental breakdown. Other effects of extreme isolation include chronic, severe headaches, developmental regression, and an inability to control urges, as well as to concentrate, to control anger, rage, primitive drives, and instincts, to plan beyond the moment, or to anticipate the logical consequences of one's behavior.

In January 2004, al-Dossary was moved to isolation in "India Block," where he deteriorated quickly. He was often left naked in the metal cell under the cold air-conditioning vents directly above his metal bed, without even a pillow, a blanket, or a plastic mat to sleep on. To avoid the chill from the air-conditioning, he cowered near the toilet. For weeks, he had neither toilet paper nor water to wash with, so he cleaned himself with the toilet water.

Letters from his family were confiscated and destroyed.

"I became like a house of cards that always falls down; whatever side you try to build it from, it will still fall down. I almost collapsed completely," he wrote. "Oh, those days and nights. I felt that time had ended at that time and did not want to move forward. I felt that the whole world with its mountains and all its gravity was bearing down on my chest. I had no helper and protector except Allah. I was at the end of my tether, all the doors had closed on me, and I had lost hope in everything except Allah. . . . In this state of darkness, injustice, and oppression, Allah was with me. He blessed me, in the severity of all this psychological stress in this very depressing cell, by helping me to memorize the whole Koran, in spite of the harshness of my circumstances, what I was suffering, and the intensity of this disgraceful psychological stress. This was Allah's mercy on me."

On May 25, 2004, al-Dossary was moved to the newly opened Camp 5, which consisted entirely of solitary cells where the air-conditioning was kept at frigid temperatures and enormous fans mimicked the sound of an airplane engine to prevent prisoners from screaming to each other through the concrete walls.

He met with attorney Joshua Colangelo-Bryan in March 2005 and told him everything he had been through. When the lawyer left, al-Dossary was threatened by an angry soldier. "It's best that you forget everything that's happened to you and don't mention it again to anyone if you want to stay safe," the soldier told him, al-Dossary later wrote. After that, he was given something peculiar tasting to eat and began to experience dizziness, headaches, vomiting, and fainting. His left arm went numb.

But he was careful to emphasize that not all U.S. soldiers treated him badly. Once, he wrote, a black soldier brought him cookies and hot chocolate. Another young soldier's eyes welled with tears after he heard what al-Dossary had endured.

"There are some soldiers who have humanity, irrespective of their race, gender, or faith," al-Dossary wrote.

Though he maintains that he has no terrorism connections and doesn't hate the United States, the Federal Bureau of Investigation and Pentagon say there was no mistake in his case and that al-Dossary went to an al-Qaeda training camp in Afghanistan in 1989, something that Colangelo-Bryan disputes. "Jumah did go to Afghanistan for a long weekend on a Saudi government–sponsored trip after the Soviets had left," he told me. "The Saudis were sending lots of people there to see Afghanistan after the Soviets had been driven out with support of the Saudis and the United States."

The Pentagon also said that he was "present at Tora Bora," but it didn't say when he was there, why this was a crime, what he supposedly did there, or who he was with. Al-Dossary maintained that he had never been to Tora Bora in his life.

Stories circulating on the Internet suggested that al-Dossary had come to the United States on a tourist visa in 2001 and delivered a heated political speech at a mosque in Lackawanna, New York, just outside Buffalo. But Colangelo-Bryan said that was not a basis for holding his client.

"Jumah did give a sermon at a mosque there, where he talked about injustice in the world," the lawyer said. "He did not urge any violence against the U.S. or any other country or person, and there have been no allegations that he did." The United States did not allege that al-Dossary had engaged in any recruiting at Lackawanna or elsewhere.

The Defense Department detained him year after year, its official position being that he was right where he belonged: in a seven-by-eight-foot cage.

That's what the military said about everyone I met in Guantánamo.

CHAPTER SIXTEEN

WHAT THE PENTAGON SAID

There were some very bad men at Guantánamo Bay, maybe even men who deserved to be called "evil." Some of the detainees were truly the worst of the worst, like Khaled Sheik Mohammad, a.k.a. KSM, the alleged mastermind of the September 11 attacks on the United States, or Yemeni Ramzi Binalshibh, a key aide to KSM and the Hamburg roommate of September 11 lead hijacker Mohammad Atta, or Abu Zubaidah, the man who allegedly organized the aborted "millennium bomb plots" in Jordan and Los Angeles in late 1999. I'm grateful that these men and others are no longer free to terrorize the world.

But I continue to believe that terrorists should receive public trials before they're locked up. Hiding them away from the world at Gitmo, or anywhere else, without charging them was shady and wrong. It made America look like a lawless thug state and tarnished our nation's image as a beacon of justice in the world.

I wanted to understand why the Pentagon was insisting that men like Dr. Ali Shah Mousovi and Haji Nusrat were among the "worst of the worst." I'd heard that the Defense Department had strategically transferred fourteen "high-value" detainees from secret Central Intelligence Agency prisons around the world to Gitmo in September 2006, after a flood of negative press and international calls to close down the military detention center, so that the claim could honestly be made that there were dangerous terrorists at Gitmo.

At its peak, Gitmo had 754 detainees. Four were said to have committed suicide. A fifth allegedly died of colon cancer. Would the military concede that those released without charge after years of detention were mistakes? And regarding the alleged suicides, why weren't there open, transparent investigations into those deaths? Why were the men's organs removed by the military before the bodies were transferred home?

I e-mailed a Department of Justice attorney responsible for coordinating habeas visits to Gitmo and asked him to put me in touch with a Pentagon representative. He referred me to Commander Jeffery Gordon, a Pentagon spokesman with the Office of the Secretary of Defense.

Some of the habeas lawyers thought I was naïve to assume that Gordon would be cooperative or straightforward. But I was open to hearing something that would diverge from what I had witnessed at Gitmo.

I e-mailed Gordon and told him that I was interested in getting the military's perspective on Guantánamo Bay. He responded immediately with a lengthy e-mail, copied to several military officials.

Instead of agreeing to help me understand the military's perspective and to answer my questions, he wrote a bitter missive chastising me for the article in the *Washington Post*, which he denounced as "biased and fundamentally flawed." He told me that he had contacted *Post* editors after my article ran and requested the same amount of space to write a rebuttal, a request that had been turned aside.

He also reminded me that I had photographed a Gitmo soldier against that soldier's will. I didn't tell him that this soldier had readily posed for photos, while I took dozens of pictures of him drinking habeas beer, smoking habeas cigarettes, and eating habeas steaks with us. He went on to call my article "deeply offensive to the military men and women who have volunteered to proudly serve in the armed forces in defense of this nation." I didn't understand the relevance of a year-old article, or why Gordon was bringing it up.

He wrote that while he was glad I had come to him to "set the record straight," I should have come to him the year before as well.

I e-mailed him back:

> I contacted you because I wanted to get your side of the story. . . . I can only write about what I have seen and observed at Gitmo; I can't speculate about all the "bad bomb makers," and so far, all that I have seen negates what I have heard. . . . I am not attempting to "set the record straight"—I am attempting to ask you if there is another side to the story which you would like to share with me and

with readers. . . . If you truly feel that I have been "biased" by my meetings with these prisoners, and if you feel that my perceptions are "fundamentally flawed," then correct me and let me know—I'm coming to you so I can report and tell the whole story. . . .

If you are interested in helping me understand . . . how America has become a safer place, with a harrowing description of the bad guys that we have heard about so much, then I would like to write about it. . . .

Finally, I would like to say that I'm sorry my article offended you. I was offended by what I saw and was merely relating that. And while my heritage is Afghan, I was born in America, and I think part of what makes this country great is the ability to discuss and speak until we learn from one another.

In reply, Gordon asked me to answer several obscure questions before he would agree to provide any information. He asked whether I had taken the bar exam and in which state, whether I was working for any nongovernmental organizations, and whether I was providing legal representation or any other services to detainees or former detainees.

I didn't know what he was getting at, but I really wanted to talk to him, so I responded: No, I hadn't yet taken the bar. No, I didn't work for any nongovernmental organizations, and I wasn't sole counsel on any case. I did have my own case but was being supervised by Dechert.

That's when the problems started.

Gordon insinuated that I was lying. He couldn't fathom how I could have my own case even though I wasn't a member of any bar. Apparently, he had done a series of Internet searches on my name and found an article on my law school Web site discussing my habeas case. He accused me of lying to an academic institution and to a government official. I was livid.

Peter Ryan of Dechert had contacted the Center for Constitutional Rights and requested an Afghan client specifically for me, in addition to the fifteen clients whom Dechert was already representing. Peter agreed to supervise me because I wasn't yet barred, but I would be responsible for preparing for meetings with the prisoner, gathering evidence on the prisoner's behalf, and so on. I wouldn't be acting as interpreter; it would be my case. Had Gordon done his homework, he'd have known that law students and nonbarred attorneys are permitted to practice under the supervision of a practicing attorney. Instead, he called me unethical.

Gordon surely knew the answers to the questions he had asked me and was attempting to entrap me. I e-mailed back and said that further communication wasn't a good idea.

His response: "Well, you didn't quite start off on the right foot with the *Wash Post Outlook* cover story last year, which was one of the strangest things I've seen in the past couple years."

He and I have a different idea of what is "strange." Strange is American soldiers torturing prisoners. Strange is giving "rewards" of $5,000 to $25,000 per prisoner, and stranger still is the U.S. military's making arrests without first investigating allegations put forth by locals who stand to gain financially from them. Strange is holding men for more than five years without ever charging them. Strange is the military's removal of organs from prisoners who committed suicide before sending their bodies home for burial. Strange is calling a paralyzed eighty-year-old man an "enemy combatant." Strange is that while U.S. soldiers throw the Qu'ran in buckets of feces, the administration had figuratively done the same to the U.S. Constitution.

Gordon accused me again of having lied. He said that I was being unethical and mentioned that he knew alumni of my law school, as if he were going to expose me or something. "I have several close friends and a relative who are also alumni of UofM [sic] Law School and am certain they would agree with maintaining integrity of the school's Web site and all their public information products."

His e-mails were always very lengthy and somewhat irrelevant and led me to believe that he had a lot of time on his hands. He told me how he'd once enrolled in a class at a law school.

"Although I am not an attorney, I did complete a cert program at a law school and thus am keenly aware of the ethical issues involved in representing oneself to the public, in particular to government officials and academic institutions," he wrote.

I figured that he had enough time on his hands to try to make me look bad, and at first, I did feel intimidated. It's not pleasant being threatened by a Pentagon commander.

Still, I took allegations of ethical impropriety seriously. I responded by e-mailing him, the dean of my law school, and Dechert attorneys directly to explain what he was saying and why it was wrong. The dean of the School of Law replied in my support, as did the attorneys at Dechert.

The ordeal made me think back to my meeting with Abdul Salam Zaeef. It seemed unfortunate that a former Taliban representative had treated me, a female visitor from America, better than the Pentagon public relations office. Zaeef had at least entertained my questions about the Taliban's mistreatment of women without becoming incensed and threatening me.

My communications with Gordon were futile, except that they gave me a good taste of what it felt like to be scared by the government and its power.

CHAPTER SEVENTEEN

THE POLICE CHIEF

Abdullah Mujahid thought that the feminist movement had shortchanged American women. Once they were loved just for being "nurturing mothers and wives, precious sisters, and little girls." But now, Mujahid perceptively noted, women in our country carry an ever-growing load of responsibilities; in addition to caring for a family, they're expected to work.

"If a woman chooses to work because she likes and wants to, she should," the thirty-five-year-old Afghan detainee said to me and Carolyn Welshhans, a lawyer from Dechert's Washington, D.C., office, at a meeting in March 2007. "But women shouldn't have to get jobs. We are happy to take care of our women, protect them. And women in my country are happy to depend on their husbands and fathers."

It sounds good. But as I listened to Mujahid, I thought that "depend" was the wrong verb. Afghan women don't just "depend" on men; they're at men's mercy. Men dictate when and

Farid Ahmad holds his brother
Abdullah Mujahid's framed
photograph; Gardez, Afghanistan.
Jean Chung/WPN for Boston Globe.

whom a woman may marry, how she may dress, with whom she may interact, and whether she'll ever be able to read a book or write a letter. But I kept all of that to myself because I sensed that Mujahid was gently trying to bridge our worlds and paint a better image of his countrymen for the two women from America.

We didn't have our first real conversation with Mujahid until our third meeting with him. He was a strongly built man with closely cropped hair without a single strand of gray. He was well mannered and gracious, like Dr. Ali Shah Mousovi, but somehow reserved and slightly guarded. The first time I met him, I assumed, because of his strong physical presence, that he would take control of the meeting, but in fact he said little. He only politely answered questions, never steering the discussion or even hinting at an initial mistrust, as most prisoners do. So, the afternoon of our third meeting in Camp Iguana was unique.

"Afghan men really believe that women should spend their lives comfortably. We love our mothers and wives," Mujahid said. "They're so delicate, and they need someone to protect and care for them. There's nothing wrong with this. I just don't think women should have to worry about feeding their families and making money."

"What if they enjoy working, like we do?" Carolyn gently challenged him.

"There's nothing wrong with a woman working, but being forced to . . ." Mujahid's words trailed off, as if he were about to say that it would be like child labor.

Still, I thought to myself that an Afghan women's movement would at least give girls the right to an education. And Mujahid agreed. Before his July 2003 arrest, he had been the police chief of Gardez, the same town from which Dr. Ali Shah hailed. When I visited Afghanistan, I met an official from the Ministry of Education who described Mujahid as a zealous supporter of girl's schools. In fact, as soon as the Taliban were pushed out of Gardez, Mujahid had financed the construction of numerous schools for girls out of his personal savings, then spent time encouraging hesitant parents to enroll their daughters.

Mujahid was curious about how Americans perceived Muslims and Afghans and whether the young blond lawyer sitting before him had any prejudgments of her own.

"What did you think about Muslim men before you came here?" he asked Carolyn.

"Actually, the first Muslims I ever met were at Guantánamo Bay," she told him, "and the experience has completely opened my eyes."

He asked how.

"I was a little apprehensive before I came," Carolyn told him. "I didn't know what to expect. But every prisoner has treated me with dignity, respect, and kindness."

Carolyn admitted that she had once lumped all Gitmo detainees together, as an indistinguishable mass of numbered

Muslim men. While she felt that they deserved representation, she had come in with a headful of biases.

"I was afraid of being rejected as an American and as a woman," she admitted.

Mujahid nodded. "The problem," he said, "is that the Taliban's short rule of Afghanistan has given all Afghan and Muslim men a horrible name. But the Taliban and what they did to our country does not offer a true picture of Afghanistan or of Afghan men. It was a terrible time for us, and anyone who had the money fled."

"You're right," Carolyn said. "And as I got to know each prisoner here, one by one, they've chipped away at my biases. With every prisoner I met, I realized that each was a unique individual. Every man was as different from the next as any two people could be."

She described how Abdullah Wazir Zadran, a good-looking twenty-eight-year-old Afghan shopkeeper from Khost, reminded her of her younger brother Jeff, who was the same age and had the same light brown eyes.

"Jeff is younger than I am, and we're very close," she said. "Seeing Zadran chained to the floor made me think of my brother and that it could have been him, thousands of miles from home, without access to his family, friends, or a fair hearing."

The boyish-faced shopkeeper was Carolyn's only client younger than her, as well as the only one who tried to boss her around. Sometimes, after some discussion of what was going on in Afghanistan or the legal issues in his case, Zadran would get a bored look on his tanned face and start telling Carolyn to do something, insisting that she bring him a book after lunch, for example. Even after she explained that books had to go through a clearance process, he would keep right on insisting.

Carolyn wouldn't get offended. She knew he was just being stubborn and trying to do things his own way. It was the kind of thing that reminded her of her younger brothers. "Although," she said, "they both know better than to boss me around."

The first prisoner Carolyn had met, therefore the one who left the strongest mental impression, was Abdul Haq Wasiq.

"He was the first I ever saw chained to the floor," she recalled. "He was the first to thank me for being a humanitarian. He was the first to refuse to meet with me when I visited again. He was the first to then change his mind again—and meet with me on another trip. He was also the first to use the word 'torture' in reference to how he was treated. He was the first to indicate how badly Guantánamo was affecting him psychologically."

The words of Dr. Hafizullah Shabaz Khail, a sixty-one-year-old Afghan pharmacist from Gardez, haunted her. "If you free one Afghan, it will be like you are bringing someone back from the dead," he said.

Meanwhile, Mohammad Zahir, a fifty-four-year-old Afghan schoolteacher from Ghazni who was badly in need of dentures, impressed her with his dry sense of humor. "Mohammad Zahir is as lonely, depressed, angry, hurt, and devastated as our other clients," Carolyn said. "He is very worried about his family. But we also have ended up laughing at least once in each of our meetings, and I think it said a lot about him that he still tries to laugh—even if most of the time he is laughing at me. Every time I meet with him, I worry that his spark will have gone out, but so far he has managed to hold onto it."

"All of the men I have met here," she told Abdullah Mujahid, "have treated me with respect and kindness."

"Religious freedom was something I always believed in," she said, "but now when I hear people speaking critically of Muslim men and Islam, I have a point of reference for disagreeing. I can now say that it is not consistent with my friend Abdullah Mujahid or Abdullah Wazir Zadran or Mohammad Zahir. I know these men, and I know they are good people with good hearts."

Mujahid listened. "I think the problem is that Americans are very removed in many ways from the Muslim world," he said finally. "There is a perception that Muslim men will gobble people up—that we are all terrorists. The West fears the Muslim world because of the actions of a few bad people, and those bad people are considered just as evil in the Muslim world as they are in America."

Really, we are more alike than different, Mujahid said. "If Americans could sit down with Muslims and get to know them, they would see how similar we are. We are just like you. We love our families. We want the best for our children. We want peace in our country. We want a future to look toward."

Again, he emphasized that most men in Afghanistan love the women in their lives and treat them well. "Men in my country give women a huge amount of respect, but the only image that is left in the minds of Americans is the Taliban's mistreatment of women," he said. "This was a single horrible regime in our history, and most Afghans hated them."

He told us about things I'd experienced myself in Afghanistan: women go straight to the front of lines, they are waved past checkpoints, they're never searched, and their cars are never stopped.

Carolyn looked at him intently. "Americans have done something very wrong to you, something you'll never forget," she said. "I'm asking whether it would be possible for you to try to understand that not all Americans are like the ones who have kept you here for so long."

I don't know whether I could have been as forgiving as Mujahid was in his reply. "I know that even every soldier here is not bad. Most have nothing to do with my arrest or lack of investigation," he said. "I know this. And I do not hold a negative judgment of individual Americans."

Mujahid was brought to Guantánamo Bay in mid-2003. A provincial police chief working to improve public safety, he was a strong supporter of Afghan democracy. He had welcomed U.S. soldiers to his neighborhood and maintained close contact with U.S. military officials. He had also helped orchestrate the removal of Taliban insurgents from Gardez.

When Hamid Karzai became president, Mujahid was promoted to a more senior position in Kabul. Like many others, he thought that this time peace would last in Afghanistan. He didn't realize that he wouldn't be a part of the new peace process. In July 2003, he was arrested in his father's home for mysterious reasons and taken to Bagram, then eventually to Gitmo.

The murkiness surrounding his arrest has never been cleared up, and the reasons for his continued detention are equally mysterious. The military said he had been colluding with al-Qaeda and had attacked U.S. forces in Gardez. His attorney has knocked down the allegations as hearsay one by one. But as her client was cleared of one set of accusations, the military would come up with new ones. In 2005, the Department of Defense (DOD) decided to accuse him of something fairly far-fetched. It alleged that he had played a pivotal role in a separatist group called Lashkar-i-Tayiba, which operated cells in Indian-occupied Kashmir.

The allegation seemed absurd. Mujahid had had nothing to do with the struggle between India and Pakistan over the disputed Kashmiri territory. But when Carolyn did an Internet search on Mujahid, she found that there was in fact a man named Abdullah Mujahid who was intricately tied to the Kashmiri separatist group. It just wasn't her client. According to press reports, the Abdullah Mujahid of Lashkar-i-Tayiba died in November 2006, while her client was still at Gitmo. It was a bad case of mistaken identity, and Carolyn quickly pointed it out to the military.

"The ability to disprove these allegations rather easily calls into question the credibility of other allegations," she said.

But that was just one of many obstacles Mujahid faced. During his combatant status review tribunal, he requested that eight witnesses be allowed to submit testimony on his behalf. Four of them were Gitmo detainees, including Ali Shah Mousovi, and the other four were high-profile officials in the Karzai cabinet. But the military almost never gave detainees access to the witnesses they believed might help their cases. Instead, the presiding officer routinely said that attempts had been made to find the requested witnesses but they could not be contacted. Mujahid got the same song and dance.

"The Afghan government was contacted on or about November 26, 2004. As of this date, the Afghanistan government has not responded to our request. . . . Without the cooperation of that government, we are unable to contact those witnesses and obtain the testimony that you requested," the tribunal president announced.

The *Boston Globe*, however, investigated and found three of the four requested witnesses within three days. Two were found immediately in Afghanistan; the third was a professor at the National Defense University in Washington, D.C. The fourth witness had reportedly died.

On February 22, 2007, the military abruptly announced that it had decided to clear Mujahid to be released and returned to Afghanistan. The DOD sent Carolyn an e-mail that said, in part, "Your client has been approved to leave Guantánamo, subject to the process for making appropriate diplomatic arrangements for his departure."

Carolyn was ecstatic and thought it would be only a matter of weeks before Mujahid was heading home. I delivered the good news to Mujahid's brother, Farid Ahmad, in Gardez. He was overjoyed; the family thought their prayers had been answered. When we gave Mujahid himself the news, a meek smile spread across his face.

"Thank you for all your efforts," he said. He told us he didn't dare to hope that he might go home and be reunited with his family until it happened, until he was on that eastbound flight back to Afghanistan. He asked us please not to raise his family's hopes either. He knew how his arrest had broken their lives.

"I don't want them to be disappointed," he said. "I've been lied to so many times."

All the while, though, his eyes were saying something different. They shone. I thought that for the first time, Mujahid had hope. He believed the good news about going home.

I didn't think much about the rationale for his fears, but over time, I understood. As the weeks turned into a month, and a month became three, then four, then six, then eight, I was bombarded by calls from Mujahid's anxious brother. Every time I answered the phone, he had just one question: when?

"When is my brother coming home? Have you heard anything?" Farid would ask impatiently. "Is there any news?"

I would have to apologize and tell him that we had no idea. "The military has not disclosed dates, only that he's cleared for release," I'd say.

Slowly, as the months dragged on, Farid grew sullen. He was disappointed and upset that he had allowed himself to believe that his brother was coming back. Mujahid's hope gradually dissipated too. One grim morning, he was particularly depressed. He didn't understand why he was still being held when it had already been decided that he would be released.

I brought him a selection of Odwalla fresh juices on the last trip in June 2007 and told him to drink the carrot juice—it was good for him.

"The doctors in Afghanistan tell us that carrots are good for your eyes," he said. "I never knew whether I should believe them or if it was a strange myth. What do our doctors know?"

"The doctors in America say the same thing," I said, pushing the bottle toward him. "It is good for your eyes."

He took a hesitant sip.

"You don't like it?" I asked.

"It's not that. But why should I care about my eyes?" he replied. "All I see are the walls of my cell all day long. You go ahead and have it. Your eyes see the sky and the ocean."

I wished I knew how to distract him from his sadness. "Okay, then have some Pepsi!" I said, handing him a plastic bottle.

He chuckled.

Mujahid had another reason to feel despondent. Right after the military declared that he had been "approved to leave," they moved him into Camp 6, where he was held in solitary confinement for twenty-two hours a day. When they took him outside for recreation, he was put in a small outdoor cage by himself.

Otherwise, he was held in a concrete box fifty-six feet square. In that small space, his steel toilet was positioned strategically in front of the small window in the door through which guards regularly peered in at him. Next to the toilet was a concrete slab that served as a bed. If he was "cooperative," he got a thin foam mattress to lay on the concrete. When he longed to speak to another human being, he crouched on the ground and put his mouth to the crack beneath the door and shouted someone's name to get his attention, then quickly put his ear to the crack and listened for any response.

But other prisoners were also trying to shout to one another, and it was often hard to communicate. When Mujahid gave up on that, he'd go to sleep. That was how he passed days: Sleeping, then sleeping some more. Thinking about when he would be released. Shouting to others in the adjacent cells— Abdullah Wazir Zadran, Chaman Gul, Wali Mohammad.

If he was given permission to have his box of personal correspondence, he would reread letters from his family. Then, he would sleep again.

"That's what I do all day," he murmured.

"Telling him that he has been approved to leave, but then moving him to solitary confinement and doing nothing, is a new, cruel form of torture for him," Carolyn said to me. "It is unconscionable that Mujahid has not been returned to Afghanistan. Our government has claimed that it does not want to hold prisoners any longer than is necessary. Yet, more than several months later, he remains in Guantánamo and in solitary confinement."

It was always hard to leave Abdullah Mujahid, as it was to leave so many of the prisoners. Sometimes I wished he were more hostile or angry, more doubtful of a lawyer's ability. I wished that he would turn us away once in a while. But he never did. He was always gentle, almost to the point of submissiveness. The last time I saw him, he was peering through the Camp 6 meeting room window as we were ushered out by guards. I got close and gave him a smile. He grinned back, the biggest smile I'd seen so far.

Meanwhile, Carolyn accepted a new job. Once she left Dechert, she wouldn't be able to work on the prisoners' cases or visit them any longer. She fretted about how to tell Mujahid and other clients that she wouldn't be coming back. I knew it would be hard because it had taken them so long to trust her and to believe that she was on their side. She worked tirelessly for them and wrote them long, detailed letters to help them pass the time. She didn't like to think about leaving the men she had grown to care so deeply about, and she hoped that they'd be released before she left. She especially hoped that Mujahid would remember their conversations.

"I hope they've helped support his belief that there are good people in the United States," she said. "We've had many discussions about the differences between Afghanistan and America, although I think Abdullah Mujahid would say that we have actually discussed the similarities. Because it is his constant argument that we are all not so different."

CHAPTER EIGHTEEN

THE POETS

By the time I first arrived at Guantánamo, they had become something of a legend—two brothers who had found a unique way of surviving three years of imprisonment: writing poetry.[1] Poetry was a lifeline to sanity for many detainees; it allowed them to express the suffering and confusion they felt. But Abdul Rahim Muslim Dost and his brother Badr Zaman were a phenomenon. They had written tens of thousands of lines of verse—on Styrofoam cups, on bits of paper—and circulated them through the prison or written them down in the margins of Red Cross stationery, hoping to slip them past the military censors to their families in Afghanistan.[2]

Both Pakistani and American government officials refused to discuss the brothers' case, so I searched public sources, from newspaper reports to public records and Web site accounts, for anything on them. They had been released before lawyers obtained access to Guantánamo in 2004, so I asked friends, acquaintances, and released prisoners in Afghanistan and Pakistan about them. Gradually, I was able to piece together some of the remarkable stories of their creativity. I never met them, but I heard so many speak of them with fondness and admiration that in the end, I felt that I, too, had come to know them and their remarkable gift.

> *Just as the heart beats in the darkness of the body,*
> *so I, despite this cage, continue to beat with life.*
> *Those who have no courage or honor*
> *consider themselves free,*
> *I am flying on the wings of thought,*
> *and so, even in this cage,*
> *I know a greater freedom.*
>
> —ABDUL RAHIM[3]

No one knows exactly what got the two brothers into the most trouble: internal Pakistani politics, their advocacy for an independent Pashtunistan, or a joke about President Bill Clinton. During the three years they spent at Guantánamo, their U.S. interrogators focused laserlike on the last: what had they said about Clinton?[4]

It was, admittedly, a bad joke. It popped up in one of the dozens of articles the two had written as journalists in Peshawar. In 1998, during the Monica Lewinsky scandal, Abdul Rahim wrote a short parody that was published in a Peshawar newspaper. Clinton had offered a $5 million reward for the capture of Osama bin Laden, who had been identified as a threat to the United States for the terrorist training camps he

ran in Afghanistan.[5] What, Abdul Rahim asked, could the
Afghans offer in return as a reward for the capture of the man
dallying with Miss Monica Lewinsky? They could offer as
much as five million afghanis, the joke being that Afghanistan
was so poor that five million pieces of its currency were
worth the vast amount of $113.[6]

"It was a lampoon . . . of the poor Afghan economy" under
the Taliban, Badr Zaman said in an interview after his release.
The article told Afghans how to identify Clinton if they spotted him. "It said he was clean shaven, had light-colored eyes,
and had been seen involved in a scandal with Monica Lewinsky," Badr said.[7] For three years, more than 100 interrogators,
including some from Washington, D.C., didn't get the joke.[8]
"Again and again, they were asking questions about this article. We had to explain that this was a satire," Badr Zaman said
in an interview with *Newsday* in October 2005. "It was really
pathetic."

U.S. interrogators may have focused on the joke about Clinton, but the real reason the two brothers were turned over to
the United States seems to have had more to do with internal
Pakistani politics. Few Americans know that Pakistan has ma-
nipulated the United States into taking care of members of
the Pakistani opposition who have nothing to do with Osama
bin Laden or the so-called war on terror. But this is most likely
what happened to the Dost brothers.

As was true for many Afghans of their generation, their lives
were heavily bound up in political events in their country. They
had fled Afghanistan for Peshawar during the Soviet occupation and joined an anti-Soviet political group called Jamiat-
i-Dawatul Qur'an wa Sunna. Abdul Rahim became editor of
its magazine, according to an account by *Newsday* reporter

James Rupert. Even then, "we were not fighters," Badr told Rupert. "We took part in the war only as writers."

The two became popular figures in Peshawar literary and political circles and were known for their writings. Badr Zaman, who had gone to graduate school at the University of Peshawar and earned a master's degree in English literature, was a fan of Geoffrey Chaucer's *Canterbury Tales* and Jonathan Swift's *Gulliver's Travels.*[9] He later became an English professor. Abdul Rahim was a magazine editor, a religious scholar, and an avid writer; by one account, he authored more than thirty books.[10] Even at Guantánamo, according to newspaper reports, Abdul Rahim was able to write a book on Islamic law, translate an anthology of Arabic poetry into Pashto,[11] and with the help of Arab prisoners, translate the entire Qu'ran into his native tongue.

In 1989, the Soviet army withdrew from Afghanistan, and the two brothers broke with their group, which had become involved with the Wahhabite interpretation of Islam. Abdul Rahim began writing lampoons of the group's leader, a cleric named Sami Ullah, portraying him as a corrupt pawn of the Pakistani government, working against Afghan interests. In November 2001, as U.S. forces attacked Afghanistan, the mullah's brother, Roh Ullah, "called us and said if we didn't stop criticizing the party he would have us put in jail," Badr told *Newsday.* On November 17, only six weeks after the September 11 attacks, agents from Pakistan's feared Inter-Services Intelligence (ISI) raided the brothers' family home and arrested them.[12]

Hayat Ullah, one of Ullah's brothers, insisted to *Newsday* that his family was not behind the arrests, even though he acknowledged that Abdul Rahim was a political rival. "We have many powerful rivals," Hayat Ullah reportedly said. "If I were going to get ISI to pick up an enemy, why would I choose an ordinary person like him?"

In an interview after his release, Badr said that his arrest had had nothing to do with al-Qaeda or with terrorism but rather with his political opponents' desire to shut him and his older brother up. They were columnists for several magazines and had been zealously pushing for the creation of a sovereign Pashtunistan, an autonomous state for ethnic Pashtun tribes on both sides of the Afghan-Pakistani border. This angered Pakistani officials, who have been trying for years to subdue the Pashtun separatist movement.[13]

Whatever the reasons for their arrest, the brothers were held in a filthy Peshawar jail for three months before being driven blindfolded and handcuffed to Peshawar's International Airport and passed to American soldiers.[14] "They chained our feet," Badr said to James Rupert of *Newsday*. "Dogs were barking at us. They pulled a sack down over my head. It was very difficult to breathe . . . and I saw the flash of cameras. They were taking pictures of us." They were dragged aboard a military plane, shackled down, and flown to Bagram Air Force Base and later to Kandahar in southern Afghanistan.[15]

Badr said his worst experiences were at these prisons, where he was forbidden to bathe,[16] threatened by dogs, deprived of sleep, and photographed naked[17]; he also had his beard and eyebrows shaved and suffered various other indignities.[18] He heard the moans of other prisoners as they were beaten and their holy book was desecrated. But he says that neither he nor his brother was tortured at Gitmo.[19]

The brothers were flown to Guantánamo in May 2002.[20] According to Badr, U.S. interrogators told them that Pakistani Intelligence alleged that they were al-Qaeda operatives, Taliban supporters, and a dangerous threat to former president Clinton.[21]

Soon after their imprisonment, Badr and Abdul Rahim were separated. But Badr found a way to discover his older brother's whereabouts. When they were first brought to Guantánamo Bay, everything was still under construction, and prisoners were kept in open-air cages or sometimes in makeshift tents. The prisoners were given plastic buckets to use for their bodily wastes. When the buckets were full, the guards selected detainees to clean and empty them. Badr was lonely and desperate to see his brother, so he volunteered for the chore. Making his way from tent to tent through the camp collecting buckets, he finally found his brother. Always the poet, Abdul Rahim greeted Badr with a bucket full of excrement and with poetry on his lips[22]:

> What kind of spring is this
> where there are no flowers
> and the air is filled
> with a miserable smell?[23]

Badr was stunned that his brother was composing and reciting poetry at Guantánamo Bay. But gradually he began to cling to the words. It meant that his brother's mind was still thriving, and it helped him persevere. Writing was difficult because detainees weren't allowed paper or pens. Abdul Rahim improvised, using his fingernails to etch prose into Styrofoam cups.[24] The better ones, he memorized. Later, he was able to use stationery provided by the Red Cross and even mail some of his poetry home.[25] In three years at Guantánamo, Abdul Rahim wrote more than twenty-five thousand verses in Pashto.[26]

"Poetry was our support and psychological uplift," Badr said in his post-release interview. "Many people have lost their minds. . . . I know forty or fifty prisoners who are mad. But we took refuge in our minds."[27]

After being separated for more than a year, the brothers were brought together and placed in adjacent cages. Their poetry soon became an underground sensation in the camp, as fellow prisoners passed the poems from cage to cage using a pulley system fashioned from prayer cap threads.[28] Many of the prisoners memorized the catchy verses, whispering them to each other in Pashto or translating them into Arabic. The poems made them laugh; sometimes they captured all their torment in a few powerful lines and moved them to tears.[29]

A favorite poem in the camp was about the androgynous appearance of the guards who patrolled the cell blocks. Badr said that he and the other prisoners couldn't distinguish women from men. The poem poked fun at the women with men's haircuts and the men without beards, all of them dressed in identical fatigues. The prisoners never saw long tresses on a woman or a rugged masculine face. The poem ends, "They may have weapons and missiles, but we can find no sign of manhood in this army."[30]

During their imprisonment, the brothers were both asked endlessly about Clinton. But they didn't crumble mentally as many did. Instead, the interrogators found that the brothers, who were fluent in English, could communicate easily with the guards and were always cooperative. The two never resisted the questioning, even though they had to explain their joke over and over. As soon as one set of interrogators figured out the political humor, a new set came in and had to be convinced all over again.[31]

When they finally convinced the prison authorities that they were not what the Pakistani ISI had claimed, they were given white prison jumpsuits and moved to the communal Camp 4, where prisoners could teach each other to read and write and to speak English, and where they had access to ample paper. The brothers spent their time writing, reading, and reflecting.

Here's a line from one of Abdul Rahim's favorite poems:

> *Bangle bracelets*
> *befit a pretty young woman*
> *Handcuffs befit*
> *a brave young man.*[32]

The brothers sent as many verses as they could home in letters.[33] Abdul Rahim's eldest son neatly catalogued whatever made it past the censors in a black binder in the home library in Peshawar. The contents of the poetry varied with the brothers' day-to-day emotions. In the beginning, it was filled with despair and hopelessness, but as time wore on, the poems grew stronger. Badr and Abdul Rahim wrote for each other as well, to keep their spirits up.[34]

The Islamic holiday of Eid was particularly difficult. Eid is a time when parents and relatives give children gifts and money, and everyone wears their new Eid clothes. Badr wrote a poem from the perspective of a child who is separated from his father on Eid day.

> Eid has come,
> but my father has not.
> He has not come from Cuba.
> I am eating the bread of Eid with my tears.
> I have nothing.
> Why am I deprived of the love of my father?
> Why am I so oppressed?[35]

When I spoke to Afghan prisoner Abdullah Wazir Zadran, I realized that this poem expressed many of the prisoners' feelings of loss during the holiday. Unfortunately, at Guantánamo, the U.S. military seemed to go out of its way to torment the prisoners on Eid. Zadran told me and Rebecca Dick of Dechert's Washington, D.C., office that the guards put up two posters all over the prison camp. One depicted "beautiful, happy, Muslim children" on Eid day. "They are laughing, wearing new clothes, and holding gifts and money," he said. The second is of a group of young Muslim children wearing tattered, dirty clothing, crying, with no gifts or money. The caption reads, "These are your children on Eid Day."

The three-year nightmare came to an end in September 2004, when Badr Zaman was selected to be transferred to the custody of the Afghan government along with seventeen other Afghans. Soon after, in April 2005, his brother Abdul Rahim

Badr Zaman with his children and nephews, whom he takes care of now. *Courtesy of Badr Zaman.*

was also released, and the two were reunited in Peshawar.

Yet, their release was not complete: the U.S. authorities had confiscated the bulk of their prison writings. Abdul Rahim felt that the loss of his writing was worse than the imprisonment. "Why did they give me a pen and paper if they were planning to do that?" he asked in an interview. "Each word was like a child to me—irreplaceable."[36]

In interviews, he pondered how he might recover his work. "I wrote from the core of my heart in Guantánamo Bay. In the outside world, I could not have written such things," he said in one interview.[37] And in another, he commented, "If they give me back my writings, truly I will feel as though I was never imprisoned."[38]

In addition to the thousands of poems, books, and literary reflections, Badr is demanding monetary compensation for three years of lost wages. "If they don't compensate us, then we might seek justice in court," he said. "My business suffered because of my arrest, and my family suffered as well, having two members taken [to Cuba]."[39] He also claimed that the Pakistani ISI had looted thousands of dollars' worth of emeralds, rubies, and sapphires from the home where the brothers had conducted their gemstone-dealing business.[40]

As he tried to readjust to freedom, Badr admitted that it was difficult to forget his captivity at Gitmo. As he went about his daily life, minute details of his detention often came to mind:

the sounds of the chains rattling around his feet, the smell of the plastic waste buckets, the razor blade shaving his beard off, the sounds of solitude.

The reunion with his older brother was comforting. They had reassured each other through the hardest moments of their lives together, and only his brother truly understood the suffering, he said. But their freedom was short-lived.

The two brothers wrote a book about their experiences, a 450-page tell-all entitled *The Broken Chains of Guantánamo*, which blamed their arrest and detention on the corruption of the Pakistani ISI.

Several former prisoners I talked to couldn't understand why the brothers would run such a risk in the volatile political climate of Pakistan. Writing a book critical of the Pakistani secret police was playing with fire.

Sure enough, shortly after their book was published in 2005, Abdul Rahim disappeared. It's believed that he was taken away by the Pakistani secret police. His family, which has been pleading for his release, doesn't know where he is or whether he's still alive.

Amnesty International issued an appeal to its 1.8 million members worldwide to lobby for the journalist's immediate release. When I visited Afghanistan and Pakistan, I heard rumors that he had disappeared at the hands of the ISI. I made dozens of calls to Pakistani government and military officials, but invariably, my calls were mysteriously disconnected, or I was told to call back later. Or the Urdu speaker on the other end of the line suddenly became unable to understand my English.

Frustrated, I got in touch with John Sifton of Human Rights Watch in New York, who explained why it was so hard to get information from the Pakistanis. His reasoning also explained why it had been similarly challenging to communicate with the Pentagon.

"It's hard to get information from governments for two simple reasons," Sifton told me. "One, the system of detention and interrogation operated by Pakistan and the United States, for terrorism suspects, is illegal, and both governments know it; they are ashamed to have the details known to the larger public. Two, some innocent victims have been sucked into the system, making the abuses all the more inexcusable."

Sifton argued that the United States and Pakistan don't play by the rules when it comes to detainees captured in Pakistan. "Detainees are arrested without warrants, held incommunicado, tortured, there are no extradition hearings, no publicity, no transparency whatsoever. The entire detention and interrogation practice jointly run by the United States and Pakistan exists outside the rule of law."

Badr now fears that he, too, will be arrested. He has given up not only his once brazen criticism of local politicians, but journalism altogether. For months, I tried to call him many times, but he keeps his mobile phone turned off and changes the number frequently. According to locals who have tried to help me locate him, Badr has abandoned his family home, moves frequently, and remains in hiding.

Freedom has done what the Guantánamo prison failed to do: it has silenced the voices of Abdul Rahim and Badr Zaman. But somewhere in the recesses of Guantánamo, their voices still live in the thousands of verses scrawled on bits of Styrofoam, Red Cross paper, and prison stationery, an epitaph for all the innocent victims of politics.

CHAPTER NINETEEN

SERIAL NUMBERS

I have been to the prison camp more than three dozen times, and each time, I have been struck by the ordinariness of it all, as well as by the radical disconnect between the beauty of the surroundings and the grim reality they mask.

I still remember my feelings of anxiety before the first trip and the stern, forbidding place I expected to find. Instead, I found sunshine and smiling young soldiers, boozy nighttime barbecues, and beaches that called to you for a late-night swim. I also found loss and tears.

And, in a sense, I've found a new part of myself. The trips to Guantánamo have brought me closer to who I am, to my heritage and what it means to me. In that sense, the camp and the relationships I've forged there will always be a part of me.

Over two years, I met nearly all the Afghans who had legal representation. And, under the supervision of Peter Ryan, I took on the representation of Hamidullah al-Razak, a charming

263

264 MY GUANTÁNAMO DIARY

middle-aged man and zealous supporter of Afghanistan's post-Taliban democracy.

The scores of prisoners I met are largely invisible to the world outside the camp. They're nameless, faceless entities, cataloged and referred to by serial number as a way of dehumanizing them. A name makes a person—or even an animal—individual and unique. Serial numbers are for inanimate objects.

The military didn't go so far as to tattoo these numbers on the prisoners' arms, but it had other ways of humiliating them. It's well known, for instance, that soldiers at Gitmo shaved the beards of the Muslim prisoners to punish them for minor infractions. What stronger image does this evoke than of the Third Reich and the Nazis shaving the beards and heads of Jews? Eventually, the Jews were stripped of their names.

It's easy to mistreat something called No. 1154. It's easy to shave its beard, to kick it around like an object, to spit on it, torture it, or make it cry. It's harder to dole out such abuse when No. 1154 retains its identity: Dr. Ali Shah Mousovi, a pediatrician who fled the Taliban, worked for the United Nations encouraging Afghans to participate and vote in the new democracy. It's harder to hate No. 1154 when you realize that he's more like you than he is different. His wife, an economist by profession, waits month after month, year after year for the news that her husband is coming home; his two sons and young daughter grow up without him.

The numbers denied the humanity of those assigned them: No. 1009, No. 1103, No. 902, No. 0002, No. 1021, No. 693, No. 0004, No. 345, No. 560, No. 928, No. 953, No. 969, No. 713, No. 976, No. 1001, No. 914, No. 801, No. 848, No. 304, No. 1037, No. 1074, No. 702, No. 892, No. 1453, No. 0003, No.

10006, No. 1458, No. 0061, No. 753, No. 306, No. 1104, No. 371, No. 1094, No. 0639, No. 657, No. 907, No. 909, No. 849, No. 1101, No. 899, No. 1003, No. 701, No. 0062, No. 1022, No. 694, No. 1095, No. 1459, No. 954, No. 1010, No. 755, No. 745, No. 820, No. 10007 . . .

It's easy to skim over numbers. And there are hundreds like them.

But at the prison camp, I listened to the numbered men tell their stories, and I quickly understood why the military had stripped them of their identities. Habeas lawyer Sabin Willett put it well. He represented Uighur prisoner No. 293, Adel Abdul-Hakim. Uighurs are ethnically Turkic Muslims who live in oil-rich northwestern China and have faced persecution from the Chinese government over their land for centuries. Abdul-Hakim was one of thirty-eight prisoners who the military admitted was not an enemy combatant but kept imprisoned nevertheless. Abdul-Hakim feared that if he were repatriated to China, he would be tortured or killed.[1]

"The facelessness of the men at Guantánamo makes their abuse palatable," Willett said to me via e-mail. "But if Adel actually turned up in the U.S., there would be pictures. His picture would be in the newspaper the next morning, and he'd be on *Good Morning America* the

No. 293, Adel, with his niece. *Courtesy of Sabin Willett.*

morning after that. And if Americans actually got a look at him, they'd be shocked. If they looked at him, if they heard him speak, if they met him, they'd ask, 'This is who we are holding down there? This guy? This is what our "war on terror" means? Adel?' And they'd feel that old Abu Ghraib shame, all over again."

There were hundreds of men just like No. 293, Adel Abdul-Hakim, and No. 1154, Dr. Ali Shah Mousovi. Each serial number represented a man: a human being with a family, an individual who valued his freedom like any American and deserved a fair trial. These men were other individuals' fathers, husbands, brothers, and sons. They had wives, sisters, and daughters whose lives will never be the same.

I listened to No. 1001, Hafizullah Shabaz Khail, protest that he was a university-educated pharmacist and a staunch supporter of Hamid Karzai's ascendancy. I watched No. 0004, Abdul Haq, pace back and forth in a panicked frenzy, refusing to come out of his tiny cell. I saw No. 1021, Chaman Gul, crouch in his cage and weep for fear that his family would forget him, then I later watched him bury his face in a dozen roses as he worried about his aging mother. No. 560, Wali Mohammad, used humor to mask his pain. When No. 061, Murat Kurnaz of Germany, was told that German officials might be put off by his long, straggly red beard, he responded thoughtfully, "If they fear a long beard, than Santa Claus is an enemy combatant."

The first time I met my client, No. 1119, it was clear to me that he missed the company of women. "I am happy you are here," he told me. "Even if they throw me in the ocean with a sweet lady like you, I would be happy."

There was No. 1002, Afghan schoolteacher Abdul Matin, accused of owning a Casio watch. No. 975, Bostan Karim, wouldn't shake my hand and only peeked at me quickly when I wasn't looking. And after watching No. 890, Rahmatullah Sangaryar, wipe away tears all morning, I bought him flowers over lunch—only to have them confiscated by the guards.

Flowers were thereafter declared contraband. I could understand how utensils or hair clips could be construed as threatening, but flowers? The ban struck me as simply malicious. I was always careful to have the thorns removed from roses and always brought the flowers back out with me after a meeting. The ban made zero sense, except as a way of depriving the prisoners of another basic pleasure.

No. 1103 was Mohammad Zahir, a fifty-four-year-old schoolteacher from Ghazni. Whenever he caught a glimpse of a lock of my hair, he would interrupt to say how pretty it was. One day, he told me that he thought the shawl I was wearing was ugly.

"Ugly?" I said, surprised. It was a beautiful, intricately embroidered shawl.

"It would be much prettier if it was red or green or had some color," he replied, "but it's simple and white with plain colors."

"I know what you're up to," I said, smiling at him. "You just want to see my hair."

He laughed, but I never took the shawl off. It would have felt odd to do that after I had been wearing it for so long in front of all the prisoners. About fifteen minutes later, as Zahir was listening to talk about habeas petitions, he bent over and picked up a single long strand of dark hair from the hardwood floor. My hair. He dangled it between his thumb and index finger.

"Now I see your hair," he said. "It is beautiful."

He twisted up the strand and put it in his front pocket.

I remember some stories fondly; others make me sad or angry. I never met Ethiopian detainee Benyam Mohammad al-Habashi, but his declassified diary entries about being held in a Central Intelligence Agency ghost prison before he was brought to Gitmo still haunt me. After he was arrested in Pakistan, he was flown to a prison in Morocco in April 2002.

> They cut off my clothes with some kind of doctor's scalpel. I was naked. I tried to put on a brave face. But maybe I was going to be raped. Maybe they'd electrocute me. Maybe castrate me.
>
> They took the scalpel to my right chest. It was only a small cut. Maybe an inch. At first I just screamed. . . . I was just shocked, I wasn't expecting. . . . Then, they cut my left chest. This time I didn't want to scream because I knew it was coming.
>
> One of them took my penis in his hand and began to make cuts. He did it once, and they stood still for maybe a minute, watching my reaction. I was in agony. They must have done this 20 to 30 times, in maybe two hours. There was blood all over. "I told you I was going to teach you who's the man," [one] eventually said.

They cut all over my private parts. One of them said it would be better just to cut it off, as I would only breed terrorists. I asked for a doctor.

Doctor No. 1 carried a briefcase. "You're all right, aren't you? But I'm going to say a prayer for you." Doctor No. 2 gave me an Alka-Seltzer for the pain. I told him about my penis. "I need to see it. How did this happen?" I told him. He looked like it was just another patient. "Put this cream on it two times a day. Morning and night." He gave me some kind of antibiotic.

I was in Morocco for 18 months. Once they began this, they would do it to me about once a month. One time I asked a guard: "What's the point of this? I've got nothing I can say to them. I've told them everything I possibly could."

"As far as I know, it's just to degrade you. So when you leave here, you'll have these scars and you'll never forget. So you'll always fear doing anything but what the U.S. wants."

Later, when a U.S. airplane picked me up the following January, a female military policewoman took pictures. She was one of the few Americans who ever showed me any sympathy. When she saw the injuries I had, she gasped. They treated me and took more photos when I was in Kabul. Someone told me this was "to show Washington it's healing."

But in Morocco, there were even worse things. Too horrible to remember, let alone talk about. About once a week or even once every two weeks I would be taken for interrogation, where they would tell me what to say. They said if you say this story as we read it, you will just go to court as a witness and all this torture will stop. I eventually repeated what was read out to me.

When I got to Morocco, they said some big people in al-Qaeda were talking about me. They talked about Jose Padilla, and they said I was going to testify against him and big people. They named Khalid Sheikh Mohamed, Abu Zubaidah and Ibn Sheikh al-Libi [all senior al-Qaeda leaders who are now in U.S. custody]. It was hard to pin down the exact story because what they wanted changed from Morocco to when later I was in the Dark Prison [a detention center in Kabul with windowless cells and American staff], to Bagram and again in Guantánamo Bay.

They told me that I must plead guilty. I'd have to say I was an al-Qaeda operations man, an ideas man. I kept insisting that I had only been in Afghanistan a short while. "We don't care," was all they'd say.

I was also questioned about my links with Britain. The interrogator told me: "We have photos of people given to us by MI5. Do you know these?" I realized that the British were sending questions to the Moroccans. I was at first surprised that the Brits were siding with the Americans.

On August 6, I thought I was going to be transferred out of there [the prison]. They came in and cuffed my hands behind my back.

But then three men came in with black masks. It seemed to go on for hours. I was in so much pain I'd fall to my knees. They'd pull me back up and hit me again. They'd kick me in the thighs as I got up. I vomited within the first few punches. I really didn't speak at all though. I didn't have the energy or will to say anything. I just wanted it to end. After that, there was to be no more first-class treatment. No bathroom. No food for a while.

During September–October 2002, I was taken in a car to another place. The room was bigger, it had its own toilet, and a window which was opaque.

They gave me a toothbrush and Colgate toothpaste. I was allowed to recover from the scalpel for about two weeks, and the guards said nothing about it.

Then, they cuffed me and put earphones on my head. They played hip-hop and rock music, very loud. I remember they played Meat Loaf and Aerosmith over and over. A couple of days later they did the same thing. Same music.

For 18 months, there was not one night when I could sleep well. Sometimes I would go 48 hours without sleep. At night, they would bang the metal doors, bang the flap on the door, or just come right in.

They continued with two or three interrogations a month. They weren't really interrogations, more like training me what to say. The interrogator told me what was going on. "We're going to change your brain," he said.

I suffered the razor treatment about once a month for the remaining time I was in Morocco, even after I'd agreed to confess to whatever they wanted to hear. It became like a routine. They'd come in, tie me up, spend maybe an hour doing it. They never spoke to me. Then, they'd tip some kind of liquid on me—the burning was like grasping a hot coal. The cutting, that was one kind of pain. The burning, that was another.

In all the 18 months I was there, I never went outside. I never saw the sun, not even once. I never saw any human being except the guards and my tormentors, unless you count the pictures they showed me.

No. 977, Izatullah Nusrat, son of eighty-year-old Haji Nusrat, also stands out in my mind. He was a younger, softer-spoken version of his father, but he had Haji's sleepy eyes, tall, hefty build, and smile. He warmed up to me right away and reached for my hand.

"My father was very happy with you," he said.

He warmed up quickly to Peter too. After we'd gone over his case, he said softly, "My innocence is as evident as it is that a black cow will give white milk. It's as clear as that." The military thought so too. They issued a notice clearing him for release, but they continued to hold him. It frustrated Izatullah, but he never lost faith in Peter. "I have a path back home, and you are at the head of my path. I trust you," he told him.

I remember one meeting in particular, and I know that Izatullah will also remember it for the rest of his life. The military granted us permission to show him a home video of his family in Sarobi, Afghanistan. He was overwhelmed when he saw his children on the tape and began laughing and crying at once. It was strange. I had never seen two such intense emotions expressed at the same time.

When the video was over, the six-foot Afghan looked up at us with watery eyes. For a moment, he was at a loss for words. He held up his thumbs and glanced at us in silence. Finally, he spoke. *"Manana*—Thank you. What you have done for me today is something I will never forget. For the rest of my life, until I die, I will remember this act of kindness," he said. "I had not seen my children in five years. Today, you have allowed me to see them, to hear them. For that, I will always be grateful."

"This was something very small," Peter said to him modestly. "We would like to put you on a plane and send you home to be with them again."

Still image of Izatullah's children from the video we showed him. *Video by Idries Khattak.*

Izatullah shook his head. "For me, as a prisoner, far away for so many years, this is not small. This is huge. I am indebted to you for the rest of my days." He asked to watch the video again.

"We can watch it all day," Peter said.

And every time it got to the part with his children lined up to face the camera, Izatullah inched closer to the portable DVD player's small screen, listening intently to every word, exclaiming over the children's shy gestures. They fidgeted with their clothing. Their eyes darted about. Their high voices and small movements made him laugh even as tears streamed down his face.

When the guards came to bring some requested documents to the door, Izatullah's eyes never moved from the video. The tears kept rolling, and the tissues he clenched became a wet ball.

At the end, he looked up again. "Did you see their teeth?" he asked. "Their little teeth fell out." He told us that he no longer recognized the younger ones, who were just infants when he was arrested.

"What's the cute redhead's name?" I asked.

Izatullah told me that the little boy was Ashmat. "He followed me everywhere," he said. "He was always with me." The last time he saw Ashmat, he said, "I was sitting with guests, and Ashmat was in my lap. He was two at the time. He never left my side. My brother, Abdul Wahid, came in to tell me there were some American soldiers who wanted to see me, so I got up to see them. Ashmat was close behind me, and so was Abid, who is three. When I was talking to the soldiers through an interpreter, Ashmat sensed that something wasn't right. Abid took a few steps back in fear, but Ashmat winced, then held his hands up and asked me to pick him up. I lifted him in my arms while I spoke. But when they led me away, I had to put him down. I looked back once. He was standing alone. This was my last memory of them. Today was the first time in five years that I have heard my children's voices."

When we asked Izatullah how he coped and whether he was depressed, his answer was surprising. "We are very unfortunate people, but it would only add to our misfortune if we allowed ourselves to get depressed," he said. "We have families—wives, children, and parents—waiting at home for us. We don't want to ruin ourselves with unhappiness and depression. We ask Allah for *sabr*—patience—and we try to keep one another in good spirits."

Izatullah also told us about the first time he had heard that a group of reported al-Qaeda and Taliban prisoners had been sent to Gitmo. "I remember feeling glad that Americans were capturing them. People who terrorize humanity should be sent to prison," he said.

Father and son had a change of heart when they were arrested and brought to Cuba. "We saw that there were so many others like us. With that, the whole system quickly lost credibility in our eyes. Maybe there are some al-Qaeda, but America, with all of its intelligence, can certainly in five years do an investigation to find out if the reports against people are true or false."

The guards signaled that time was up, and Peter and I began to pack up. "The next time I speak to you, I hope to be speaking to you on the telephone from Afghanistan, inshallah," Peter said.

I also think often of another Afghan, whose first name was Mohammad. When months went by with no progress on his case, he lost hope of a legal solution and decided that he didn't want a lawyer. "Guantánamo is not a place of law," he reasoned. "It is a jungle."

The thirty-eight-year-old was different from many of the prisoners in a fundamental way. He wasn't a pediatrician, a schoolteacher, a businessman, or even a goatherd. He admitted that at the time of his arrest, he was working for the Taliban. He also had a part-time job working on his family farm but made no bones about leaving the Taliban on his resume.

"The American government under President Bush has committed horrible atrocities, but that doesn't mean that all people working for the U.S. government support Bush's ideologies or support his actions," he said. "I'm sure there are many, many good people who work for the American government right now. Similarly, the Taliban ran the government of Afghanistan for seven years. There are many people who made up that government. Some people were weak minded and led to do things that were not right. There were others who disagreed with the policies of their government. I cannot speak for all of them, but I can say that I am not a political figure. I worked under their government as a checkpoint guard."

I was a little shocked when I first heard about his associations, and I began to wonder whether the soft-spoken, gentle-natured man sitting across the table eating Hostess Twinkies and KFC chicken strips could in reality be a monster. The mention of Taliban instantly conjured images of bearded men caning women in the streets of Kabul.

Mohammad wore tan-colored prison garb and a black skull cap over his thinning hair. During our meeting, I found him exceptionally sharp. He tactfully suppressed his emotions and kept his tone of voice even, calm, and in control. He had a lot to say and gently steered the meeting with slight voice inflections. He was always thinking, and only his subtle body language hinted at despair or, sometimes, gave a glimmer of optimism. Even as he watched a video of his dying father telling him that "getting letters from him was like giving a thirsty man water," he tried to remain stoic.

Most of the time, we listened to him talk as he doodled on scratch paper, drawing perfectly symmetrical flower petals and a mountainous Afghan horizon. Meanwhile, I sketched cartoon bunnies and practiced writing my name in Pashto with his help. Rebecca Dick of Dechert's Washington, D.C., office drew cats. All the while, we talked politics. Sometimes Mohammad spoke in a Socratic, questioning style. Other times, he launched into rhetorical soliloquies along lines like these:

> America said it came to fight the Taliban's abuse of human rights. But America has shown the world that they don't respect those rights either. They have shunned international law. They bombed weddings. They bombed Janaza funeral prayers, and killed people mourning the deaths of their loved ones. They bombed houses and killed little girls and boys. What crime did these people commit? There was never al-Qaeda or the Taliban found in these places.
>
> America said it was concerned about women's rights under the Taliban. Does America care about

my daughters or my wife? Who is feeding them while they have imprisoned me here? Does America care about the widows who have no source of income and the thousands of little girls without fathers?

The world will find out the truth about Guantánamo. One day they will read about it in history books. They will watch it in movies. This is very bad for America that they are doing this. May God show them the right path and some humanity.

The problem with the American government is that their decisions are twisted. They are driven by greed. They follow their stomachs, they follow oil, and where they can make the most money. And then it is the poor Afghans who suffer at your hands. We were very happy when the Americans first came. We considered you our friends from the time of the Russians. But then the bombs began to fall from the sky. They shattered what was left of our poor country and imprisoned us without charge or evidence.

Is America really in a position to be establishing democracies? They have much they need to change about themselves first. I am not saying that all Americans are bad. Please don't get me wrong. There are good among us all. But, there are two people in this war on terrorism who have gotten a bad name: The Americans and the Taliban.

All the detainee meetings left me feeling helpless. The men I met showed me the human face of the war on terrorism.

Though they were systematically dehumanized, to me they became like friends, or brothers, or fathers and uncles. I often see their faces in my dreams at night.

Once I dreamed that my father, Baba-jaan, was at Gitmo. He was being led away out of Camp Echo by two guards. I don't remember what he was wearing, but like all the others, he put on a brave face and called out to me, "I love you, *bachai*—my daughter." I stood there at a loss as he disappeared. I thought of that dream when I saw the Afghan men in their cages. Any one of them could have been my dad, or somebody else's.

I can honestly say that I don't believe any of the Afghans I met were guilty of crimes against the United States. Certainly, some of the Guantánamo detainees were, just not the men I met. Some might have been allied with Afghan warlords, and some might have worked under the Taliban. Perhaps, had I met some of these prisoners in Afghanistan five years ago, they would have wanted to cane me for not covering properly. But there was no evidence they had committed crimes under U.S. law.

I wish we could have just handed most of them the freedom they so desperately craved.

EPILOGUE

Tehran, October 12, 2006

The phone rang at a little after 3 PM. Waheeda knew at once that it was good news. Her brother-in-law, Ismael, was calling from Gardez, giddy with excitement.

"Doctor Sahib is coming home today, inshallah!" he exclaimed. He'd just heard a public announcement: a group of Afghan prisoners would be arriving from Guantánamo later that day. Among the sixteen names was that of her husband, Ali Shah Mousovi.

Even as Ismael's message echoed through Mousovi's Tehran home, the doctor was aboard a plane headed east, toward home. Blindfolded and shackled, he pictured his family in his mind and wondered what it would be like to see them after so long. The minutes seemed endless.

Then, at last came the vibrations of wheels descending and locking into place and the aircraft gliding down the tarmac of Bagram Air Force Base. Mousovi heard the cabin doors being opened.

One by one, the men were led off the windowless plane, loaded into vehicles, and driven about thirty miles south to Kabul. There, American soldiers handed them over to the Afghan Peace and Reconciliation Committee, a Kabul-based organization headed by former

---

This account has been reconstructed with the help of Dr. Ali Shah Mousovi and his family.

Afghan president Sibghatullah Mujadidi. Their blindfolds and shackles were removed. The men said a prayer together, and afterward, some spoke with journalists and Afghan officials. When it was Mousovi's turn, he stood up but found himself at a loss for words.

"Someone who has spent four years only speaking to walls—it is difficult for him to talk in the presence of leaders," he began. "You must be assured that all those sitting here and most of those still in Cuba, none of them have done anything to deserve [what happened to them in] Cuba." Most had nothing to do with terrorism, he said. They had been turned over, because of tribal, ethnic, religious, and political animosities, to the American military who "without any investigation, arrested people and put them in jail."[1]

After a short ceremony, the former detainees were reunited with family and friends who stood waiting outside. Still wearing their Gitmo prison garb, the weary but contented men walked quickly into the arms of their loved ones.

Ali Shah Mousovi scanned the crowd for his brothers' faces. When he spotted them, they began to cry.

"Those were the hardest years of our lives," one brother who lives in Washington, D.C., told me later. "I will never forget that day. I cried like a baby when I saw him there."

From Kabul, Mousovi was whisked to Gardez, where he was given a hero's welcome by crowds of well-wishers who had flocked from neighboring towns for his homecoming.

"There weren't any gift shops at Guantánamo Bay," Mousovi joked. "All I have is this prison uniform, if you want it!"

In fact, Mousovi said he would probably keep the uniform for the rest of his life. His brothers, however, urged him to trim the beard he had grown in Cuba and dye it black again. Mousovi was hesitant, but his brothers knew that it would be good for him, particularly be-

fore he saw his wife and children in Iran. He finally agreed, and with his beard shorn close and dyed black, he instantly looked decades younger.

That evening though, his brothers watched with concern as he lay down to rest and curled his body into a defensive, almost fetal position. It was very unlike the relaxed way he had always slept before.

Ali Shah Mousovi at his Gardez home.

Once arrangements were made, Mousovi was off to see his family in Iran. His homecoming was not a small family affair. Dressed in a tan suit, he was greeted at Tehran International Airport by hundreds of well-wishers and journalists. The crowds flocked around him; friends, neighbors, and locals placed flower garlands around his neck and congratulated him.

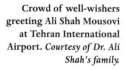

Crowd of well-wishers greeting Ali Shah Mousovi at Tehran International Airport. *Courtesy of Dr. Ali Shah's family.*

Ali Shah Mousovi with daughter, Hajar, at Tehran International Airport. *Courtesy of Dr. Ali Shah's family.*

Dr. Ali Shah with his mother at Tehran International Airport. *Courtesy of Dr. Ali Shah's family.*

Abu-Zar cut through the crowds and reached out for his father. Mousovi did a double-take, looking at his eldest boy, now a tall lanky teenager with a beard. After that initial look-over, Abu-Zar remained glued to his father's side. And then, one by one, the doctor and his teary-eyed family embraced.

Mousovi's younger son, Kumail, ran around with a camcorder, recording the end of a bitter chapter in the family's history. Paparazzi followed as the family slowly made its way out of the airport and Mousovi stopped in front of a waiting car to speak to the crowd of onlookers and local news reporters who had gathered around him.

Ali Shah with his two sons, Kumail and Abu-Zar, and his wife, Waheeda, at their Tehran home a few months after his release. *Courtesy of Dr. Ali Shah's family.*

"I am returning from prison. I don't have stories of adventures or vacation. I have nothing exciting to speak of. I was a prisoner. There are many more just like me. Unfortunately, we all saw only hardship," he said.

Then, he and his family got into the car and drove off.

When I visited Afghanistan in the winter of 2006, Mousovi was still in Iran, but we spoke once in a while by telephone. "It's so great that I can pick up a phone and call you now, Doctor Sahib," I told

him in one of those calls, addressing him with a term of high regard and admiration.

"I will never forget the love you showed me while I was a prisoner," he said. "I hope to see you one day soon in Afghanistan."

When I went back to Afghanistan a year later to collect affidavits and exonerating evidence for my client, Hamidullah al-Razak, I was happy to learn that Ali Shah Mousovi was there too. He'd come from Iran to house-hunt in Kabul, to finally set up his clinic and build a life for his family in their war-torn country.

"I want my children to have a love, to have meena—affection—for Afghanistan," he explained. "I want them to see to their homeland while it is free."

When I called his brother Ismael hoping to get together, I learned that Mousovi and his family had gone to Gardez for a wedding. So, I decided to hitch a ride to southern Afghanistan with a local aid worker. The drive was beautiful, with stunning mountains and the changing colors of autumn drenching the landscape.

Our car pulled up to Mousovi's house, and he came out to greet us, Ismael following close behind.

"Mahvish-jaan, I can't explain how happy you've just made me," Mousovi said, clutching my hand.

I was itching to give him a big bear hug, the kind I'd give my friend Georges from Miami. Georges would show me just how happy he was to see me by giving me a monster squeeze and picking me straight up off the floor. I think I fantasized a dramatic reunion like that with Dr. Ali Shah. But Afghan culture and society throws up so many intricate barriers between men and women that I had to settle for the tight grip of his hand and his carefully chosen words. It was the same at Guantánamo. There were many, many times when I wanted to console prisoners with a hug. But other than with Haji Nusrat, it never happened; the culture inhibits it.

I smiled at the doctor and chose my words as carefully as he had. "Dr. Sahib," I began, "I'm so glad to finally see you here in your home. It means more to me than I can explain to you."

"May Allah always keep you happy," he said and then, "Raza, raza—Come, come," as he ushered me into the house, where I met his mother, a little old lady who immediately embraced me tightly and proceeded to plant kisses all over my face and head. She held my hand for the next several hours. "I feel like my daughter has come to visit," she announced. I channeled the affection I felt for Ali Shah toward his kind mother.

The doctor told the story of the moment we first met, when both of us were nervous about whom we would be meeting. I expected a terrorist; he, perhaps an abusive interrogator. I walked in and saw a nervous pediatrician standing at the back of the room. He saw me under an Afghan shawl and mistook me for his sister. "I really thought it was Parveen, that she had come to see me somehow," he said.

The sight of Dr. Mousovi at his house was slightly surreal. I had only known him as a gentle, white-bearded man with chains around his feet. Seeing him at home with his family, just as I'd always prayed he would be again, allowed me to feel the weight of everything I'd held back during our Camp Echo meetings. He'd been the first prisoner I met, and the impact of that initial meeting was greater than most of my meetings with other prisoners. He was the first to break down my biases and to show me what sort of injustice my country had committed against good, kind people. I realized that I hadn't allowed myself fully to feel all the effects of that until now, when I saw Dr. Ali Shah safe and free.

Being at his house was like being at the home of an uncle. I poured green tea for the doctor and his mother into small, clear tea glasses, and they filled bowls with red pomegranate seeds. I helped

*his mother carry in dishes of rice, yogurt, meat, and eggs. They were
wonderful hosts; there were no formalities. We talked, walked in and
out freely, sometimes sat on the couch, sometimes on the floor. And
following custom, everyone encouraged everyone else to eat.*

*I couldn't stay late because I'd been told that it wasn't safe to drive
through the south at night, but I ended up lingering anyway. It was
hard to leave. Mousovi and his mother kept pressing me to stay for
the wedding of a relative from the extended family. His nieces presented me with sparkly orange wedding bangles, and his mother gave
me a pretty embroidered white shawl.*

*When I had to go, his mother embraced me tightly, while Dr. Ali
Shah sat on the floor on his knees looking on. "Our hearts don't
want you to leave," he said. "This is your home too."*

*I wasn't good at this impromptu poetic word game, and I was a
bit overwhelmed at seeing him so happy, so I simply said, "I'll see*

Dr. Ali Shah, his mother, and I at his Gardez home. *Photo by Lal Gul.*

you again soon, and we'll stay in touch." As he walked me out, he told me how much our friendship meant to him.

"We'll have this special thing forever, though it started in the most unlikely of places," he said.

"I know what you mean," I replied. "You're like family."

I wished him fun at the wedding that night. "Weddings are happy occasions," he said. "You coming to my house today was like the happiness of two weddings for us."

I think that made up for the bear hug.

Some of the men I met at Guantánamo have been released, but many have not. Haji Nusrat's captivity had a bittersweet ending.

In August 2006, the eighty-year-old was released as unexpectedly as he'd been arrested. Like Ali Shah Mousovi, he was given a hero's welcome in Yakhdan, his native village in Sarobi, by hundreds of visitors who had streamed in for the homecoming.

Nusrat's family immediately began to entertain well-wishers, including a few Americans—U.S. military officers stationed at a Sarobi base who dropped by to see what all the commotion at his home was about. The American soldiers were treated just as warmly as the Afghan guests, invited in and offered green tea.

"They greeted me and said they were sorry for what had happened to me," Nusrat told me later. "I told them I had forgiven them."

I trekked to Sarobi in November 2006. I was greeted by Abdul Wahid, Nusrat's son, a tall man with light brown eyes, who led me into a guesthouse room lined with red cushions. I took my shoes off and sat down as someone brought in pastries and nuts and Abdul Wahid poured tea.

I could hear the sound of Haji Nusrat's voice outside. He was speaking to some visitors, who continued to stream in four months

Haji Nusrat. *Author photo.*

after his release. He didn't know I was coming, so when he stuck his head through the window to see who his next visitor was, his face lit up in surprise. His sons helped him into the room, and he sat next to me on the cushioned floor.

"Bachai, you kept your promise. I knew you would," he said.

"I'm so happy to see you here," I told him. He was so different from the way he'd been at Gitmo, much calmer and more peaceful.

"Bachai, what happened to me was cruel," he said. "I suffered a big injustice. It was not a small injustice."

I asked him about his release.

"My release," he said leaning back into the pillows, "left me ne khushala, ne khapa—not happy, not sad. I didn't want to leave my son behind."

When he was led out of Camp 4, Nusrat said, "Izatullah came up to the edge of the fencing and said, 'Khudai-pa-aman—May God's peace be with you.' I gave him my hand, and then I had to leave him."

"He must have been happy for you, but also sad," I said.

"No, my son was happy. He was happy that his father was being released. I was sad."

I spent the day at Nusrat's because Afghans are so insistent that a guest stay as long as possible. An Afghan guest is typically offended if tea is not offered. Then, the host usually insists that the guest par-

take of the next meal. So, when lunchtime came around, there was no question that I would be staying. We went into another room, where I was surprised to see a satellite TV, and had an elaborate communal meal. Nusrat sat next to me on the floor. I was a little surprised, again, to see him drink Nestle bottled water instead of tap or boiled water. He handed me a can of Pepsi, and his sons and grandsons brought in two-foot pieces of fluffy bread. They laid out chicken, lamb, rice, spinach, soup, and potatoes on a floor mat.

As people bustled about, I talked quietly to Haji. Then, he remembered something and started yelling for his son, who had stepped out of the room.

"Waa Abdul Wahiddaa!" he yelled. "Come in here and bring that box."

I was amused at the way he ordered his eldest son about. Abdul Wahid waited on his father hand and foot and never complained.

"Waa Abdul Wahiddaa!"

Finally, the twenty-seven-year-old came in holding a box wrapped in sparkly blue-and-white paper and tied with long, colorful ribbons. As he walked toward us, holding the box out to me, Nusrat stopped him.

"Give it to me. I want to give it to her," he grumbled.

Abdul Wahid passed him the box, and Nusrat passed it to me.

"As I have said before, you are like my own child," he said. "Our friendship will be strong and will last forever. Don't ever let it go."

"Of course not, I wouldn't," I responded. I thanked him for the gift. I opened it, careful not to rip the shiny wrapping. It was a thick brown embroidered shawl. I knew I would treasure it for years to come.

Nusrat introduced me to his extended family and other guests who had stopped by for lunch and told them the story of how we met.

Haji Nusrat and his son Abdul Wahid having lunch in Sarobi. *Author photo.*

Then, we ate out of assorted plates and bowls of food, using the bread in place of utensils. Haji placed small saucers of salt and pepper in front of me and put pinches of both on my chicken and spinach. As we ate, I asked Baba, as he now insisted I call him, about his health. He paused between slurps of brothy soup and asked a favor.

"Can you take me to America with you so that I can have an operation on my neck?" he asked.

I thought it was a joke. "What? You want to go to America?" I asked, not believing that he would ever want to go to the United States after his experience. "Why not England, France, or Germany?" There was silence as all heads turned toward us. But the old man really wanted to go to the United States, despite everything.

"Why not? I never had disliked America or Americans. I never considered them my enemy, and I didn't do anything to them," he said, opening up one of his tirades. "It was my own Afghans who betrayed me. Not the Americans. The Americans were foolish to believe lies and not to investigate, but they came to Afghanistan not knowing anything or who they could trust. My real enemy was some dishonorable lying Afghan who probably sold me to the Americans."

Abdul Wahid joined in. "We have never been against the Americans. We support the current government. I work with the new democracy," he said. "My father would like to go to America for medical treatment, that's all." He explained that his father's paralysis could be cured with surgery. They had taken him to Islamabad, Pakistan, many years before for an operation, but it had been unsuccessful, and the surgeons said that the old man needed to go to Europe or America for treatment.

Nusrat showed me the surgical scars on the back of his neck.

"Bachai, if you can help me get a visa, maybe I will be able to walk again," he said. "But I need permission to be a guest in America to get the treatment first."

I told him that it might be difficult for him to get a U.S. visa because his classification as an enemy combatant hadn't been rescinded upon his release. If there was any possibility of getting a visa for the purposes of seeking medical treatment, he would need some medical documentation from his doctors stating that treatment for his paralysis was not available in Afghanistan. I told him I'd look into it when I got home. He seemed happy with that and encouraged me to eat more.

"Why are you eating like a bird? You need to gain some weight," he said.

A few hours later, I was ready to head back to Kabul, but the family insisted that I stay for dinner, spend the night, and leave in the morning. Nusrat said he wanted me to spend a few months with him. I said everything I could think of to convince them to let me go, promising that I'd stay longer the next time I visited, but after some back-and-forth, Haji finally relented. "Next time you come, you spend at least one month with my family," he said. "If I find out you ever came to Afghanistan and didn't visit, I will be upset with you."

I assured him I wouldn't do that.

Before I left, I took some pictures to take back to Izatullah at Gitmo.

"Make sure you tell him you saw me with your own eyes. Tell him there is no difficulty and by the grace of the Almighty, he will be among us very soon," Nusrat said.

As I collected my things, he added, "Allah has made you a great woman. You should marry a great Afghan man."

"You think so?"

"Yes, I do. Marry a man of your wathan."

I didn't want to tell Haji that my fiancé was a white-bread American from California. I knew he wouldn't understand. Somewhere along the way, I'd reached a level of equilibrium in my cultural balancing act. I no longer struggled with the classic East versus West identity crisis; I wanted to be accepted as a viable product of both worlds. I handpicked the characteristics that suited me from both cultures and left out the ones I didn't care for. But I knew that others wouldn't always understand, and if I'd told Nusrat about my fiancé, I think I would have eroded my own sense of peace with where I now found myself.

At the same time, I felt, at some level, as though I was deceiving him. It was the same way I felt at Guantánamo. I'd never told any of the prisoners that I was engaged to an American man, someone with no roots in Afghanistan, or any Middle Eastern country for that matter. I knew that they all expected me to be a good Pashtun girl

*who played by their centuries-old rules. I'd tried to tell the truth
once, when my client Hamidullah al-Razak kept plying me with personal questions. I tried to dodge them initially, but part of building a
relationship and trust with your clients is engaging them not just on
a legal level but on a personal one as well. So, I finally relented and
told him about my fiancé. I was happily surprised when he accepted
it easily, and I felt better about not having lied to him. But on the following trip, I was met by a cross-armed, stern-faced Mohammad Zahir, a fifty-four-year-old Ghazni schoolteacher, who wasn't thrilled
by the rumor he'd heard, and I had to backtrack on my story. I felt
badly about lying, but Gitmo is such a delicate and intense environ-
ment that I felt it was wisest.*

Haji and I. *Photo by Abdul Wahid.*

But I really cared about Haji Nusrat. I knew that he had been tortured, humiliated, beaten, and imprisoned without charge for many years, that he'd been through so much at the hands of Americans. And yet, I didn't have it in me to try to reason with him and explain my position.

I knelt back down and told him he looked better than I'd imagined. I was happy to see him free, and I prayed that his son would join him in Afghanistan soon too. He took my hands in both of his and gave them a squeeze.

"You're a good daughter. You kept your promise, bachai," he said. "Today, you made me happy. God is great, and God is merciful."

"Take good care of yourself, and I'll see you and Izatullah next time I am here, inshallah" I replied.

On the night of October 9, 2006, guards informed four men in Camp 3, Block 1 that they would be sent home on the night of October 11. Goatherd Taj Mohammad was one of them. He was ecstatic. The night before his flight, he could hardly contain himself. He could barely speak and prayed nonstop, asking everyone in adjacent cells to pray as well that the news was true.

The next night, guards accompanied by Red Cross workers came to fetch the men. They were all given white uniforms and white shoes for the flight home and transfer of custody in Afghanistan. I suppose it would make for a bad photo op if the U.S. military released "non-compliant" detainees in tan and orange prison garb. Once the men were dressed and ready, the guards unlocked their cages one by one, as other prisoners looked wistfully on.

When I met with Abdullah Wazir Zadran on the morning after Taj's departure, he said the place would be very quiet without him.

Zadran was happy for his friend, but I sensed a twinge of envy too. The two had become close while imprisoned together.

Taj stays in touch with Abdul Salam Zaeef in Kabul and asked Zaeef to pass on his contact information to me. I tried calling him, but we ended up playing phone tag; he travels an awful lot for a goatherd and is often not in town. When he was, I had a friend of mine go to his village

Taj Mohammad in Kunar after his release. *Photo courtesy of Nimatullah Karyab.*

and take a picture of him nine months after his release. He also wrote me to say that he'd like a copy of this book—in Pashto and in English.

When I do get hold of him, I plan to find out whether he's still interested in taking a second wife, from America.

The families of Salah al-Aslami and the two Saudi prisoners who the U.S. military said committed suicide at Gitmo on June 10, 2006, continue to mourn their deaths. Al-Aslami's young widow, Hayat Warshad Ali, still hasn't recovered and remains bedridden in the family home.

The U.S. military has never conducted a conclusive investigation. To date, the Department of Defense (DOD) has also refused to release the suicide letters that were supposedly written before the men hanged themselves. The DOD has also continued to turn down requests for anatomical samples of the organs removed from the victims' bodies.

Al-Jazeera journalist Sami al-Haj remains at Guantánamo. He will have been on hunger strike for one year as of January 7, 2008. Sami's imprisonment and force-feeding has continued to cause public outrage worldwide. U.S. Rep. Keith Ellison of Minnesota spoke out publicly in support of al-Haj, calling for a hearing to prove the basis for the journalist's imprisonment and that of hundreds like him.

"If he's a bad actor, prove it. If not, let him out," Ellison said to the Associated Press in November 2007, declaring that it seemed al-Haj was being held only for being a journalist and a cameraman.[2]

In late June 2007, Bahraini prisoner Jumah al-Dossary sliced his abdomen with a metal shard, almost severing a major artery. It was the thirty-three-year-old's twelfth suicide attempt. He was rushed to the hospital after guards found him unconscious. A few weeks later, al-Dossary was released from Gitmo and handed over to the Saudi government (he is a dual citizen of Bahrain and Saudi Arabia).

Today, he alternates between a Riyadh rehabilitation center with resortlike amenities and his family home, spending two weeks at a time in each, which he will continue to do until his health improves.

His attorney, Joshua Colangelo-Bryan, believes his transfer out of Gitmo indicates his innocence.

"If the U.S. administration believed that Jumah was a threat to our national security, he would still be at Guantánamo," Colangelo-Bryan said. "The fact that he was voluntarily sent home shows clearly that there is no basis to believe that he poses any threat."

NOTES

Chapter 2

1. Brent Mickum, "Tortured, Humiliated and Crying Out for Some Justice," *The Guardian*, January 12, 2005, and Associated Press images.

2. See www.globalsecurity.org/military/facility/guantanamo-bay_delta.htm.

3. Ibid., and Associated Press images.

4. See www.globalsecurity.org/military/facility/guantanamo-bay_delta.htm.

5. Ibid.

Chapter 3

1. See www.globalsecurity.org/military/facility/guantanamo-bay_delta.htm.

2. Ibid.

3. Ibid.

Chapter 5

1. See "Current Population Survey, Annual Social and Economic (ASEC) Supplement," U.S. Census Bureau, http://pubdb3.census.gov/macro/032007/hhinc/new02_001.htm.

Chapter 8

1. See www.globalsecurity.org/military/facility/guantanamo-bay_delta.htm.

Chapter 10

1. United Nations World Population Prospects Report for 2006, www.un.org/esa/population/publications/wpp2006/WPP2006_Highlights _rev.pdf.

2. See www.savethechildren.org.

3. See www.cia.gov/library/publications/the-world-factbook/ print/af.html.

Chapter 11

1. See http://news.bbc.co.uk/1/hi/world/south_asia/3280439.stm.

2. See http://news.bbc.co.uk/2/hi/south_asia/3051501.stm.

3. Mark Denbeaux, "A Profile of 517 Detainees through Analysis of Department of Defense Data," Seton Hall University, School of Law, http://law.shu.edu/aaafinal.pdf.

4. Autopsy details and interview quotets are based on European press reports.

5. All statements by pathologists are from European media reports.

Chapter 12

1. Information provided by counsel at the Center for Constitutional Rights.

Chapter 15

1. Translation by Mahmood Khatib.

Chapter 18

1. A note on sources: All published statements made by Guantánamo detainees during attorney-client meetings were recorded and submitted to the Department of Justice for classification review.

2. Thomas Coghlin, "Writing Poetry Was the Balm That Kept Guantánamo Prisoners from Going Mad: Former Inmates Say They Wrote Thousands of Lines," *San Francisco Chronicle*, July 17, 2005.

3. N. C. Aizenmann, "In a Jail in Cuba Beat the Heart of a Poet: Afghan," *Washington Post Foreign Service*, April 24, 2005, A19.

4. James Rupert, "Writers Jailed in 2002 for Political Satire," *Newsday*, October 31, 2005.

5. Rupert, "Writers Jailed."

6. Rupert, "Writers Jailed."

7. Rupert, "Writers Jailed."

8. Coghlin, "Writing Poetry Was the Balm."

9. Rupert, "Writers Jailed."

10. Sadaqat Jan, "Ex-Guantánamo Detainee Held Again," Associated Press, December 27, 2006.

11. Coghlin, "Writing Poetry Was the Balm."

12. Rupert, "Writers Jailed."

13. Coghlin, "Writing Poetry Was the Balm."

14. Coghlin, "Writing Poetry Was the Balm."

15. Rupert, "Writers Jailed."

16. Aizenmann, "In a Jail in Cuba," A19.

17. Coghlin, "Writing Poetry Was the Balm."

18. Yusufzai Ashfaq, "Journalists Release Guantánamo Bay Report," *Oneworld.net*, August 1, 2006.

19. Rupert, "Writers Jailed."

20. Aizenmann, "In a Jail in Cuba," A19.

21. Rupert, "Writers Jailed."

22. Chicago Public Radio, "Habeas Shmabeas," *This American Life*, March 10, 2006; Aizenmann, "In a Jail in Cuba," A19.

23. Harpoon Rashid, "Ex-inmates Share Guantánamo Ordeal," BBC News, Peshawar, May 2, 2005.

24. Coghlin, "Writing Poetry Was the Balm."

25. Aizenmann, "In a Jail in Cuba," A19.

26. Coghlin, "Writing Poetry Was the Balm."

27. Coghlin, "Writing Poetry Was the Balm."

28. Aizenmann, "In a Jail in Cuba," A19.

29. Coghlin, "Writing Poetry Was the Balm."

30. Coghlin, "Writing Poetry Was the Balm."

31. Rupert, "Writers Jailed."

32. Aizenmann, "In a Jail in Cuba," A19.

33. Rashid, "Ex-inmates Share."

34. Aizenmann, "In a Jail in Cuba," A19.

35. Coghlin, "Writing Poetry Was the Balm."

36. Aizenmann, "In a Jail in Cuba," A19.

37. Coghlin, "Writing Poetry Was the Balm."

38. Aizenmann, "In a Jail in Cuba," A19.

39. Rashid, "Ex-inmates Share."

40. Rashid, "Ex-inmates Share."

Chapter 19

1. Uighur names are changed to avoid harassment of their families by the Chinese government.

Epilogue

1. "Sixteen Afghans Return Home from Guantánamo Alleging Torture," Agence France-Presse, October 12, 2006, http://humanrights .ucdavis.edu/projects/the-guantanamo-testimonials-project/testimonies/ prisoner-testimonies/exhausted–16-afghans-freed-after-guantanamo.

2. Ben Fox, "Jailed Gitmo Journalist Gains Support," Associated Press, November 1, 2007.

Mahvish Rukhsana Khan is a recent law school graduate and journalist. She has published in the *Wall Street Journal*, the *New York Times*, the *Washington Post*, and other media. She lives in San Diego.

PublicAffairs is a publishing house founded in 1997. It is a tribute to the standards, values, and flair of three persons who have served as mentors to countless reporters, writers, editors, and book people of all kinds, including me.

I. F. STONE, proprietor of *I. F. Stone's Weekly*, combined a commitment to the First Amendment with entrepreneurial zeal and reporting skill and became one of the great independent journalists in American history. At the age of eighty, Izzy published *The Trial of Socrates*, which was a national bestseller. He wrote the book after he taught himself ancient Greek.

BENJAMIN C. BRADLEE was for nearly thirty years the charismatic editorial leader of *The Washington Post*. It was Ben who gave the *Post* the range and courage to pursue such historic issues as Watergate. He supported his reporters with a tenacity that made them fearless and it is no accident that so many became authors of influential, best-selling books.

ROBERT L. BERNSTEIN, the chief executive of Random House for more than a quarter century, guided one of the nation's premier publishing houses. Bob was personally responsible for many books of political dissent and argument that challenged tyranny around the globe. He is also the founder and longtime chair of Human Rights Watch, one of the most respected human rights organizations in the world.

• • •

For fifty years, the banner of Public Affairs Press was carried by its owner Morris B. Schnapper, who published Gandhi, Nasser, Toynbee, Truman, and about 1,500 other authors. In 1983, Schnapper was described by *The Washington Post* as "a redoubtable gadfly." His legacy will endure in the books to come.

Peter Osnos, *Founder and Editor-at-Large*

Mount Laurel Library
100 Walt Whitman Avenue
Mount Laurel, NJ 08054-9539
856-234-7319
www.mtlaurel.lib.nj.us